Public Sector Budgets

To: Dana Ott

Public Sector Budgets

A Comparative Study

Attiat F. Ott
Clark University

Edward Elgar

Published by
Edward Elgar Publishing Limited
Gower House
Croft Road
Aldershot
Hants GU11 3HR
England

Edward Elgar Publishing Company
Old Post Road
Brookfield
Vermont 05036
USA

British Library Cataloguing in Publication Data
Ott, Attiat F.
Public Sector Budgets: A Comparative Study
I. Title
339.5

Library of Congress Cataloguing in Publication Data
Ott, Attiat F.
Public sector budgets: a comparative study
p. cm.
Includes bibliographical references and index.
1. Budget. 2. Budget—United States. 3. Budget—Case studies.
I. Title
HJ2005.088 1993
350.72'2—dc20 93-22654
CIP

ISBN 1 85278 618 3

Printed and bound in Great Britain by
Hartnolls Limited, Bodmin, Cornwall

Contents

PART THREE: BUDGET POLICY

Tables

Figures

Preface

A public sector budget is an important document that shapes for all times the rights and obligations of every citizen. In a free society, the individual and government enter into a social contract whereby private resources are exchanged for public resources for the common good. The process through which this exchange takes place is as important as the actual outcome.

The volume focuses on both the process and the outcome. Contributors to this volume bring forth in their respective chapters (Chapters 7, 9, 10, and 11) perceptions and knowledge of the workings of the public sector in different countries. Their contributions not only add a dimension often neglected in books about budget making but also further our understanding of why budget outcomes differ under different systems of government and the degree to which such outcomes have been shaped by constitutional limits or constraints.

This volume has its antecedent in Ott and Ott's 'Federal Budget Policy', first published by the Brookings Institution in 1965, subsequently revised in 1969 and 1977. David Ott died in 1975 before the last revision of the Brookings volume was completed. The federal budget process and budget policy have changed a great deal since then. These changes have been incorporated in Part One of this volume. Still, this part bears the mark of David's understanding of the federal budget and the budget process.

I would like to record my appreciation to contributors to chapters in this volume for their participation. I am grateful to Robert Kilpatrick of the Office of Management and Budget for comments helpful in revising Chapter 4; to the director and staff of the Congressional Budget Office for the many studies of the U.S. federal budget which have made the task of researchers on the federal budget easier; to the staff of the U.S. Bureau of the Census for the use of their county governments data file. Special recognition is due to the John M. Olin Foundation for funding support of the research activities of the Institute for Economic Studies at Clark University.

Preparing the manuscript for publication drew on the skills of so many at the Institute for Economic Studies. In particular the expertise and patience of Barbara Dodds in carrying out this task is greatly acknowledged.

Attiat F. Ott

Contributors

Attiat F. Ott is a Professor of Economics and Director of the Institute for Economic Studies, Clark University, Worcester, Mass. She is the author and/or co-author of several books, articles and monographs in Public Sector Economics, Macroeconomics and Health Economics.

Peter Smith is a Senior Lecturer in the Department of Economics and Related Studies, University of York, United Kingdom. His principal research interests are Public Sector Efficiency and Fiscal Federalism and he has published widely on both topics.

Gladstone A. Hutchinson is an Assistant Professor of Economics in the Department of Economics and Business, Lafayette College, Easton, PA. His primary research interest is Public Sector Efficiency in developing countries. His published work reflects this.

Ute Schumacher is a Senior Research Associate at the Institute for Economic Studies, Clark University, Worcester, Mass. Her primary research interests are Public Finance and International Economics. She has published articles on profitability of manufacturing industries in the U.S. and privatization of public enterprises in Jamaica.

Ronald J. Shadbegian is an Assistant Professor, Department of Economics, University of Massachusetts, Dartmouth, Mass. His research interests are Public Finance and Monetary Economics. He has published articles in both areas.

Kamal Desai is a Research Associate, Institute for Economic Studies, Clark University, Worcester, Mass.

1. Introduction

In a democratic institution, decisions affecting the welfare of its members are often delegated to a few. This voluntary outcome ensures efficiency by reducing the net costs of reaching decisions under the rule of unanimous consent.

Nations who have chosen the democratic form of government rely on elected representatives to reach decisions affecting the welfare of each individual within the collectivity. Depending on the decision rule that is adopted — a simple majority or super majority — the individual welfare may be increased along with everyone else's or sacrificed to enhance the welfare of another. A societal decision that benefits everyone will be undertaken irrespective of the chosen voting rule. When trade-offs exist, the rule adopted becomes crucial. The closer the voting rule to that of unanimity, the lower is the decision cost on the individual and vice versa. To safeguard individual interests against the rule of low majority, constraints on the power of the elected representatives are usually imposed. The most significant constraint which helps balance the cost and benefits of representative government is the right to limit the power of government exercised in free elections and through referendums, and, in rare instances, by amending the Constitution.

Since the government possesses no resources of its own, it must acquire them from private owners. By virtue of its existence it interferes with entitlement to and the use of society resources. For the government to perform a role in the economy (no matter how small), some private interests have to give way to the public interest.

The public and private interests may not necessarily conflict. When they do, the likelihood for reconciliation is much greater in a representative democracy with a high voting rule than is the case with a low one. An optimal decision rule, however, is one that balances at the margin the costs and benefits of the decision rule.

This volume is about budget decisions. It is a comparative study of budgeting in alternative models of government. By focusing on the experiences of selected countries, we aim to uncover the interrelationships between budget outcomes and budget modality. The volume consists of three parts: Part One (Chapters 2 to 7) is devoted to the study of the U.S. public sector. The political economy of budgeting at the federal level and the federal budget structure comprise most of this part. Since the U.S. is organized as a federal system of government, Chapter 6 addresses the issues relating to this form of fiscal organization. Chapter 7 is devoted to an analysis of the U.S. fiscal federalism. Part Two (Chapters 8 to 12) offers an overview of the issues and case studies of budgeting in two federal systems of government, Canada and Germany, and one unitary form of government, the U.K. The implications of the form of government for the size and growth of governments are explored in the last chapter of this part (Chapter 12).

Budget policy is the subject dealt with in the last part of the volume. Chapter 13 outlines briefly the policy issues to be addressed. The two recent topics that are shaping the current debate about the role of government and the consequences of its fiscal actions for current and future generations' welfare are: the large size of the public sector's budget deficits and the government role in economic progress. Chapter 14 is devoted to an analysis of public sector deficits, while in Chapter 15 we explore the links between public sector capital formation and economic growth.

The choice of budget policy of an administration is often the leading domestic issue in national elections. Budget decisions involving tax increases, expenditure reduction, and the underlying budget deficit are not only controversial issues, but also complex ones. Economists disagree among themselves over some aspects of budget policy and over the appropriate budget posture. Politicians, too, disagree, and their disagreement does not necessarily reflect diversity of views among the economics profession. Every year a budget battle is waged — a tug of war ensues between the Legislative branch and the Administration. In a federal system of government, another battle has to be fought between the national and subnational governments. But almost always, a budget is produced and budget actions taken. In the budget-making process, the national interest and constituents' interests somehow get reconciled; at least until the next budget cycle.

PART ONE

Public Sector Budgeting in the United States

2. Introduction and Background

The making of a nation's budget, at least initially, belongs to the executive branch of the government. The legislative branch then approves or disapproves the budget submitted by the executive. From transmittal to execution, it is shaped by the system of government. In a parliamentary system, the legislative branch's power to alter the executive budget is quite limited. Indeed, under the parliamentary system of Canada, Germany and the United Kingdom, the government budget is accepted (or rejected) as a whole without amendment or modifications. Thus, a single budget reflecting the nation's priorities as formulated by the executive is assured.

In the United States budget-making practices, the President 'proposes' and the Congress 'disposes'. The U.S. Congress is free to change the President's budget priorities or substitute one of its own. Not infrequently, especially during the 1980s, one heard the phrase 'dead on arrival' — describing the President's budget transmittal to Congress. After the congressional phase of budgeting is completed, what emerges is a budget that bears little resemblance to the original budget proposal. Even though the Congress participates as an equal partner with the executive in the budget-making process, the political judgement still places the responsibility (credit or blame) for the budget program on the shoulders of the executive, in the person of the President.

Part One of this volume is devoted to the study of public sector budgeting in the U.S. Because the U.S. is a federal system with multiple units of government, there is not a single budget for the sector as a whole nor is there a uniform budget practice or process that is followed by the various levels of government. In contrast, most countries, for example the United Kingdom, have a central government that directs all public activities in the country. In the United States, the constitution guarantees certain powers for the states and thus limits the powers of the central government over lower levels of government.

Expenditure priorities and revenue structure also differ in a federal fiscal system. Demand for public services, tax bases and efforts is not uniformly distributed across communities. Hence, the fiscal structure that evolves over time reflects not only the institutional setting but also the distribution of preferences and wealth across communities. These differences are reflected in their budget processes.

Federal, state and local governments' practices in budget making are governed by the constraints they face. For example, state governments are required by the constitution to balance their budgets while no such constitutional limits exist at the federal level. Municipal governments and school districts depend on federal and state aid to carry out their functions, hence their budget making depends on the form and amounts of aid received. This dependence, especially in recent decades, perhaps explains why the state-local governments have retained the old fiscal year — from July 1 to June 30 — when the federal government changed its fiscal year to October 1 to September 30. Agencies at the state and local government levels, when planning for own budget choices for the upcoming fiscal year, would know nine months in advance the level of federal aid allocated to them at the conclusion of the federal budget process.

Budget making at all levels of government in the U.S. involves three steps: executive preparation and submission; legislative action, and execution and control. By far the most formal, extensive and complex budget making is that at the federal level. Part One of this volume is devoted entirely to federal budgeting. In Chapter 3, budget concepts used for federal budget presentations are reviewed. A detailed account of the federal budget process is presented in Chapter 4. A review of federal budget trends is given in Chapter 5. Because federal fiscal actions affect budget activities of the state and local governments, Chapter 6 addresses those significant features of fiscal federalism. Quantitative analysis of the U.S. federal structure is presented in Chapter 7.

3. The Federal Budget: Concepts and Uses

1 INTRODUCTION

Government fiscal activity can be reported in a number of ways. The form selected, for the most part, is dictated by legal requirements and policy guidelines. Since 1969, the unified budget concept has been used in presenting the federal budget. The U.S. budget for fiscal year 1993 contains, in addition to the current budget concept, alternative presentations of budget activities. In this chapter several of the most important concepts used or proposed for budget presentation are examined. Advantages and disadvantages of each are discussed. The U.S. federal budget for FY 1993 is used as the basis for alternative budget presentations. We begin first with the current budget concept, known as the 'unified budget', or consolidated budget. The next section describes the federal sector as measured in the National Income and Product Accounts and compares it with the unified budget presentation. Also in this section the full employment and cyclically adjusted budget concepts are discussed. In the following section, two alternative ways of presenting the budget accounts are given. One alternative divides the budget between current accounts and capital accounts; the second applies the same principles of budgeting used at the state level to the federal budget. Although the alternative presentations of the federal budget contain essentially the same information as the unified budget, they do not correspond exactly; the presentations are approximates for the purpose of illustrating alternative budget concepts. Related budget concepts are discussed at the end of the section. This includes current services estimates, tax expenditures and the credit budget. The chapter concludes with a brief discussion of generational accounts, a proposed method for assessing the impact of budget decisions on different generations.

2 THE UNIFIED BUDGET CONCEPT

Prior to FY 1969, the U.S. federal budget emphasized different budget concepts in different years, with resulting confusion among the news media in their attempts to report on it, among congressmen in public statements and congressional debate, and certainly among the citizenry in discussing and evaluating federal budget policy. Charges of 'gimmickry' were leveled at the federal government from time to time when there were changes in the budget concepts being used.

In the midst of growing public concern over the citizens' ability to understand and evaluate federal budget policy, President Lyndon B. Johnson appointed the President's Commission on Budget Concepts in March 1967 to conduct a thorough review of the concepts used in presenting the federal budget and to make appropriate recommendations. The report of the Commission (in October 1967) suggested a budget format that would reduce confusion, but at the same time provide the necessary information for decisions on fiscal policy that affect the level of economic activity and for decisions on the allocation of resources among federal government programs.[1] (See appendix for a discussion of major differences between the current budget concept and the Commission's recommendation.) This proposal was in large part adopted as the official format beginning with the FY 1969 budget. Over the years, the budget format has undergone several changes, but the Commission's report continues to provide the basic framework for federal budget concepts and presentations. The current, unified budget, concept is comprehensive, encompassing the full scope of federal programs. The unified budget is essentially on a cash basis — receipts are recorded when collected; outlays when money is actually spent. By its focus on aggregate cash outlays and receipts, the unified budget provides the best information on the federal sector's effect on the national economy.

The unified budget consists of two major groups of funds: federal funds and trust funds. By distinguishing between trust funds and federal funds, the budget presentation, in effect, resurrects an old budget concept — the 'administrative' budget, which was abandoned at the recommendation of the President's Commission on Budget Concepts. (The principal differences between the administrative budget and the unified budget are first, the unified budget includes both federal and trust funds while the administrative budget included only the federal funds, and second, the unified budget eliminates interagency transactions.)

Federal funds comprise all governmental transactions not earmarked by law as belonging to the trust funds. They are used for the general purposes of the government as opposed to specific functions. Federal funds are of several types. The general fund receipts include virtually all income taxes and many excises. Its outlays are funded from fund receipts and from general borrowing from the Treasury. Special funds (for example the reclamation fund) contain federal receipts earmarked for specific purposes, other than for carrying out a cycle of operation. Revolving funds such as the postal service funds, finance a cycle of business-type operations. These funds charge for their services and use the proceeds to finance their expenditures. Revolving funds proceeds are recorded as 'offsets' to expenditures made by the funds. A special class of revolving funds are the intragovernmental funds which carry out their activities in a businesslike fashion within and between government agencies.[2]

Trust funds, such as the social security trust fund and the highway trust fund, consist of funds that are designated by law as trust funds. Trust funds also include funds established to carry out 'the stipulations' of trust agreements where the federal government is the fiduciary. Trust funds' receipts are earmarked and must be used for purposes specified by law. While trust funds' outlays may not exhaust trust funds' receipts, surpluses are permitted to accumulate to be used for future years. In the unified budget accounts, surpluses of trust funds are used to finance the federal funds deficit hence reducing the government need to borrow from the public. Within the category of trust funds, there is a special subcategory of revolving trust funds. These funds are credited with trust-type receipts earmarked by law to carry out a cycle of business-type operations.

Table 3.1 shows receipts, outlays and balances of each fund group. Interfund transactions and offsetting receipts are separately identified. As shown in the top part of the table, federal funds' and trust funds' receipts are almost equal in size — \$713.8 billion of federal funds, \$708.4 billion of trust funds. This comparison however masks the role of interfund transactions and other transactions with the public. Of the \$713.8 billion of federal funds, \$3.8 billion are in the form of intragovernmental transactions. The trust funds receive \$205.8 billion or 29 per cent of the funds income in the form of transfers from the federal funds, \$82.4 billion in the form of interest and the rest, \$123.4 billion, in the form of other transfers (see Table 3.2). In addition to netting out interfund transactions, offsetting receipts are deducted from total funds' receipts to arrive at the unified budget receipts.

Deductions for offsetting receipts arise for two reasons. First, budget receipts of government enterprises are treated as offsets to expenditures (negative expenditures) if the activity generating the receipts is market-oriented as opposed to being essentially a government activity — that is, one involving compulsion or regulation. Thus, the receipts of the Tennessee Valley Authority from the sale of electricity are counted as expenditure offsets and enter the budget as negative expenditures, while patent and copyright fees are counted as receipts and not netted out, since they come from a regulatory activity of the government. Second, in order to avoid counting the same transaction twice, transactions between (or among) government agencies must also be netted out. These intragovernmental transactions are also included as offsetting receipts.

The second part of Table 3.1 presents outlays, and the resulting budget deficit. In the unified budget the concept 'outlays' is used to denote disbursement of funds. Thus outlays include net lending by the government as well as government spending. In FY 1993, total outlays across all fund groups was given as \$1,759.4 billion, 75 per cent of which are federal

Table 3.1 **_Budget summary, fiscal year 1993_**

Item	Billions of dollars[a]
Receipts	
Federal funds	713.8
Trust funds	708.4
Interfund transactions	—205.8
Total budget receipts	1,216.4
Deductions for offsetting receipts	
Proprietary receipts from the public	—48.5
Intragovernmental transactions	—3.8
Total budget receipts, unified basis	1,164.1
Outlays	
Federal funds	1,170.3
Trust funds	589.1
Interfund transactions	—205.8
Total budget outlays	1,553.6
Deductions for offsetting receipts	
Proprietary receipts from the public	—48.5
Intragovernmental transactions	—3.8
Total budget outlays, unified basis	1,501.3
Surplus/Deficit	
Federal funds	—456.5
Trust funds	119.3
Total budget deficit, unified basis	—337.2

Note: a: Estimates.

Source: *The Budget of the United States Government, Fiscal Year 1993*, Part 3, pp. 24, 32 and 54.

funds' outlays, the remainder (25 per cent) are trust funds. After netting out interfund transactions and offsetting receipts, total budget outlays on a unified basis amount to $1,501.3 billion. As shown in Table 3.1, the unified budget deficit is equal to the sum of federal funds' deficit and the trust funds' surpluses. In FY 1993, the unified budget deficit was estimated to be in the order of $337.2 billion compared to a deficit in federal funds accounts in the amount of $456.5 billion.

Because the unified budget concept requires fund groups' transactions to

Table 3.2 *Income, outgo and surplus or deficit by fund group, fiscal year 1993*

Item	Billions of dollars[a]
Federal funds	
Incomes from public	709.9
Outgo to public	964.5
Deficit	–254.6
Receipts from trust funds	3.8
Outgo to trust funds	
Interest	82.4
Other	123.4
Total Deficit	–456.5
Trust funds	
Receipts from the public	502.7
Outgo to the public	589.1
Deficit	–86.4
Receipts from federal funds	
Interest	82.4
Other	123.4
Surplus/Deficit	119.4

Note: a: Estimates.

Source: *The Budget of the United States Government, Fiscal Year 1993*, Part 3, p. 24.

be consolidated, the 'consolidation' tends to obscure the interrelationship between a fund's receipts from the public and a fund's outgo to the public. Table 3.2 reports the income, outgo, and balances of each fund group separated by the type of transaction. Federal funds' transactions with the public show income collected from the public to be in the order of $709.9 billion, compared to disbursement of $964.5 billion for the benefits of individuals. The federal funds' deficit measured by its transaction with the public amounts to $254.6 billion, almost one half of the total deficit recorded for total funds transactions. With respect to the trust funds, it is evident from the table that the surplus in the funds reflects interfund transfers, in the form of interest on accumulated balance (prior years' surplus of the funds) as well as other transfers from the federal funds. Table 3.3 reports unified budget receipts by major type, outlays by functional category and the consolidated budget deficit.

Table 3.3 *Unified budget receipts, outlays and budget deficit, fiscal year 1993*

Item	Billions of dollars[a]
A. Government receipts	
Income, estate, gift, customs duties	648.6
Social insurance taxes and contributions	446.7
Excise taxes and misc. receipts	68.8
Total receipts	1,164.1
B. Outlays by function	
Defense and international	314.2
Science, space, technology	17.0
Energy, natural resources, agriculture	40.8
Commerce and housing credit	63.6
Transportation	35.1
Education, training, employment and social services	49.6
Health and Medicare	237.5
Income security	197.3
Social security	302.3
Veterans' benefits and services	34.3
Other	36.6
Net interest	214.6
Undistributed offsetting receipts	—41.6
Total outlays	1,501.3
C. Surplus/Deficit	—337.2

Note: a: Estimates.

Source: *The Budget of the United States Government, Fiscal Year 1993*, Parts 2 and 3.

Activities Outside the Unified Budget

As mentioned above, the unified budget concept adopted in 1969 calls for the budget to include all of the federal government's fiscal transactions with the public. Beginning in 1971, however, various laws were enacted which effectively removed several entities from the budget. Most of these entities made direct loans to the public. The terms 'on-budget' and 'off-budget' are now common in the budget process. These are used to distinguish between various activities of the federal government. Under current law the 'off-budget' federal entities consist of the two social security trust funds (old-age and survivors' insurance and disability insurance), and the Postal Service

Fund. As will be discussed in the budget process chapter (Chapter 4), the transactions, outlays, receipts, and surpluses or deficits of a federal entity that is off-budget do not appear in the budget; its budget authority is not included in total budget authority, and its activities are not subject to congressional budget authorization.

In 1985, the Balanced Budget and Emergency Deficit Control Act of 1985 (commonly known as the Gramm—Rudman—Hollings Act) placed 'on-budget' all of the entities that were then off-budget. The two social security funds, as of 1986, were moved off-budget, but the funds' deficit or surplus is included in the calculation of deficit targets mandated by the Act.

The Omnibus Budget Reconciliation Act of 1989 moved the Postal Service Fund off-budget and exempted the fund from the deficit targets mandated by the 1985 Act. In fiscal year 1993, off-budget receipts were estimated to be equal to $325.8 billion, on-budget receipts $843.4 billion. Off-budget outlays were estimated at $264.0 billion and on-budget outlays at $1,234.3 billion.

3 THE FEDERAL SECTOR OF THE NATIONAL INCOME AND PRODUCTS ACCOUNTS

The federal sector of the National Income and Product Accounts (NIPAs) corresponds in concept to the system followed in the NIPAs — a system of dual-entry accounts used by the Department of Commerce to estimate the current productive activity of residents of the United States. On one side, the NIPAs show the market values of the currently produced final output of goods and services, classified by type of expenditure: consumer expenditures, gross private domestic investment, federal, state, and local government purchases of goods and services, and net exports. The total of these items is called the gross domestic product (GDP).[3] On the other side, the accounts measure and classify the stream of income generated in the process of producing GDP: wages and salaries, proprietors' income, rental income, corporate profits, and net interest.

The federal sector in the NIPAs, sometimes referred to as the national income accounts budget, is not a budget in that it is not a financial plan for proposing, determining or controlling fiscal activities of the federal government. Rather, the design of the federal sector concept in the NIPAs was intended to be consistent with the conceptual structure of the entire system of integrated accounts. Since GDP is a measure of final output, only government purchases of goods and services that are part of final output are included. Other federal expenditures such as transfer payments, interest payments and grants to state and local governments, which are part of the federal sector in the NIPAs are netted out when all sectors are consolidated into a summary account for the nation as a whole.

Differences Between the NIPAs and the Unified Budget Concept

The NIPAs' treatment of federal government activity differs from that of the unified budget principally in four ways: timing of adjustments, netting and grossing of receipts against spending, exclusion of lending and financial activities, and coverage. Timing differences arise because, in the unified budget, receipts are counted when the cash is collected, and most expenditures are counted when checks are issued (except interest, which is recorded when it accrues). In the NIPAs, personal taxes and social insurance generally are recorded when they are paid, and corporate profit taxes and business taxes are recorded on an accrual basis (when income is earned or when a liability to pay the federal government is incurred). Expenditures in the NIPAs are reported in several ways — on an accrual basis for construction and interest, on a delivery basis for other goods purchased such as defense purchases, and on a checks-issued basis for grants-in-aid, subsidies, and transfer payments. An adjustment must therefore be made in order to reconcile the differences in the timing of receipts and expenditures between the two concepts.

Netting and grossing differences occur because the unified budget records certain transactions as offsets to outlays, but they are recorded in the NIPAs as receipts and outlays. In the NIPAs both receipts and outlays are increased by the amount of the federal government's contributions to its employees' retirement plans because these amounts are counted as part of the compensation of employees (these payments by the government to itself are netted out in the unified budget). Also the NIPAs impute certain items, such as social insurance to employing agencies to finance federal employees' unemployment benefits. The unified budget does not, since federal employees' unemployment benefits are financed by direct appropriations. Lending and financial transactions are treated differently in the unified budget and in the NIPAs. The NIPAs exclude financial transactions of the federal government such as current loans, loan repayments, loan asset sales, and loan guarantees, since they generate no current income or output. For example, the sale of a government asset such as Conrail is counted as a receipt in the unified budget but is not counted in the NIPAs. Similarly, direct lending by agencies such as the Farmers Home Administration is excluded from the NIPAs since none of these agencies' transactions give rise to purchases of final output. As we shall see later on in the chapter, the Federal Credit Reform Act of 1990 introduced several changes in the way lending transactions of the federal government are recorded in the federal budget. In the case of direct loan obligations and loan guarantee commitments made after 1991, the Act requires that the budget records the estimated subsidy cost when the direct loan or loan guarantee is disbursed. The non-subsidized cash flows are recorded in non-budgetary accounts as a means of financing the deficit. This new procedure recognizes that part of the federal lending activity is an

Table 3.4 *Relation of the unified budget to the national income and product accounts' concept, fiscal year 1991*

Item	Billions of dollars[a]
Unified budget receipts	1,054.3
Plus: Government contributions for employee retirement (grossing)	47.2
Other netting and grossing	21.3
Timing adjustments	–5.0
Geographic exclusions	–1.7
Other	0.1
Equals: NIPA receipts	1,116.2
Unified budget outlays	1,323.0
Plus: Lending transactions	–14.0
Deposit insurance and other financial transactions	–66.7
Government contributions for employee retirement (grossing)	47.2
Other netting and grossing	21.3
Defense timing adjustment	3.1
Other timing adjustments	–2.0
Geographic exclusions	–6.8
Bonuses on outer continental shelf land leases	0.9
Other	–0.6
Equals: NIPA expenditures	1,305.4

Note: a: Estimates.

Source: *The Budget of the United States Government, Fiscal Year 1993*, Part 3, p. 19.

exchange of assets of equal value, but that the other part is a subsidy granted by the government to the private borrower. This change will have no effect on NIPAs' treatment of lending activities of the federal government — neither the subsidies nor the loan transactions are recorded.

The budget and the NIPAs' concepts also have coverage differences. The NIPAs exclude U.S. territories for purposes of computing the gross domestic product and related services, but include off-budget federal entities. Table 3.4 shows the major differences between the unified budget and the federal sector in the NIPAs. In Table 3.5, federal sector receipts and expenditures in the NIPAs are reported.

Table 3.5 *Federal transactions in the national income and product accounts, fiscal year 1991*

Item	Billions of dollars[a]
Receipts	
Personal tax and non-tax receipts	474.5
Corporate profit tax accruals	103.2
Indirect business tax and non-tax accruals	75.6
Contributions for social insurance	462.9
Total receipts	1,116.2
Expenditures	
Purchases of goods and services	445.8
Defense	(325.9)
Non-defense	(119.9)
Transfer payments	505.3
Domestic (to persons)	(534.2)
Foreign	(—28.9)
Grants-in-aid to state and local governments	146.3
Net interest paid	185.2
Subsidies less current surplus of government enterprises	22.8
Wage disbursements less accruals	*
Total expenditures	1,305.4
Deficit	—189.2

Notes: * $50 million or less.
a: Estimates.

Source: *The Budget of the United States Government, Fiscal Year 1993*, Part 3, p. 18.

For economic analysis and for the conduct of fiscal policy, the NIPAs' budget concept is preferred to the unified budget. By eliminating such things as purely financial transactions (those involving the exchange of assets) and by using the accrual method, the NIPAs' concept provides a better measure of budget actions than does the unified budget. As shown in Table 3.6, in fiscal year 1988 converting from the unified to the NIPAs' budget concept made relatively little difference in the deficit: the unified budget shows a deficit of $155.1 billion compared with a NIPAs' deficit of $145.8 billion, a difference of $9.3 billion, but the two measures were not always so close.

In fiscal year 1968, for example, the exclusion of $6 billion in loans from

Table 3.6 *Receipts, expenditures and deficits in the unified budget and in the NIPA (in billions of dollars)*

Item	1988	1989	1990	1991
Receipts				
Unified budget	909.0	990.7	1,031.3	1,054.3
NIPA	955.1	1,047.1	1,087.9	1,116.2
Difference	46.1	56.4	56.6	61.9
Expenditures				
Unified budget	1,064.1	1,144.2	1,251.8	1,323.0
NIPA	1,098.5	1,162.1	1,245.6	1,305.4
Difference	34.4	17.9	−6.2	−18.0
Deficit/surplus				
Unified budget	−155.1	−153.5	−220.5	−268.7
NIPA	−145.8	−134.3	−168.0	−189.2
Difference (absolute)	9.3	19.2	54.5	79.5

Notes: Data reported in this table reflects the benchmark revisions of the NIPAs in December 1991. The revisions included a number of conceptual changes affecting the size of the federal sector in the NIPAs. Between 1980—90 the deficit was reduced by $1.6 billion on average.

Source: Based on United States Department of Commerce, *Survey of Current Business* (Sept. 1991).

the NIPAs' budget, and the inclusion of more than $4 billion in receipts as a result of adjusting receipts to an accrual basis, produced a NIPAs' deficit of only about half the size of the unified budget deficit of $25 billion. During the early 1980s, deficits have differed by some $20—30 billion from each other. Over the past few years the NIPAs' and unified budgets have differed substantially. In FY 1990, the unified deficit was 25 per cent higher than the NIPAs' deficit; in fiscal year 1991, the unified deficit was 42 per cent higher than the federal deficit in the NIPAs.

Perhaps the most important reason given for preferring the NIPAs' concept to the unified budget is the need for consistency when comparing data. In economic analysis, the gross national product or gross domestic product is commonly used as an indicator of the level of economic activity. To see how changes in fiscal decisions affect the level of economic activity, it is desirable to use as a measure of government policy a data series that is conceptually consistent with the GDP estimates. As shown above, the NIPAs' budget concept does correspond to the system of accounts used to measure GDP while the unified budget does not.

The Full-Employment Budget and the Cyclically Adjusted Budget

Federal receipts and outlays are not determined solely by tax laws and appropriations bills. They are also determined in part by the level of economic activity. When the economy is in a recession both corporate and personal tax receipts fall due to the decrease in corporate profits and personal income. This reduction in income taxes triggers an automatic stabilizing influence on the economy. Government outlays rise during the recession as more people become eligible to receive benefits from income maintenance programs such as unemployment compensation and food stamps. The fall in budget receipts together with the rise in outlays increase (reduce) the level of the budget deficit (surplus).

In other words, the direction of causation runs both ways: the budget affects the aggregate level of activities in the economy; the economy affects the state of the budget balance. In order to disentangle these two forces, economists have developed the concept of the full-employment budget. This is a hypothetical construct designed to insulate the budget totals from the effects of changes in the level of economic activity. It shows what outlays and receipts would have been if the labor force were fully employed.[4] The full employment concept — popular in the 1960s and the 1970s — lost favor with policy makers in the 1980s. Basically, objections to the concept have arisen over the arbitrary choice of the full-employment unemployment rate. Economists have long held that a 4 per cent rate of unemployment defines a state of full employment in the economy. In the late 1970s and early 1980s, with the onset of double digit inflation and unemployment rates, the theoretical development of a vertical Phillips curve (i.e. the absence of a trade-off between inflation and employment in the long run) and the national rate of unemployment concept, the full employment concepts for output and the budget were dropped.[5] Since the emphasis of the full employment concept has been on identifying the component of the budget deficit that reflects discretionary actions and not the cycle-induced changes in the budget, the new concepts developed to replace it address this function rather than the creation of an alternative budget concept. The two budget concepts now in use are: the structural or 'standardized-employment' budget and the cycle-neutral or 'cycle-adjusted' budget. The standard employment budget estimated by the Congressional Budget Office (CBO) beginning FY 1984, is an estimate of what budget receipts, expenditures and deficits would be if the economy were continuously operating at its potential (CBO estimated this to be at an unemployment rate of 6 per cent).[6] The difference between the unified budget deficit and the standardized employment deficit would then measure the cycle effects on the budget. The Council of Economic Advisers (CEA) in their 1985 report provides an alternate definition of the structural deficit. According to the report, the structural component is the amount of the deficit that would remain even if the unemployment rate were at the inflation threshold level. For 1983 the inflation threshold level of unemployment was estimated to be 6.5 per cent.[7]

The cyclically adjusted budget concept was developed by Thomas Holloway and first appeared in his 1984 paper: 'Simplified Reduced Form Methods to Estimate Cyclical And Inflation Components of the Budget'. Since then, the Department of Commerce, Survey of Current Business, has published estimates of the cycle-adjusted deficit on a NIPAs' basis.[8]

To calculate a cycle-adjusted budget a reference trend for real output is needed. Cyclically adjusted receipts, expenditures, and surpluses or deficits are estimates of what these measures would be if the economy were moving along a trend growth path — a path free from cyclical fluctuations. Accordingly, the cycle-adjusted budget magnitude is free from cycle effects. Several methods are proposed for constructing the cycle-adjusted trend: a peak-to-peak reference trend, a trough-to-trough reference trend, and a reference trend based on middle expansion.[9] The Bureau of Economic Analysis offers two measures of the cyclically adjusted budget: one a middle expansion trend GNP and one based on a six per cent unemployment rate trend GNP. Both calculations are reported in the *Survey of Current Business*.[10]

To summarize this discussion of alternative measures of the budget gap, Table 3.7 reports the deficit for the NIPAs' budget, the cyclically adjusted budgets for fiscal years 1986-1990.

4 ALTERNATIVE BUDGET PRESENTATION

The Capital or Divided Budget Concept

From time to time, proposals have been made that the federal government should adopt another method in presenting its budget. One such proposal is the capital or divided budget. The basic idea of the capital budget is the separation of the consolidated budget into two parts, the 'current' and the 'capital' accounts. The general format of a divided budget is shown in Table 3.8 with dollar entries obtained from the budget for FY 1993. The current account component of the budget would include all expenditures except purchases of assets by the government and investment in human capital; all receipts except sales of government assets or similar type of income. The capital account part would show as expenditures purchases of government assets as well as investment in human capital and show sales of government assets and funds transferred from the current account to cover depreciation as receipts. As indicated in Table 3.8, the divided budget shows a deficit of $129 billion in the current account and $209 billion in the capital account, a consolidated deficit of $338 billion. It is to be emphasized that the allocations of budget aggregates reported in the table

Table 3.7 *Alternative measurement of the federal budget deficit, 1986–90*

Item	1986	1987	1988	1989	1990
Cyclically adjusted budget[a]					
Receipts, billions of dollars	840.1	921.0	947.1	1,025.5	1,100.8
% of trend GNP	19.6	20.4	19.8	20.1	20.3
Expenditures, billions of dollars	1,027.9	1,068.3	1,119.6	1,189.6	1,278.1
% of trend GNP	24.0	23.7	23.4	23.3	23.5
Surplus or deficit (—), billions of dollars	—187.9	—147.3	—172.5	—164.1	—177.3
% of trend GNP	—4.4	—3.3	—3.6	—3.2	—3.3
NIPA deficit	—206.9	—158.9	—145.8	—134.3	—166.0
Addendum:					
GNP, billions of dollars	4,286.4	4,514.6	4,786.7	5,101.5	5,432.5

Note: a: Calculation based on 6 per cent unemployment rate trend GNP.

Source: United States Department of Commerce, *Survey of Current Business* (May issues).

are for illustrative purposes only, as the segregation of budget totals between the current and capital accounts are to some extent arbitrary.

The capital budget proposal has been and still is quite controversial. Opposition to the concept centers on the fundamentals behind the divided budget. Under the proposal, investment outlays would be separated from all other outlays. Government investment would be financed by borrowing while all other outlays would be financed by current taxation, or current accounts receipts. Advocates of a capital budget argue that first, it would provide the information and incentives necessary to promote efficiency in government and secondly, it would eliminate the often involved and cumbersome discussion of the burden of the public debt. In addition, the distortion of consumer choice over time caused by debt rather than tax financing of government spending would be eliminated. Its critics argue that a capital budget would distort the setting of budget priorities, frustrate stabilization policy, and raise a host of problems in its implementation. Before turning to these criticisms, let us first consider the merits of the capital budget as they relate to the burdens and distortions created by debt financing.

In a full-employment setting, debt-financed public expenditures may impose a burden on future generations, either because government borrowing displaces private borrowing and thus reduces private capital formation or because government use of resources through borrowing results in extra taxation imposed on future generations to service the debt. This debt service has no counterpart when the resource is transferred through taxation. If a capital budget were adopted, only outlays of the investment type would be financed by debt issues. Since future generations are expected to benefit from these outlays, no burden would be imposed on them as taxes were increased to service the debt. In this case the capital budget would balance future taxes with future benefits.

The distortion of individuals' choice over time under debt financing occurs because individuals have less than perfect foresight about the relation of their future tax liability (connected with servicing the debt) to their current tax liability. In effect, they shift the burden of the debt-financed outlays to future generations, while no such shift is possible with current taxation. Thus, under conditions of full employment, individuals are able to increase their total consumption, including consumption of government goods and services, through debt finance. Future consumption will be reduced not only because of the lower levels of private capital formation, but also because of the additional future taxes that must be levied to service the debt. If debt finance was restricted to investment-type activities, this distortion would not take place — current benefits of government expenditures would be paid for by current taxes and future benefits by future taxes.

Opponents of the capital budget believe that it would not promote efficiency. Because investment outlays would be financed by debt, the budget constraint is relaxed — budget decisions would be biased in favor of capital spending. The arguments against the capital budget were summed up by Kermit Gordon (1966). He pointed out that, unlike the budgets of business firms (where capital budgeting is used), the purpose of the federal budget is not to measure profit or show the ownership of assets. Rather it is to present in detail the financial dimensions of the President's plan for conducting the affairs of the nation. A divided budget, by excluding capital-type outlays from the President's budget, would produce confusion rather than clarity. Moreover, the fiscal principle of balancing the ordinary (current account) budget and borrowing to finance capital outlays would introduce biases in favor of 'investment in bricks and concrete' and against that for 'people and knowledge' and would not guarantee a level of aggregate demand consistent with stabilization purposes.

The problem with the capital budget, as this critique implies, does not, however, stem from the concept *per se* but rather from the 'standard' conception of a capital budget. A divided budget disaggregates the total but does not change that total. What the adoption of a capital budget would do is to change the budget presentations. Under present practice, the federal budget focuses on the President's program rather than on the way the expenditures are financed. Capital budgeting would retain the existing structure but arrange the information in such a way that emphasis is placed on the type of activities as well as the sources of funds used to finance these

Table 3.8 A capital budget: an illustration (in billions of dollars)

A. Current Account	
Receipts	
Income, Estate, Gift, Custom Duties	648.6
Excise taxes and misc.	53.7
Other receipts	446.7
TOTAL	1,149.0
Outlays	
Purchases of current goods and services, transfer payments, net interest and grants to state and local governments (other than for purchasing of assets)	1,236.4
Depreciation of government assets	20.4
TOTAL	1,278.8
Surplus/Deficit	—129.1

Table 3.8 continued

B. Capital Accounts: Physical and Human Capital	
Purchases of government assets	
Direct	97.3
Defense	(76.5)
Non-defense	(20.5)
Grants to state and local governments for purchases of assets	29.6
Outlays for R&D	95.1
Defense	(46.2)
Non-defense	(28.8)
Outlays for education and training	42.5
Direct	(20.7)
Grants to state and local	(21.8)
TOTAL Purchases	244.5
Receipts	
Sales of government assets	11.4
Depreciation transferred from current accounts	20.4
Rents from leases of government assets	2.7
TOTAL Receipts	35.5
Surplus/Deficit	–209.0
TOTAL Surplus/Deficit	–338.1
Memorandum:	
Surplus/Deficit capital account (Physical capital only)	(91.4)
Surplus/Deficit current account (including spending on R&D and education and training)	(246.7)

Source: Calculated using data on federal capital outlays reported in *The Budget of the United States Government, Fiscal Year 1993*, Part 3.

activities. As to the preference for investment in bricks instead of humans this need not arise. Government expenditures on education and public health have long been recognized as investments in human capital. They are just as 'legitimate' as investments in physical capital. While it would not be easy to separate government outlays on human resources between consumption and investment, it would be desirable to make a start in this direction. A divided budget would help rather than hinder spending on human capital. It would help to offset the current tax-induced bias against investments in human capital — it might lead to modification of government practices such as the disallowance for tax purposes of depreciation on human capital; and the nondeductibility of educational expenses.

Capital budget presentation for the federal government seems to be gaining support. Recent developments — high levels of federal deficits and the emerging consensus that the U.S. capital stock has been eroded — are the motivations behind the renewed interest in the capital budget. The Federal Capital Investment Program Information Act of 1984 (Title II of public law 98-501) requires that the federal budget include projections of federal physical capital spending and information regarding recent assessments of public civilian capital needs.[11] In its 1989 report *Managing the Cost of Government: Proposals for Reforming Federal Budgeting Practice*, the General Accounting Office (GAO) went so far as to propose the adoption of the capital budget. According to the GAO's report the consolidated budget presentation of government activities has 'biased' decision making against capital investment by requiring recording of the entire cost of an asset in the year of acquisition and failed to distinguish operating deficits from capital financing requirements.

Unlike our presentation of a divided budget outlined above (Table 3.8), the GAO's proposal would divide the consolidated budget into three separate fund groups; each fund's activities would then be divided into capital and operating budgets. The GAO's budget presentation is given in Table 3.9. As shown in the table, the unified budget receipts, outlays and deficit are disaggregated to distinguish asset acquisition and capital financing requirement from outlays on current accounts and their financing requirements. The financing requirement as reported in the unified budget, $337.2 billion, is now decomposed into an operating budget deficit of $311.1 billion and a capital budget deficit of $26.1 billion. It is obvious then, that most of the unified budget deficit (92.3 per cent) is attributable to the budget gap on current accounts — consumption-type expenditures by far outpaced tax efforts of the federal government.

The GAO proposal may take some time to be implemented. The basic problem encountered in developing this budget concept has to do with the allocation of depreciation charges to the trust funds. Because trust funds (such as the highway and airport trust funds) finance their investments through earmarked taxes, recording both earmarked receipts and depreciation would require double counting with respect to assets acquired by the trust funds.[12] Other objections voiced against the GAO proposal are the same as those presented earlier regarding the capital budget concept.

Since decisions on government investment policies are part of the budget decision-making process, the adoption of a capital budget for the federal government would raise three questions: Given the state of the economy, what is the appropriate tax, money, or debt policy? Do the benefits of the public investment project accrue to present as well as future generations or do they only benefit future generations? And, are the benefits and costs identifiable and unambiguous?

The feasibility of capital budgeting may hinge on the ability of budget makers to identify the benefits and beneficiaries of investment projects, and the effect of debt-financed capital outlays on countercyclical fiscal policy. Until now the concept of capital budgeting for the federal government has been rejected. But in the light of the recent developments a capital budget may not be too far off in the future.

Table 3.9 *GAO: a divided federal budget presentation, fiscal year 1993 (in billions of dollars)*

	Total	General Fund	Trust Fund	Enterprise Fund[a]
	A. Operating Budget			
Receipts				
General receipts	1138.3	690.3	468.0	—
Offsetting collections				
proprietary receipts from the public	47.6	18.6	28.1	0.4
reimbursements to appropriations	99.9	21.3	7.0	71.6
Total revenues	1,285.8	730.2	483.0	72.0
Outlays				
Functional outlays	1,573.6	893.8	568.1	111.5
Additional operating costs				
asset consumption	20.4	20.4	—	—
pension liabilities	—	28.9	–28.9	—
Total before transfers	1,594.0	943.1	539.2	111.5
Interfund transfers	3.1	201.9	–198.8	—
Total expenditures	1,596.9	1,145.0	340.3	111.5
Surplus/Deficit	–311.1	–414.8	142.7	–39.4

Table 3.9 continued

	Total	General Fund	Trust Fund	Enterprise Fund[a]
		B. Capital Budget		
Receipts				
Government receipts	25.7	—	25.7	—
Offsetting receipts				
proprietary receipts from public	0.9	0.1	0.8	—
reimbursements to appropriations	16.7	8.4	*	8.3
Total revenues	43.3	8.5	26.6	8.3
Outlays				
Functional outlays	93.0	56.4	24.2	12.3
Additional costs				
asset consumption	–20.4	–20.4	—	—
pension liabilities	—	—	—	—
Total investments before transfers	72.6	36.1	24.2	12.3
Interfund transfers	–3.1	—	–3.1	—
Total Outlays	69.5	36.1	21.1	12.3
Surplus/Deficit	–26.1	–27.6	5.5	–4.1
Surplus/Deficit total Divided budget basis	–337.2	–442.4	148.2	–43.5

Notes: Totals may not add up due to rounding.
* $50 million or less.
a: Enterprise entities include the U.S. Postal Service and Tennessee Valley Authority.

Source: *The Budget of the United States Government, Fiscal Year 1993*, Part 3, p.54.

State-Budget Format for the Federal Government

In political discussions, especially during the presidential elections, presidential candidates and in particular state office holders often contrast the fiscal discipline exercised by the state government as manifest in balanced budgets at the state level with the ever increasing budget imbalances at the federal level. Some politicians have even gone as far as to argue that the federal deficit would disappear if the federal government were to adopt budget practices or protocol similar to those exercised by state governments.

Before presenting what a state-type budget format would mean for the federal budget, it is perhaps useful to point out a fundamental difference between budget making at the federal and state levels. In the United States, most state governments are subject to the constitutional requirement of a balanced budget. Many states, especially in recent years, have also been bound by constitutional limits on taxes and spending. These limits result in budget procedures that differ significantly from those at the federal level as no such limits are imposed on the federal government. Indeed, efforts to amend the U.S. Constitution to ensure a balanced federal budget have failed time and again for lack of support among policy makers as well as by the economics profession.

State government activities are divided into three types of accounts: general government, special (trust) funds and capital funds. The focus of the state budget is on the general government account. Using the budget of the state of California as an example, the unified budget total as given in the U.S. budget document for FY 1993 was rearranged so that it would correspond (as far as possible) to that state-type budget presentation. An overview of what the federal budget presentation would be like if this practice was followed is given in Table 3.10. As shown in the table, the information content, although similar to that of the divided-capital budget, is much more difficult to emulate, particularly in regards to allocating amortization of prior debt to expenditures by function in the general fund. Moreover, because of the stabilization role of the federal government (no such role is assigned to state governments), the federal budget focus has to be on the consolidated budget accounts and not on simply the general fund accounts.

Other Budget Concepts

A series of congressional acts aimed at improving budget accountability and control led to the development of other budget concepts: the current services budget or base-line budget estimates, tax expenditures, and the credit budget.

Current services estimates

The current services budget shows what receipts and outlays would be without policy changes. These budget estimates are neither recommended amounts nor forecasts of budget aggregates, rather they form the bases

Table 3.10 *State-type presentation of the federal budget, fiscal year 1993 (in billions of dollars)*

	General Fund	Special Fund	Capital Fund[a]	Total Incl. Bond Funds[b]
Revenues				
Government receipts	647.5	441.6	—	1,089.1
Other receipts	40.7	29.2	—	69.9
Offsetting collections				
proprietary rights	12.7	24.3	—	37.0
reimbursements to appropriations	45.6	0.2	—	45.8
interfund transfers	3.8	108.6	—	112.4
TOTAL	750.3	603.9		1,354.3
Outlays				
Functional outlays	1,277.3	525.4	88.8	1,891.5
Surplus/Deficit	–527.0	78.6	–88.8	–537.2

Notes: a: Capital outlays include capital projects and the associated amortization.
b: An amortization of prior debt was estimated and allocated as expenditures of the general fund.

Source: *The Budget of the United States Government, Fiscal Year 1993*, Part 3, pp. 57–8.

against which the administration or congressional budget proposals can be compared. Both the Office of Management and Budget (OMB) and the Congressional Budget Office (CBO) calculate current services estimates. These estimates are based on two assumptions: that the level of budget receipts is that which would be generated under existing tax law (including scheduled changes) and the level of budget outlays is that needed to maintain ongoing programs after adjusting for inflation. The difference between the unified budget proposal and current services budget estimates reflects the administration's budget initiatives. Currently, in accordance with the Gramm—Rudman—Hollings Act (GRH) of 1985, the President's budget shows two sets of estimates — current services and base-line estimates conforming with the GRH deficit targets.

Tax expenditures

The Congressional Budget Act of 1974 requires that in the unified budget presentation, tax expenditures are to be identified and estimates of their magnitudes provided by functional category. Tax expenditures, as the name suggests, are not budget outlays; rather these are provisions in the tax code that grant subsidies in the form of tax incentives to promote certain activities and to assist certain groups. For example, capital formation is encouraged by permitting businesses to claim some portion of the cost of an investment as a credit on their income tax returns; home ownership is encouraged by allowing home owners to deduct mortgage interest and property taxes from their taxable income. As is clear from these two examples, tax expenditures involve no transfer of funds from the government to the private sector. The federal government forgoes some of the revenue that it otherwise would have collected, and the beneficiary taxpayers (persons and firms) pay lower taxes than they otherwise would have.

Tax expenditures may be defined more formally as those revenue losses attributable to provisions of the federal income tax laws that allow a 'special exclusion, exemption, or deduction from gross income or [which provide] a special credit, preferential tax rate, or deferral of tax liability'.[13] Provisions resulting in tax expenditures have also been defined as exceptions to the normal structure of the tax system.

Unfortunately, these definitions are necessarily somewhat ambiguous. The first does not classify all exclusions, exemptions, or deductions as tax expenditures, but only those that are in some way 'special'. The second definition suggests that these provisions are 'special' in that they represent departures from the 'normal' structure of the income tax, but the normal structure is not specified.[14] This is not the place to go into all the considerations involved in determining which tax provisions should be called tax expenditures and which should not. Suffice it to say that there is general agreement on most of the provisions that qualify as tax expenditures. One representative list is given in Table 3.11.

The credit budget

In addition to direct spending and tax expenditures, the federal government engages in activities that affect aggregate demand for credits. Federal credit activity takes three forms: direct loans, loan guarantees, and federal sponsorship (GSEs). A direct loan is a cash payment by a federal agency to a borrower to be repaid with interest over the duration of the loan. Direct loans are usually made at subsidized interest. A guaranteed loan does not involve cash payment by the government; rather it represents an obligation to repay the lender both the principal and interest in case of default. GSEs — shorthand for government-sponsored enterprises — are private corporations chartered by the U.S. government to perform certain public functions (examples are: Federal National Mortgage Corporation, Student Loan Market Association, Federal Home Loan Mortgage Corporation, and Federal Agriculture Mortgage Corporation). Most GSEs

Table 3.11 *Estimated tax expenditures in the income tax (top twenty ranked items, fiscal year 1993)*

	Revenue loss billions of dollars
Net exclusion of employer plan pension contributions and earnings	51.2
Exclusion of employer contributions for medical insurance premiums and medical care	43.1
Deductibility of mortgage interest on owner-occupied homes	42.9
Step-up basis of capital gains at death	28.1
Accelerated depreciation (Normal tax method)	26.5
Deductibility of nonbusiness State and local taxes other than on owner-occupied homes	23.8
Exclusion of OASI benefits for retired workers	19.4
Deductibility of charitable contributions	18.0
Deferral of capital gains on home sales	13.9
Deductibility of state and local property tax on owner-occupied homes	12.6
Exclusion of interest on public purpose state and local debt	11.7
Exclusion of interest on life insurance savings	8.7
Exclusion of untaxed Medicare benefits	8.0
Exception from passive loss rules for $25,000 of rental loss	6.6
Net exclusion of IRA pension contributions and earnings	5.5
Exclusion of workmen's compensation benefits	3.7
Preferential treatment of capital gains (normal tax method)	3.7
Exclusion of social security benefits for dependents and survivors	3.6
Deductibility of medical expenses	3.4
Exclusion of interest on industrial development bonds	3.3

Source: *The Budget of the United States Government, Fiscal Year 1993*, Part 3, p. 39.

are financial intermediaries providing credits to private borrowers. Since GSEs do not generate their own resources, they must borrow money to supply credit. GSEs' borrowing usually comes from the U.S. Treasury. Their own debt is treated by banks as equivalent to Treasury debt.

Over the years, federal credit activities have been treated as either on-budget or off-budget items. Prior to the 1969 budget (when the unified budget concept was adopted), credit activities were recorded on-budget — disbursements as spending, loan repayments as receipts — unless the law stipulated them to be offset against spending in the loan account, thereby creating revolving funds, e.g. the Export-Import Bank.

In the pre-unified budget era most federal loans came to be included in revolving funds. Loan guarantees were treated as non-budgetary contingent liabilities, hence not recorded at the time they were made. They were recorded in the budget as spending only when disbursements occurred. However, loan guarantee premiums were recorded as budget income (or offsetting collections) at the time the guarantee was made. GSE activities were excluded from the regular (administrative) budget and neither treated as direct loans nor as loan guarantees. Because of differences in budgetary treatment of federal credit activities, the President's Commission on Budget Concepts sought to address this issue. The Commission made two recommendations: 1. dividing the budget into an 'expenditure account' and a 'loan account' and 2. dividing the face value of direct loans between a subsidy element and an expenditure element. The subsidy part would be charged to the expenditure account and the non-subsidized part charged to the loan account.[15] Since the GSEs are private corporations, the Commission recommended that their activities be excluded from the budget.

The explosive growth of federal credit, especially in the 1970s, led to attempts at controlling credit expansion. Efforts to do so began in 1981, when the Reagan administration proposed and the Congress enacted the credit budget. The credit budget establishes targets for direct and guaranteed loan programs. Since then every budget resolution has contained targets for federal credit.

The newly created credit budget is, however, limited in scope. It includes both direct loans and loan guarantees, but does not include the lending of GSEs. Moreover, the subsidy element of the credit is not treated as a budget expenditure, and is hence exempt from limitations imposed by congressional acts on budget expenditures.

The failure of the credit budget to control federal credit activities prompted many to call for a more thorough credit reform. The goal of the reform is to 'display and control' the subsidies in the budget program.[16] The Federal Credit Reform Act of 1990 is the latest attempt at reforming federal credits. Beginning with FY 1992, the federal budget presentation incorporated the new credit accounting procedure spelled out by the Act. Under this system, federal direct loans and loan guarantees (but not GSEs), would be divided into two components: the subsidy value of all new loans and new loan guarantees would have to be appropriated on an annual basis and scored (budget score keeping) separately from the non-subsidized component. The non-subsidized portion of the loans would be recorded in the appropriate financing accounts: one account for direct loan financing, the other for loan guarantees.[17] In FY 1991, total net lending of the federal sector amounted to $496.0 billion. Of this total, federal direct loans, loan guarantees and GSE loans amounted to $105.3 billion. The largest component of this lending activity is carried out by GSEs with over $90 billion.

5 SUMMARY AND CONCLUSIONS

Several budget concepts, each with its own particular uses, have been examined in this chapter. The unified budget proposed by the President and modified and enhanced by the Congress is the financial plan of the federal government. The NIPAs' budget, which is a statement of federal spending and taxation as recorded in the national income and product accounts, measures the impact of fiscal policy on the economy. The full-employment budget and the cyclically adjusted budgets are hypothetical constructs designed to show what expenditures and taxes would be if the economy were operating at a cycle-neutral trend growth path.

Proposals for a federal capital budget were also examined. The capital or divided budget separates government accounts into two components: consumption type and investment type. Consumption activities would be financed by current taxes while capital outlays would be financed by debt. Current taxes would also be used to meet depreciation charges and for amortization of the debt. Other concepts relevant to budget presentations such as tax expenditures, current services budget estimates, and the credit budget were also discussed. This chapter concludes with a brief discussion of a new accounting concept — generational accounts — for the public sector (federal, state and local).

Generational accounts (GAs), a method developed by Auerbach, Gokhale and Kotlikoff (1992), offer budget analysts and policy makers a framework for comparing fiscal actions across various generations. By extending budget incidence calculation to overlapping generations, the technique enhances our knowledge of how budget decisions affect individuals of different generations. A basic ingredient in this type of accounting is the 'imputation' of the net fiscal surplus to members of each generation. According to the authors, GAs measure as of a particular base year 'the present value of the future taxes that the average member of each given generation is estimated to pay to the government minus the present value of the future transfers that the average member is estimated to receive'.[18]

In its initial stages of development the generational accounts are by necessity quite limited. Specifically GAs include taxes paid to the government (labor and capital income taxes, payroll taxes and excises) and transfers received (social security, health and welfare) but do not impute the value of public goods and services. This shortcoming is especially critical in view of the fact that the GAs system covers the entire public sector —

federal, state and local. Since almost all activities of the state-local governments are in the nature of merit or semi-public goods, and investment in infrastructure (physical and human), the GAs system fails to account for spillovers across generations.

The second limitation is that the accounts begin as of a given year — all previous gains or losses are forgone, hence a comparison of one generation with another (the objective of GAs) is not possible. Most critical perhaps is the absence in the calculation of second-order effects of fiscal actions. Clearly a tax cut aimed at lifting the growth path of the economy may have intergenerational distributional effects which are quite different from a policy that relies on changes in government spending financed by a combination of taxes and debts. The authors recognize these limitations as well as others. The GAs concept, nonetheless, is a step in the right direction. When fully developed it might even shed some light on some of the more controversial budget questions such as the burden of the debt, intergovernmental equity in the distribution of tax burdens or the design of optimal tax-transfer structures.

APPENDIX

Highlights of the Recommendations of the President's Commission on Budget Concepts

Prior to 1969, the administrative budget was the official budget of the U.S. government although other presentations such as the Consolidated Cash budget or the National Income Accounts budget were frequently used especially in conjunction with the size of the deficit. The Commission on Budget Concepts recommended strongly that the President's budget presentation give no attention to a surplus or deficit calculated on the basis of the administrative budget, because such amounts do not reflect total budget transactions.

The Commission also recommended using the single concept 'outlays' to denote disbursement of funds. This would include net lending by the government as well as government spending. The Commission recommended, however, that lending activities of the federal government be clearly distinguished from expenditures in the budget summary. This recommendation was based on the belief that the economic impact of government lending differs from that of government spending on goods and services and from that of transfer payments such as social security benefits. When the federal government makes a loan, the Commission reasoned, the recipient incurs a liability; his spending behavior is thus likely to be different from the spending behavior of a recipient of social security benefits or of a federal wage payment.

The Commission also recommended putting all receipts and expenditures on an accrual basis, that is, counting expenditures when the government incurs a liability to pay for goods and services and counting receipts when the private sector incurs a liability to make payments to the federal government. The logic of this concept is that the economic impact of the budget occurs when goods are produced for federal government use and when taxpayers incur a tax liability to the government.

With respect to federal entities (off-budget) such as the Export-Import Bank, the Commission strongly recommended that the budget should include all programs and activities of these agencies. Only GSEs were to be excluded because of their private corporate status.

NOTES

1. President's Commission on Budget Concepts (1967).
2. Office of Management and Budget (1992), p. 23.
3. The GDP concept replaced GNP as a measure of national income and products in 1991. The distinctions between GDP and GNP are discussed in the August 1991 issue of the *Survey of Current Business*.
4. From the early 1960s, an unemployment rate of 4 per cent was used to define a condition of full employment, although this definition was frequently criticized, especially in the 1970s. In its 1977 annual report, the Council of Economic Advisers suggested a 4.9 per cent rate as more appropriate to take account of changes in the composition of the labor force since the mid-1950s. In the 1980s a 6 per cent unemployment rate was believed to represent the full-employment unemployment rate.
5. Fellner, among others, has criticized the use of full employment output as the benchmark for calculating the budget gap. According to Fellner the size of an economy's output potential depends on a large number of variables which are not specified in the methods used to obtain that output path. For details see Fellner (1982), p. 3.
6. Congressional Budget Office (1983), pp. 17—18.
7. Council of Economic Advisers (1984), p. 36.
8. Holloway (1984).
9. For later years, the *Survey* publishes a cyclically adjusted budget estimated at a 6 per cent unemployment rate trend GNP. For peak-to-peak, see Ott (1983) and de Leeuw *et al.* (1980).
10. For discussion of the use of the capital budget within this framework, see Bailey (1972).
11. For detail on physical or other capital presentations for the federal government, see Office of Management and Budget (1992), Part 3.
12. Ibid.
13. Congressional Budget Office (1976), p. 381. See also Senate Committee on the Budget (1976).
14. See Office of Management and Budget (1977), pp. 371, 379, 425, 433.
15. President's Commission on Budget Concepts (1967), p. 27.
16. Cuny (1991), p. 26.
17. For a detailed discussion of the Credit Reform Act of 1990, see Cuny (1991).
18. Office of Management and Budget (1992), Part 3, p.7.

REFERENCES

Auerbach, A., Gokhale, J. and Kotlikoff, L.J.(1992) 'Social Security and Medicare Policy from the Perspective of Generational Accounting' in Poterba, J.M. (ed.), *Tax Policy and The Economy*, Cambridge, MA, National Bureau of Economic Research, MIT Press.

Bailey, M.J. (1972), 'The Optimal Full-Employment Surplus', *Journal of Political Economy*, **80** (July/August), pp. 649—61.

Congressional Budget Office (1976), *Budget Options for Fiscal Year 1977: A Report to the Senate and House Committee on the Budget*, Washington D.C., U.S. Government Printing Office.

Congressional Budget Office (1983), *An Analysis of the President's Budgetary Proposals for Fiscal Year 1984*, Washington D.C., U.S. Government Printing Office.

Council of Economic Advisers (1977), *Economic Report of the President 1977*, Washington D.C., U.S. Government Printing Office.

Council of Economic Advisers (1984), *Economic Report of the President 1984*, Washington D.C., U.S. Government Printing Office.

Cuny, T.J. (1991), 'Federal Credit Reform', *Public Budgeting and Finance*, Summer.

de Leeuw, F. *et al*. (1980), 'The High Employment Budget: New Estimates 1955—80', *Survey of Current Business*, **60** (11), pp. 13—43.

Fellner, W. (1982), *The High Employment Budget and the Potential Output: A Critique Focusing on Two Recent Contributions*, Washington D.C., American Enterprise Institute.

General Accounting Office (1989), *Managing the Cost of Government: Proposals for Reforming Federal Budgeting Practice*, Washington D.C., U.S. Government Printing Office.

Gordon, K. (1966), 'Reflections on Spending', *Public Policy*, **15**, pp. 7—9 (Brookings Reprint 125).

Holloway, T. (1984), 'Simplified Reduced Form Methods to Estimate Cyclical and Inflation Components of the Budget', Washington D.C., U.S. Department of Commerce, processed.

Office of Management and Budget (1977), *Budget of the United States Government, Fiscal Year 1978*, Washington D.C., U.S. Government Printing Office.

Office of Management and Budget (1992), *Budget of the United States Government, Fiscal Year 1993*, Washington D.C., U.S. Government Printing Office.

Ott, A.F. (1983), 'Output and Budgetary Cost of Disinflation', *Western Tax Review*, **4** (2), pp. 89—108.

President's Commission on Budget Concepts (1967), *Report of the President's Commission on Budget Concepts*, Washington D.C., U.S. Government Printing Office.

Senate Committee on the Budget (1976), *Tax Expenditures: Compendium of Background Material on Individual Provisions*, Washington D.C., U.S. Government Printing Office.

United States Department of Commerce (1991), *Survey of Current Business*, **71**(8), Washington D.C., U.S. Government Printing Office.

4. The Federal Budget Process

1 INTRODUCTION

Crucial to any discussion of budget policy, which entails the setting of levels and composition of taxes and expenditures to achieve certain goals, is an understanding of the administrative and the legislative process through which expenditures and taxes are determined. This chapter describes the process for federal government expenditures and also discusses briefly the forces and individuals involved in making the decisions that go into the final budget.

The decision-making process on government receipts is much different from the process for government expenditures, and the two cannot be described in a parallel fashion. The budget document, for example, contains a vast array of data on proposed spending but virtually nothing on tax measures. Moreover, the Constitution requires that 'all bills for raising revenue shall originate in the House of Representatives; but the Senate may propose or concur with amendments as on other bills' (Article I, Section 7). For these reasons, the description in this chapter is limited to the expenditure process.

It is worth noting at the outset that the federal budget process has undergone numerous changes, especially in the last 20 years or so. (A list of major laws is given in the appendix.) For the first 132 years, Congress controlled the finances of the federal government, with minor exceptions. With the increasing involvement of the federal government in the economy and changes in the economic system, congressional control began to erode while that of the executive increased. In the 1921 Budget and Accounting Act, Congress reorganized the budgetary function of the executive branch. The trend toward executive branch dominance in the budgetary process was arrested with the passage of the Congressional Budget and Impoundment Control Act of 1974, which restored to Congress some of the power over budget making it had lost and provided it with better means and greater responsibility for controlling the budget.

The 1974 Budget Act was amended in 1985 and 1990 because of 'grid lock' over budget aggregates. In the early 1980s, it was evident that neither side in the budget equation — the executive or the Congress — was able to exercise control over the budget. A credibility gap over the deficit path emerged. The Balanced Budget and Emergency Deficit Control Act of 1985, known as the Gramm—Rudman—Hollings (GRH) Act, was enacted to address the budget imbalance and the mounting federal debt. The Act specified procedures for reducing the budget deficit. In 1987, the Supreme Court held as unconstitutional these procedures. In response to the court decision, the Act was amended in 1987.

The Balanced Budget and Emergency Deficit Control Reaffirmation Act of 1987 calls for a balanced budget by 1993. It provides a framework for reducing the deficit through 'sequestration' of funds when the budget deficit reaches specified trigger levels. A combination of exogenous shocks and internal problems led to a historically high ratio of federal deficit to GNP, hence another budget act. The Omnibus Budget Reconciliation Act of 1990 (OBRA) spells out the agreement over the deficit reached between the executive branch and the Congress. A key section of OBRA is the Budget Enforcement Act of 1990 (BEA). The BEA contains procedures designed to enforce the deficit reduction targets agreed to in the OBRA of 1990. The new enforcement procedures apply to fiscal years 1991 to 1995.

In this chapter, we give an overview of the federal budget process as it has developed since the passage of the Congressional Budget Act of 1974. Phases of the budget cycle are identified and procedures followed in each phase spelled out. Recent changes introduced in the budget process are summarized. The chapter concludes by highlighting some of the problems that still plague the federal budget process and offers suggestions for improvement.

2 THE BUDGET CYCLE: EXECUTIVE PREPARATION AND TRANSMITTAL

Although budgeting is a continuous process, the term 'budget cycle' is often used to emphasize its periodicity. There are clearly defined phases of budgeting in most budgetary systems. At the federal level in the United States, four phases can be identified: 1. executive preparation and transmittal; 2. congressional action; 3. execution and control, and 4. review and audit. Each of these phases is interrelated with the others.

The President's budget submitted to the Congress early in each calendar year (eight to nine months before the next fiscal year begins on October 1) is the climax of many months of planning and analysis throughout the executive branch. The appropriate time sequence of, and the participants in, each stage of budget preparation by the executive branch may be inferred from Figure 4.1. The timing suggested is only approximate, since it may vary under different pressures or in different departments. Also the role of the President in making budget decisions differs significantly from one President to the next. Nevertheless, the chart is indicative of the lead time required and effort involved in the preparation of the executive's budget.

Figure 4.1 *Formulation of the President's budget*

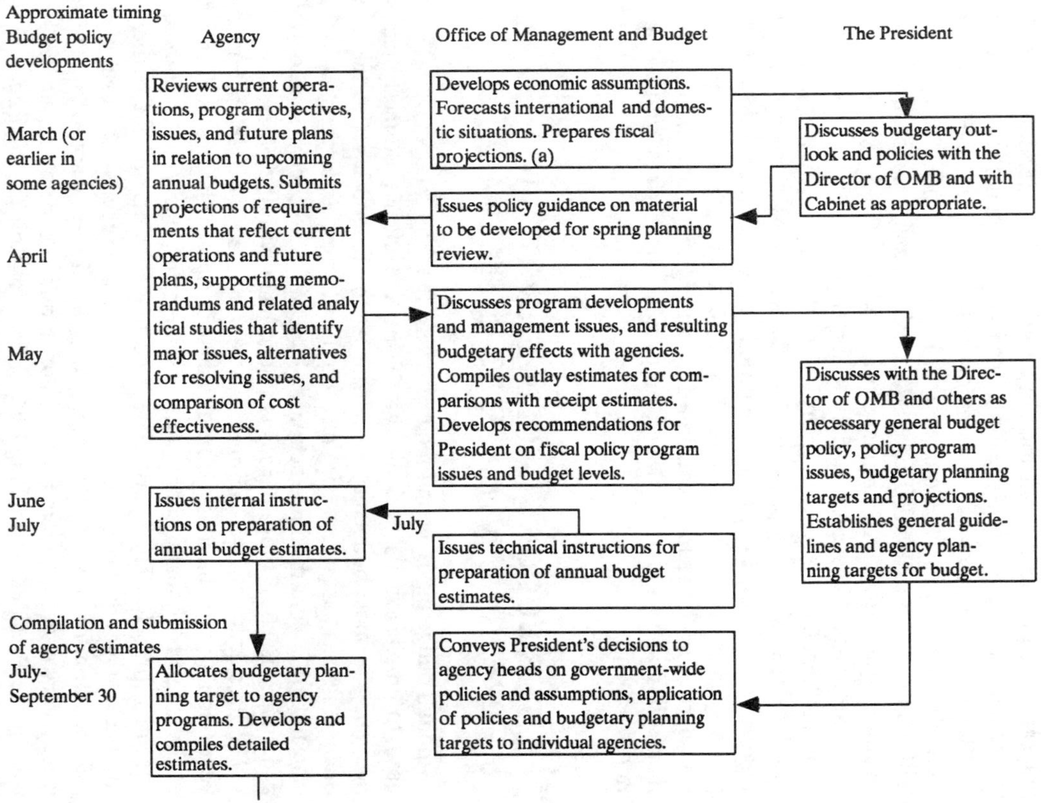

Figure 4.1 continued

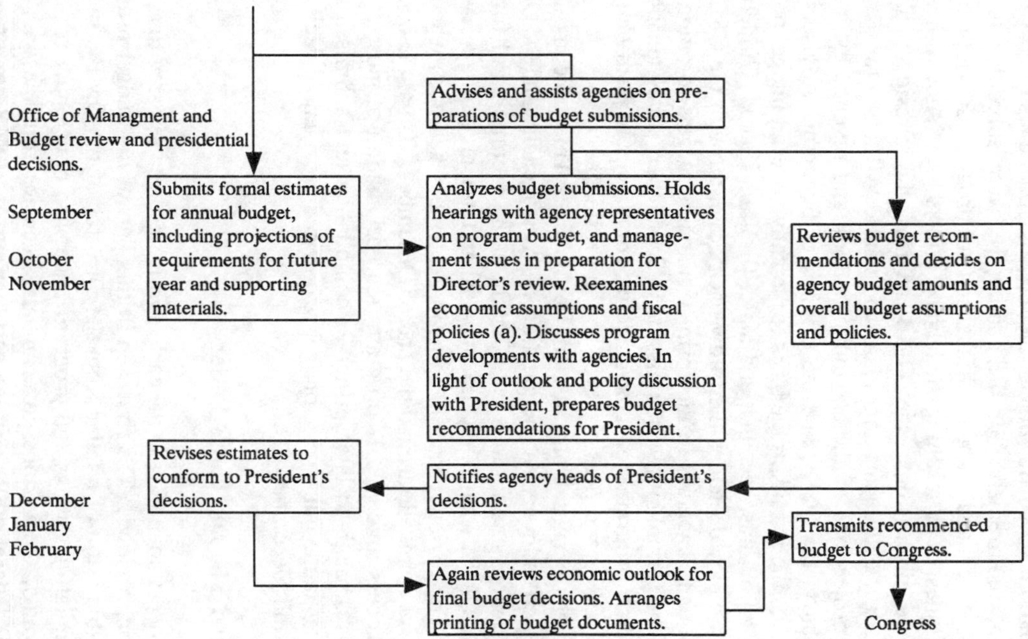

Note : a: Jointly with the Treasury Department and the Council of Economic Advisers.
Source: Compiled from discussion with Executive Office of the President, Office of Management and Budget (OMB).

Figure 4.1 illustrates a basic characteristic of budgeting in the executive branch — the two-way flow of decisions up from the agencies and then back down from the Office of Management and Budget (OMB) and the President. Budget policy development begins at the agency level. By March, or earlier in some cases, the individual organizational units in the departments and agencies make plans for their programs and expenditures. They review current operations, program objectives, issues, and future plans in relation to the upcoming budget. Budget offices in each agency provide information, supporting memorandums, and related materials when, in early spring, requirements for the coming year are submitted to the Office of Management and Budget, which discusses program developments, management issues, and resulting budgetary effects with agency heads. Following these discussions, the OMB advises the President about preliminary agency and department plans and goals. All this information, together with projections of the economic outlook and revenue estimates from the Treasury, the OMB, and the Council of Economic Advisers (in late spring), gives the President the basis for tentative overall budget policy decisions on total outlays, receipts, and major program issues. Guidelines reflecting these policy decisions then flow back down through the OMB to the departments and agencies in the form of planning targets to guide the preparation of the formal budget submission in September. They must then either modify their programs to fit the guidelines or attempt to justify higher amounts to the OMB and possibly even to the President.

The second phase runs from July to December. This time is spent compiling detailed estimates and negotiating between agencies and the OMB on budget allocations and figures, culminating in the submission of formal estimates to the OMB, where they are analyzed and prepared for review by the Director. The review process begins in September and ends when all budget issues are resolved, around the end of December. Thus, the budget formulation process involves: 1. program-issue orientation of most of the budget process through to late spring; 2. compilation and submission of agency estimates in the fall; and 3. budget review and presidential decisions in November and December.

Budget Review: The Director's Letter

The budget process beginning in the early spring has been referred to as the 'spring planning review'. The first step in this part of the budget process leads to the submission of a letter from the Director of the OMB. In this period of formulating outlays and program issues and developing requests for new programs, the various governmental agencies compete with one another for the federal dollar. In the early spring, the OMB confers with departments and agencies on the upcoming budget. An important aspect of this early consultation is to identify for each agency a set of 'program issues' — decisions that must be made regarding the scope and size of the agency's programs and program elements. These partly reflect program issues left over from the previous year's budget process, but new issues are also raised.

The program issues for each agency and department are the product of negotiations between the OMB and the agency, often at the highest levels. The Director of the OMB discusses in general terms budget policy with the President and his staff; this is reflected in his and his staff's discussions with the departments and agencies. At this early stage, then, the basic objectives of the budget process already reflect, in a broad sense, the presidential perspective. The discussions and decisions on program issues lead naturally to simultaneous consideration of the special analytical studies needed from each agency. By the early summer, the OMB director sends a letter to each department or agency head. This letter formalizes the budget targets set by the President, agreements reached on program issues, and analytical studies for each agency.

Agency Budget Preview Activities

After the Director's letter has gone out, the budget process centers in the agencies and departments. The activities there focus on: 1. initiation and completion of analytical studies needed to reach decisions on the program issues identified in the Director's letter; 2. intra-agency budget review; and 3. preparation of budget estimates and reports on analytical studies for submission to the OMB.

Through the agency budgeting office and professional staff flows the information on programs and costs needed by the administrator to decide on program objectives raised in the Director's letter as well as programs and costs for future budget years. Often it is impossible to conduct the needed analysis in the time provided, and program issues may have to be decided on diverse grounds, ranging from political pressures to the administrator's intuitive judgement. Not every agency's programs or budgets are included in the Director's letter. A large segment of budget outlays is virtually outside the budget process and often is not reflected in program objectives or issues. These outlays include such open-ended or fixed cost items as interest on the public debt, social security and other retirement programs, and veterans' pensions. The levels of these outlays are determined by provisions written into legislation authorizing the programs and by other factors not readily subject to annual budgetary control. They are, however, subject to review, and legislation is frequently proposed to change them. The crucial budget decisions, then, relate primarily to proposed changes in the open-ended programs and to programs subject to budgetary control. They take the form of an evaluation of relatively small increases in costs and activities.

The focus of the budget preview process on program issues and analytical studies should not obscure the fact that budget making is and always will be a *political* process, and at the agency level, the politics of budget making are important in several ways. Agencies and their 'line people' are expected to be advocates of increased appropriations. It is generally accepted as natural and inevitable by Congress and the OMB that agency budget offices will have a strong interest in justifying their program decisions and appropriation requests. As advocates, the agencies supply information crucial to congressional and OMB decisions — information Congress and the OMB otherwise would have to obtain for themselves.[1]

On the other hand, agencies or departments rarely ask for all the funds they believe they could use. If they did, the OMB or Congress would probably make substantial cuts. To have proposals cut sharply every year would set what the agencies would consider an unfortunate precedent, though some cuts are inevitable in an agency's budget. Moreover, the OMB has the task of weighing budget requests across the whole range of federal activity and of making recommendations to the President concerning the choices open to him.

So in making decisions on programs and expenditures, agencies cannot, for strategic reasons, aim too high or too low. Their decision making will reflect clues and hints from the executive branch, Congress, clientele groups, and their own organizations. In this way, they are able in most cases to get a rough idea of what will prove acceptable to the OMB, the President and his advisers, and congressional committees on the budget.

Thus in the late spring and in the summer, the agencies and departments prepare for the submission of their budget proposals to the OMB. Before the submission date, the agency or department usually has its own preview when internal drafts of analytical studies are submitted, criticized, and revised. Once the department or agency head is satisfied, analytical studies and budget requests are submitted to the OMB, usually in September. Then begins the formal budget review process within the OMB, which will be described later in this chapter.

The Fiscal Side of Budgeting

While the agencies' budget-making process is taking place, the President and his economic advisers are engaged in a continuing parallel process. The President and his advisers review data on economic conditions and future outlook that are prepared jointly by the Council of Economic Advisers, OMB and the Departments of Commerce, Labor and the Treasury. Following a review of these projections, the President establishes general budget and fiscal policy guidelines for both the fiscal year that will begin about 15 months later and for the two years beyond.

At the end of the spring planning review, the Director of the OMB and his staff deal directly with the President and his advisers on emerging problems, initial clearance on major program decisions, and the overall revenue and expenditure outlook. By late summer, the administration's general budget policy including estimates of the deficit for the forthcoming fiscal year begins to take shape.

Also at the end of the spring planning review, at the time the policy letter based on guidelines received from the President is sent by the Director of the OMB to agency and department heads, the general budget policy is translated into budget planning figures of some twenty agencies. These are not ceiling figures; rather, the OMB is informing the agency that, in view of the administration's program, the agency's budget will probably be somewhere near a certain figure. Agencies can bring in estimates exceeding the planning figure, but if they do, they must indicate where they could make cuts if required to adhere to the planning figure. It is at this point that the program and fiscal aspects of the budget process come together.

The Review Process

Throughout the fall and early winter, the executive branch is engaged in a crucial stage in the budget-making process — the development of the President's budget. Current services estimates are also prepared to provide the Congress with a basis for reviewing the President's budget. The agencies and departments conduct intensive examinations of their programs in the light of the planning figures or budget directives that have been passed down to them and the previous year's action by Congress. The agency or department that is well within its planning figure seldom has problems (though this situation is so rare as to be completely outside the experience of most career agency budget officers). Most, however, face a difficult decision about where to cut, or whether to cut at all, or whether to fight it out by appealing to the OMB and, if necessary, to the President.

After the review within the department, estimates are submitted to the OMB and then referred to the budget examiners. The knowledge the examiners possess about the agency, based on long-run experience, field investigation, and the like, is now brought to bear on the estimates. The examiners give considerable attention to the basis for the individual estimate, review the agency's past performance, check the accuracy of the factual information presented, and consider the future implications of the program. Furthermore, the examiners identify programs, budget, and management issues of importance to be raised for discussion with agency representatives during the hearings conducted at the OMB. At these hearings, usually held in October and November, the department or agency presents and defends its programs and budget before the examiner and other OMB staff members.

On the basis of the hearings and his knowledge of agency programs, operations and overall policies, the OMB examiner, after consultation with the Associate Director to whom he reports, submits his recommendations to the Director for the 'Director's review'. This is conducted by top staff members of the OMB — the Director, the Deputy Director, and other officials, with the Director usually serving as chairman.

Concurrent with the Director's review is the last stage of executive budget preparation — presidential review of the budget as it emerges from the OMB and preparation of the annual budget document. After the President's review, his program decisions and approved allowances are sent to each agency head, who may then accept them or appeal them to the OMB or to the President. Another hearing on some of the issues is thus sometimes obtained. At this hectic time, final conclusions are drawn on the economic outlook, prospective revenues, and total budget outlays. A reexamination of fiscal policy issues is made at this time. Consistent with the multi-year budget planning system, an evaluation of the impact of budget decisions on budget authority and outlays and the deficit in the following years are also considered. Thus, the budget formulation process involves the simultaneous consideration of the resource needs of budget programs in relation to current and projected economic conditions and statutory constraints. (For FY 1991—95, spending caps and the maximum deficit are set by law.)

During the last week of January — somewhat miraculously, considering the coordination and effort involved — the President's budget is transmitted to Congress. Because of changes in the budget process introduced by the recent acts — the Balanced Budget Acts of 1985 as amended in 1987 and the Budget Enforcement Act of 1990 — the executive branch's role in the budget process does not end with the budget transmittal to Congress. These changes and the new timetable for reporting requirements on the budget are discussed in the next section.

3 CONGRESSIONAL BUDGETING

The congressional side of budgeting begins with the submission of the President's budget, although congressional review takes place when the President transmits current services or baseline estimates.[2] This phase of budgeting has undergone a great deal of change beginning with the Budget Act of 1974. The review of congressional budgeting provided in this section will highlight changes in the process introduced by three major acts: the 1974 Act, the Gramm—Rudman—Hollings Act of 1985 and amended in 1987, and the Budget Enforcement Act of 1990.

The 1974 Act

Until 1975, Congress took action on the President's budget in a piecemeal fashion. Spending proposals were acted upon one at a time and tax measures were treated separately. This process offered Congress no opportunity to look at both sides of the budget as a unified proposal, to consider whether the resulting budget deficit was consistent with the needs of the economy and/or whether the budget priorities implied in individual spending and tax measures reflected national priorities.

The Congressional Budget and Impoundment Control Act of 1974 addressed these shortcomings. The Act gave Congress a mechanism for looking at the budget as a whole early in the budget cycle and explicitly addressing the overall budget balance (deficit). The centerpiece of this mechanism is the concurrent resolution on the budget. Specifically, the Act introduced the following changes:

1. It set up a budget committee in each House, which, using reports from the Congressional Budget Office also established by the Act and from the various committees of the Congress, studies budget options and prepares budget resolutions.
2. It required Congress, before taking action on appropriations or spending measures, to adopt concurrent *budget resolutions*, first setting target figures for new budget authority and budget outlays as well as the appropriate levels of federal receipts, the budget surplus or deficit, and the public debt, and later setting ceilings and floors on these totals.
3. It changed the fiscal year to October 1 — September 30 and provided a firm budget schedule for Congress.
4. It changed the rules on impoundment of funds by the President.

The newly created budget committees were set up to give Congress a better perspective on budget totals and fiscal policy requirements. The House Budget Committee has twenty-five members: five each from the House Appropriations and Ways and Means Committees, thirteen from other standing committees, and one each from the majority and minority leadership. The Senate Budget Committee has sixteen members whose selection has been made by the Democratic and Republican Conferences in accordance with normal selection processes.[3]

The new committees have been given general jurisdiction over the congressional budget process and related matters. Specifically, they are required to report two concurrent resolutions on the budget each year, to study the effects of existing and proposed legislation on federal spending, and to oversee operations of the new Congressional Budget Office (CBO).

The CBO — the congressional counterpart of the Office of Management and Budget — is a nonpartisan informational and analytical arm of Congress with broad authority to obtain data from executive agencies. The CBO is headed by a director, appointed to a four-year term by the Speaker of the House and the President *pro tempore* of the Senate. The Act specifies the CBO's duties according to priorities:

1. to furnish the House and Senate Budget Committees with information relating to all matters within their jurisdiction;
2. to supply the House Ways and Means Committee, the Senate Finance Committee, and the appropriations committees with all available data related to the budget and to make budget-related studies at their request;
3. to give other congressional committees available information and undertake studies on their behalf; and
4. to supply all members of Congress with relevant available information.

The CBO is also required by the Act to submit an annual report to the House and Senate Budget Committees setting forth budget alternatives and national budget priorities as well as tax expenditures. This report must be submitted by April 1. Moreover the office must issue periodic score-keeping reports, five-year budget projections, and cost analyses of legislation reported by all committees other than the appropriations committees.

Budget transmittal

In moving the government to an October 1 — September 30 fiscal year, the Act expanded the congressional 'budget season' to nine months, giving Congress a longer period to shape the budget than in the past. The congressional budget process begins around November 10 of each year with the submission of a current services budget. The Joint Economic Committee reviews the current services budget and reports its evaluation to Congress by December 31. As under prior law, the President submits his revised federal budget to Congress around the end of January.

First budget resolution

After receiving the President's budget proposals and after considering advice from the CBO and other committees, the House and Senate Budget Committees draw up, reconcile, and report a first concurrent resolution to their respective Houses by April 15 of each year.[4] Floor consideration of the budget resolution takes place under special rules devised to expedite the proceedings so that adoption of the first concurrent resolution does not take place after May 15.[5] May 15 is also the date by which legislative committees must report authorizing legislation for the ensuing fiscal year.[6]

The first concurrent resolution is a tentative budget. It sets target totals for budget authority, outlays, receipts, and the public debt to guide Congress in its subsequent consideration of appropriations and tax measures. The resolution also includes any recommendation for changes in tax revenues or in the level of the debt ceiling.

Within these overall targets, the resolution breaks down budget authority and outlays into seventeen major functions (defense, health, and so on).

The functional targets are intended to represent broad priorities and not to make judgements on the specific goals within each function. The latter is subsequently determined by congressional committees.

Congressional consideration of spending and tax measures

Congressional action on requests for appropriations and for changes in revenue laws continues to follow the old pattern: appropriations are considered within the appropriations committees and subcommittees, while revenue measures are taken up by the Ways and Means Committee. The process is the same as in the past, but subject to the guidelines of the first concurrent resolution on the budget. The budget resolution *guides* but does not *bind* Congress in acting on the appropriations and revenue bills.

After enactment of the first concurrent resolution, Congress begins processing appropriations requests for the upcoming fiscal year according to an established pattern.[7] These requests are considered first in the House of Representatives. The House Appropriations Committee, through its thirteen subcommittees, studies appropriations requests and examines each agency's performance in detail. Each subcommittee is responsible for reporting out one or occasionally two appropriations bills, of which there are thirteen or fourteen in each congressional session. Hearings are held and testimony is given by the relevant agency and its budget officers. After the hearings, the subcommittee goes into executive session and decides on the recommendations it will make. The recommendations are usually accompanied by reasons for the subcommittee's action and by comments on the agency's programs, efficiency, and personnel.

The subcommittee's recommendations and reports are then sent to the full committee for action. The recommendations are sent as a bill to the House where they are debated with the House sitting as a committee of the whole.

Following action by the House, the appropriations and tax bills are forwarded to the Senate, where a similar process is followed. The initial work on appropriations proposals is done in the thirteen subcommittees of the Appropriations Committee. As in the House, they hold hearings, make agreed-upon changes in the bill, and send it to the full committee.

On the floor of the Senate, discussion of appropriations and tax measures is more extensive than it is in the House as a result of the Senate's privilege of unlimited debate. Senate—House differences on appropriations (and on tax bills) are reconciled by a Conference Committee consisting of members of both Houses. The Conference Committee report is returned to the House and Senate for further consideration. If agreed to by both Houses, the legislation is transmitted to the President for his approval or veto.

Before the Congressional Budget Act of 1974, it was customary to report any appropriations bill out to the floor when it had been approved by the full committee. The 1974 Act, however, changed this process by directing the House Appropriations Committee to try to complete action on all its appropriations and to submit a summary report before reporting the first bill for floor action.

Also under the 1974 Act, all appropriations bills must be passed by the seventh day after Labor Day except for those cases where the necessary authorization legislation has not been enacted in time. In this case, appropriations bills may be held up until after the final action on the conference report or until reconciliation.

Second budget resolution and reconciliation process

After finishing action on all bills by September 15, Congress is required to take another overall look at budget totals. A second concurrent resolution is passed, either affirming or revising the budget targets set by the initial resolution. The resolution adopted will contain budget ceilings, by function, for budget authority and outlays. A floor for revenue measures is also set. If separate congressional decisions taken during the appropriations process are not consistent with the second concurrent budget resolution totals, the resolution may direct that changes be made in budget authority (new or carried over from previous years), entitlement, receipts, or the public debt. This resolution also instructs the committee with jurisdiction over the prescribed changes to report implementing legislation. The House and Senate Budget Committees then combine these changes and report them to the floor in the form of a reconciliation bill. By September 25, Congress completes the reconciliation process, thereby enacting the second concurrent resolution. Congress cannot adjourn for the year until the reconciliation legislation is passed.

With the enactment of the reconciliation bill, the congressional budget process is completed. At this point Congress may not consider any spending or revenue legislation that would make budget figures differ from those specified in the second resolution. However, Congress may, if the need arises, adopt a new budget resolution during the fiscal year. If action on appropriations is not completed by the beginning of the fiscal year, Congress may enact a *continuing resolution* to provide the agencies affected with authority to continue operating at previous year levels until their regular appropriations are enacted.

Amendments to the 1974 Congressional Act: The GRH Acts

Although the structure set up by the 1974 Act still stands, significant changes in congressional budgeting have taken place since then. The first major legislation is the Gramm—Rudman—Hollings Act of 1985. The Act called for automatic spending reductions or sequestration when the budget deficit exceeds a specified level.[8] The Act failed to pass constitutional tests because it empowered the head of the General Accounting Office, a legislative branch agency, to determine spending cuts to meet the deficit target. In September 1987, Congress amended the Act of 1985. The amended Act, known as the Balanced Budget Reaffirmation Act of 1987 puts the entire responsibility for estimating the deficit and determining spending cuts 'squarely' on the Office of Management and Budget.[9] The Congressional Budget Office was given reporting and checking responsibilities, although the OMB held the power of determining which of the two sets of statistics were the valid numbers.

The GRH Act of 1985 as amended in 1987 sets deficit targets as well as automatic enforcement mechanisms or sequestration. The Act allows a $10 billion margin of error over the deficit target before the cuts are triggered. The Congress can vote to suspend the Act's requirements under certain conditions of unexpected slow economic growth.[10]

When automatic spending reduction occurs, the Act requires that one-half come from defense spending and the other half from non-defense outlays. The Act, however, exempts certain benefits programs including social security and programs benefiting low-income households. Net interest payments (not directly accountable) are also exempt. For several other programs, including Medicare, Stafford Loans and Veterans' medical care, the Act limits the extent of reduction. For the other programs, reductions are achieved by sequestration of budget resources — in other words by cancelling agencies' ability to commit some funds.

Under the provisions of the Act of 1987, the OMB must issue, on August 25, an 'official' projection of the budget deficit based on policies in place as of mid-August. Previewing this official estimate, the OMB's mid-session review of the budget in late July gives the deficit estimate in relation to the deficit target. In mid-October, the OMB must make a second 'binding' estimate of the deficit. If policy changes, including all legislation enacted between mid-August and mid-October, do not push the deficit over the target deficit, sequestration will not occur. If sequestration is triggered, spending cuts must be made to reach the specified target.

It is worth noting that the deficit targets contained in the Balanced Budget Act are expressed in terms of the total deficit, even though the Act of 1985 moved off-budget the two social security trust funds: the Old Age and Survivors' Insurance and the Disability Insurance. The base line budget projections then must show separately the on-budget deficit, the off-budget deficit or surplus as well as the total deficit.

The GRH Act of 1987 introduced to the budget process a 'timetable' for balancing the federal budget and a new budget schedule. The Act of 1985 called for a zero deficit by 1991, the 1987 Act for a zero deficit for 1993. From mid-August until the end of the budget cycle, both the executive and the Congress would be operating under the 'threat' of the GRH sequestration. This 'threat' introduced a 'discipline' of sorts to budget making that was lacking in prior years. Indeed, since GRH's passage, only two sequesters took place: one in March of 1986; the second, a partial sequester, in 1989.[11] With the new procedure in place, it looked as if sequesters would become engraved in the budget process.[12]

GRH sequestration procedure as a means for settling differences over spending priorities and for reducing the size of the federal deficit lost credibility sooner than was expected. In 1990, the official estimate of the deficit for FY 1991 by far exceeded the target deficit and the cuts required to meet the GRH deficit target were exceedingly high.[13] The OMB sequester report outlined required spending cuts to bring the deficit to the target levels. (The OMB Initial Sequester Report of August 20 put the sequester at $85.4 billion. After allowing for anticipated legislation, the OMB estimated the sequester amount to reach $105.7 billion.) The cutbacks proposed by the OMB were viewed as 'politically unacceptable'. For example the report spelled out cuts in programs such as 'a halving of military forces', the 'closing' of many air traffic control installations and 'cancellations' of vaccinations against childhood disease for one million children.[14]

The bitter debates and controversy over the FY 1991 budget during the summer of 1990 were reconciled with the enactment of the Omnibus Budget Reconciliation Act of 1990 (OBRA). The Reconciliation Act set in motion new procedures to salvage the budget process. These procedures were spelled out in Title 13 of the OBRA, known as the Budget Enforcement Act of 1990. This Act amends both the Act of 1974 and the GRH Acts.

The Budget Enforcement Act of 1990 (BEA)

The Budget Enforcement Act (BEA) of 1990 introduces specific changes in both the executive and legislative budget practices. These changes are summarized below:[15]

Budget structure

The BEA divides the budget into two mutually exclusive categories: 'discretionary' spending and 'direct' spending and receipts. The discretionary category was further divided into three expanded programs: domestic, international and defense. Discretionary spending refers to those programs that are subject to annual appropriations. The other budget category, direct spending and receipts, is defined by the BEA as budget authority provided by law other than appropriations acts, entitlement authority, and food stamps.[16] Social security and the postal services are treated as off-budget items. (In FY 1991 actual discretionary spending was equal to 40 per cent of total budget outlay and 49 per cent of total on-budget outlays.)

Spending controls or caps

The BEA establishes procedures for limiting spending through 1995. Limits or caps apply to discretionary spending by setting budget authority

(BA) targets and outlay (OL) targets. For FY 1991—93, limits are specified for the three discretionary programs, and limits on each program are enforced independently. For FY 1994 and FY 1995, the spending caps apply to total discretionary budget authority and outlays.

These discretionary spending caps are not set in concrete. The BEA allows:

1. adjustments to the limits reflecting changes in inflation assumptions and other changes. The Act also permits cap adjustments due to changes in concepts and definitions resulting from legislative actions that reclassified certain programs (i.e. shifting programs between discretionary and direct spending categories);
2. adjustment to the limits after appropriations have been enacted (for 1991 to 1995) to cover special budget items (i.e. funding for the Internal Revenue Service and the International Monetary Fund and for emergency appropriations); and
3. cap adjustments to be made at the end of a congressional session for the enactment, as appropriations actions, of changes in receipts. Special allowances for budget authority in 1992 and 1993 and for outlays for 1991 to 1995 are also granted by BEA.

Pay-as-you-go control

With respect to the second budget category — direct spending and receipts — no caps are established by the BEA. What the Act provides for is a pay-as-you-go control in that legislation enacted which affects this budget category must be 'deficit neutral'. In other words, legislation reducing receipts would be offset by spending reductions and vice versa. To make sure that this requirement is met, a 'score card' is to be maintained to show the deficit impact of enacted direct spending and receipt legislation. Discretionary spending caps and maximum deficits under the BEA are reported in Tables 4.1 and 4.2. An estimate of pay-as-you-go legislation activities on the deficit is given in Table 4.3.

Sequestration reports

The Budget Enforcement Act of 1990 requires both OMB and CBO to issue sequestration reports for both the discretionary budget programs and for the pay-as-you-go budget category. These reports must contain estimates of the following three items: 1. the discretionary spending limits and adjustment to them (Discretionary Sequestration Report); 2. the amount by which direct spending or receipt legislation, enacted after the BEA, has increased or decreased the deficit (Pay-as-you-go Report); 3. the maximum deficit amount (Deficit Sequestration Report).

Compliance with spending caps is monitored throughout the fiscal year. Sequester calculations are made when the caps and/or deficit targets are

Table 4.1 *Discretionary spending limits and adjustments, fiscal year 1993 (in billions of dollars)*

Spending Limits January 13,1992	Budget Authority	Outlays
Full sequestration report		
Domestic	205.9	224.3
International	21.6	20.1
Defense	291.5	297.1
Adjustments		
Domestic	–1.7	*
International	–0.1	–0.1
Defense	–2.4	–0.3
Preview report limits		
Domestic	204.2	224.3
International	21.5	20.0
Defense	289.0	296.8
Other adjustments		
Domestic	1.8	1.1
International	1.3	0.6
Defense	—	—
Estimated end of session discretionary limits		
Domestic	206.1	225.4
International	22.8	20.6
Defense	289.0	296.8
Estimated total discretionary limits	517.9	542.8

Note: * Less than 50 million.

Source: *The Budget of the United States Government, Fiscal Year 1993,* Appendix Two, pp. 5–10.

exceeded. The timetable for congressional budgeting as modified by the GRH and BEA is summarized in Table 4.4.

To summarize

The Omnibus Budget Reconciliation Act of 1990, which was enacted after lengthy and difficult negotiations between the executive and Congress, chartered a course leading to a lower deficit path for the federal budget.

Table 4.2 Budget proposals, caps and maximum deficit amounts, fiscal year 1993 (in billions of dollars)

Item	Budget Authority	Outlays
Budget discretionary spending proposals		
Domestic	203.1	224.7
International	22.1	20.6
Defense	281.1	291.6
TOTAL	506.3	536.9
Caps[a]		
Domestic	206.1	225.4
International	22.8	20.6
Defense	289.0	296.8
TOTAL	517.9	542.8
Maximum deficit amounts[b]		
Current maximum deficit		407.2
Current estimated deficit		406.1
Excess[c]		—1.1

Notes: a: For details on discretionary spending limits see Table 4.1.
b: This is defined to be equal to the projected on-budget baseline deficits, assuming that discretionary spending complies with the caps minus any deficit increases from pay-as-you-go legislation.
c: Since no excess deficit is estimated for 1993, no sequester was estimated for fiscal year 1993.

Source: *The Budget of the United States Government, Fiscal Year 1993*, Appendix Two, pp. 5—10.

In addition to spending cuts and tax increases, the Act establishes enforcement procedures for limiting spending, hence indirectly controlling the size of the deficit. Two sets of enforcement rules govern the process. First, discretionary spending caps are established to limit both budget authority and outlays for domestic, international and defense appropriations. For the other budget programs — mandatory spending and receipts — the pay-as-you-go rules state that legislation affecting these programs must not raise the deficit. The BEA requires both the CBO and the OMB to monitor budget action to ensure compliance with the caps. The deficit target feature established by the GRH Acts was retained by the BEA. Maximum deficit amounts for fiscal years 1991—95 were spelled out and sequestration procedures established to ensure that budget estimates do not exceed the target deficits. The Act, however, allows for adjustments to the established spending caps to meet changing budgetary conditions.

Table 4.3 *Budgetary effect of pay-as-you-go legislation enacted since the BEA, fiscal years 1993—95 (in billions of dollars)*

Item	1993	1994	1995
Change in the deficit[a]			
Revenue impact	—509	—226	—764
Outlay impact	—627	—209	—241
Total change (OMB January Report)	—1,136	—476	—1,005
1992 final sequestration report			
Total change since the final report	—209	697	861
Total change since the BEA	—1,345	221	—144

Notes: a: For a listing of legislation included in the pay-as-you-go calculation see CBO, *The Economic and Budget Outlook: An Update* (Aug. 1992), p. 60.

Source: *The Budget of the United States Government, Fiscal Year 1993*, Appendix Two, pp. 5—10.

4 BUDGET EXECUTION AND CONTROL

Once the budget is approved by Congress, it becomes the financial basis for the operations of government agencies during the fiscal year. How is budget authority granted by Congress to an agency or department converted into outlays?

Apportionment and Allotment

When the appropriations bill is enacted, an appropriations warrant, drawn by the Treasury and countersigned by the General Accounting Office, is sent to the agency. The agency reviews and revises its budget in the light of the appropriations bill and, within ten days of the appropriations bill's passage, submits to the Office of Management and Budget a request for apportionment. Apportionment may be defined as the rate at which budget authority can be used, and the authority is usually apportioned by quarters over the period of appropriation, both to ensure that the budget authority is not spent faster than Congress intended and to ensure the most economical and effective use of funds.

The OMB approves or revises the agency apportionment requests; in effect, the OMB is the apportioning authority. The power of apportionment gives the executive some latitude in controlling the direction and timing of federal outlays. Within the individual agencies, the use of budget authority apportioned by the OMB is controlled through a similar device. The breakdown of apportionment by organizational units is called *allotment*.

Table 4.4 *Congressional budget timetable*

Deadline date	Action to be completed
November 10	Current services budget submitted
5 days before budget submission	CBO sequester preview report
15 days after Congress meets	President submits budget and revises targets and caps
February 15	CBO annual report to Budget Committees
March 15	Reports of Congressional Committees submitted to Budget Committees
April 1	Senate Budget Committee reports budget resolution
April 15[a]	Congress completes budget resolution
May 15	Appropriation bills may be considered in the House
June 10[b]	House Appropriations report last bill
June 30	House completes action on annual appropriation bills
July 15	President submits midsession review
August 15	CBO sequester update report
August 20	OMB sequester update report with adjustments to caps and targets
September 15	Action on second concurrent resolution on the budget
September 25	Final action on second concurrent resolution: completion of reconciliation process
October 1	Fiscal year begins
10 days after end of congressional session	CBO final sequester report
15 days after end of congressional session	OMB final sequester report (with adjustments to caps and targets)

Notes: a: If Congress fails to complete the budget resolution, the Chairman of the House Budget Committee files 302(a) allocations; Ways and Means Committee is free to proceed with pay-as-you-go measures.

b: An appropriation bill that violates caps which is enacted before July 1 triggers a sequester in that category. OMB issues sequester 15 days after enactment.

Source: Based on Doyle and McCaffery (1991), p. 33. See also CBO, *The Economic and Budget Outlook: An Update* (August 1991 and August 1992).

Obligations Incurred and Outlays

With few exceptions, the various agencies actually incur obligations only after apportionment by the OMB. The incurring of obligations, however, does not necessarily mean immediate cash expenditures. In some cases, the expenditure of funds virtually coincides with the incurring of obligations; in others, the actual expenditure of funds may lag considerably behind.

In two kinds of commitment, the time lag between obligations and outlays is very short. Outlays for the purchase of existing assets (except land, where the lag may be considerable) and for payments such as social security benefits, veterans' pensions, and unemployment compensation, coincide with — or are very close to — the incurring of the obligations. Government expenditures for services (in particular those of government employees) also typically occur close to the time of commitment.

But when the federal government contracts with the private sector to employ resources on its behalf — that is, when the federal government buys goods and services produced by the private sector — the lags of outlays behind obligations may be substantial. These lags are both administrative and operational; it takes private producers time to draw plans, negotiate with subcontractors, and deliver the product. Some of the economic impact on the private sector (as discussed in Chapter 3) thus occurs long before actual delivery of goods and payment, since the producers must employ resources in order to produce goods.

Outlays

When they occur, outlays are generally made from Treasury deposits at the twelve Federal Reserve Banks, which are part of the 'Account of the Treasurer of the United States'. This account consists mostly of the Treasury checking accounts at the Federal Reserve Banks and at commercial banks. Federal disbursing officers make payments by issuing checks against the Federal Reserve Bank accounts on the basis of vouchers approved by certifying officers of the various agencies; the amount that can be issued is set by the agency's budget authority and the apportionment of it by the OMB. The checks are usually deposited in commercial banks, which then receive a credit to their Federal Reserve Bank accounts. The Federal Reserve Bank charges the Treasury account with the amount of the check and sends the check to the Treasury, where the checks that have been cashed are verified against the record of checks that have been issued.

It is the Treasury's responsibility to maintain adequate working balances in the Federal Reserve Banks to meet payments as they are made. For this purpose, amounts are funnelled by the Treasury into Federal Reserve accounts from deposits at commercial banks made directly by district officers of the Internal Revenue Service and from receipts from debt issues.

During the fiscal year, changes in laws or economic conditions may necessitate the enactment of additional budget authority. In this case, supplemental requests are sent to Congress for its consideration.[17] On the other hand, the President may wish, for policy reasons, to withhold some of the appropriated funds. In this case, the President must send a special message to Congress requesting a 'rescission' as required by the 1974 Act. Budget authority proposed for rescission must be made available for obligations unless both the House and Senate pass a bill authorizing rescission within forty-five days of contiguous session as defined in the Act. A deferral message — a temporary withholding of funds from obligation — would remain in effect for the fiscal year (though not beyond) unless overturned by a simple majority in either House.

Audit

The individual agencies and departments are responsible for ensuring that the obligations they incur, and the resulting outlays, are legal according to authorizing and appropriations legislation. The Congress, however, may obtain an independent check through the General Accounting Office, which is headed by the Comptroller General. The GAO audits the books of the administrative offices responsible for the custody and use of public funds. It also plays an important role in supervising the accounting systems of agencies and departments and in ensuring that the methods of reporting result in full disclosure of the receipt and use of funds.

Three major types of audits are made by the GAO. The *comprehensive* audit, the most important, concentrates on the accounting and reporting system used by a particular agency and checks transactions selectively. The *general* audit examines the accounts of agency disbursing and certifying officers to determine the legality of each transaction. If illegal or improper handling of receipts or outlays is discovered, recovery procedures are instituted by the GAO against the responsible officer. Finally, the *commercial* audit is applied to government corporations and enterprises. No recovery is possible in this case, but Congress is informed of questionable or improper practices.

The annual report and the results of GAO audits are transmitted to Congress by the Comptroller General. The results of special investigations of particular agencies are referred to the House and Senate Committees on Government Operations. The Comptroller General is required, under the 1974 Act, to monitor the executive branch's message to Congress on proposed rescission. Should the President fail to comply with congressional actions that overrule impoundment of funds, the Comptroller General can ask the courts to issue an order requiring release of impounded funds. In addition, the Comptroller General is required, under the Budget Enforcement Act of 1990, to monitor compliance with the spending caps and deficit targets. As shown in Table 4.4, GAO is required to issue a compliance report 30 days after the end of the congressional session.

5 IMPROVING THE BUDGET PROCESS

The single most important achievement in the history of budget making in the U.S. is undoubtedly the passage of the Congressional Budget and Impoundment Act of 1974. The Act established a new and well-laid-out budget process. By requiring both Houses of Congress to vote on budget totals before deliberating on appropriation requests, it has eliminated a major weakness of congressional budget practice — the practice of looking at separate appropriation bills on a piecemeal basis. Moreover, by endowing Congress with three new instrumentalities (the two budget committees and the CBO), it has given Congress the access to information and the staff it needs to determine national budget priorities and policies. And finally, by focusing congressional attention on all legislation affecting aggregate spending and taxation, it has facilitated congressional appraisal of fiscal action. However, the Act left many problem issues unresolved. The most significant problem, which is at the root of current difficulties, is the 'uncontrollability' of the budget.

In any one year, much (77 per cent in 1992) of the federal budget is 'locked in' before the congressional review begins because a great deal of spending is mandatory. Programs for which expenditures are mandatory include social security and interest. This 'locked-in' feature means that only marginal changes in discretionary programs can be accommodated in any one year, unless Congress is willing to go along with the administration requests for new or increased spending.

This is precisely what happened. During the 1980s, the Reagan administration proposed and Congress enacted tax cuts and spending increases that left behind a trail of deficits. Changes in the macroeconomy — recession and shallow recovery — compounded the problem. It was neither possible to control the growth of mandatory spending nor to raise the needed revenue to finance the growth in expenditures and/or reduce the size of the deficit. In 1981 the deficit amounted to $57.9 billion; in 1985 it stood at $212 billion. The Gramm—Rudman—Hollings Act of 1985 and the Budget Enforcement Act of 1990 are two legislative responses to the uncontrollability issue. Whereas the GRH Act aimed at controlling the budget deficit by establishing deficit targets, the BEA took aim at controlling spending. The BEA sets caps on discretionary spending but left untouched (except for new initiatives) mandatory spending (the uncontrollables). BEA, moreover, does not establish targets for the deficit.

What BEA succeeded in doing is to set rules and procedures for rationing budget resources. Discretionary spending appropriations would be held within specified limits; newly legislated mandatory increases in spending have to be offset by increases in receipts. The BEA, however, failed to institute procedures for reviewing mandatory spending programs or address the remaining problems in budgeting.

Suggested Reforms

Any and all proposals for reform should begin with a clear statement of objective: to reestablish a balance between claims on the budget dollar and the availability of the dollar.

The BEA sought to address only a part of this equation. By establishing a pay-as-you-go rule for mandatory spending, the BEA may succeed in halting the growth of mandatory spending associated with new legislative initiatives, but it left other sources of growth untouched. With respect to discretionary spending, the BEA side-stepped the issue completely relying instead on caps.

Claims on the budgetary resources are reviewed in the congressional phase of budgeting during the process of authorization. Hence, the reform should begin at this stage of the game with controlling budget authority.

Authorization

All programs — discretionary or mandatory without requiring annual or multi-year authority as well as those with permanent authority — must be subjected to regular review as part of the budget process. The review process would focus on the need of competing programs in the light of 'available' budget resources. When needs exceed resources, either a system of rationing of budget authority is set in motion (such as caps) or legislation raising extra budgetary resources is introduced.

A systematic program review

The current practice of evaluating the budget program in terms of a baseline estimate tends to bias the review process. Under this practice, the executive and the Congress accept agency's prior claims on the budget resources even when national priorities call for a change in an agency's program or when available resources are not sufficient to fund all claims. Baseline budget estimates may be useful in assessing the future budget outlook (since the effects of inflation and workload are included), but 'they are open to manipulations and easily act as self-fulfilling prophecies'.[18]

To address this bias, a review procedure by agency program should be instituted. A three-year program review cycle would be designed to correspond to the three BEA program categories. Each program would be examined, evaluated, and justified in relation to other programs within the broad category spelled out by the Act and also in terms of the nation's budget priorities spelled out in the President's budget message.

Enhancing presidential controls

The current system of budgeting gives the President little opportunity for controlling the outcome. Unlike parliamentary systems of government, the U.S. Congress can act to accept, reject or modify the administration's budget. The President has no opportunity to control spending authority granted by Congress — the President cannot 'strike' from legislation provisions that in his view do not serve the national interest, nor is the President able to ensure that rescission of budget authority is implemented. Most importantly, the annual congressional resolution on the budget does not require the President's signature. The way of addressing this deficiency is the line item veto. A line item veto requires amending the Constitution. This, however, may be difficult to achieve as Congress is usually reluctant to surrender any of its powers to the executive. Lacking that, perhaps a procedure would be set up where final presidential involvement in the negotiations over the budget resolution would take place.[19]

Long-term budget planning

Although the Budget Act of 1974 requires the executive branch and the Congressional Budget Office to present five-year budget projections, the one-year budget still dominates congressional budget-making efforts. By focusing on the one-year budget, the President and Congress cannot effectively translate domestic and foreign policy issues into budgets. To do so would require a multi-year budget planning where goals for future years are set, implications for current policy initiatives recognized and budgeted for. Rivlin (1976 and 1986) argues for replacing the annual budget with a multi-year budget. This reform, when implemented, would effectively reduce the time spent by the executive branch and the Congress on budgeting. It would free managers and legislators from the day-to-day task of budget-making so that more time could be spent on program issues and operations, hence improving the overall performance of the public sector.

Constitutional Limits

The inability of the executive branch to present to the Congress a budget that balances claims against resources either for the fiscal year in question or in the near term (during the tenure of the President), and frustration over the congressional failure to deal with the budget deficit prompted many to call for instituting appropriate rules into the Constitution itself. During the early 1980s, various proposals were advanced to impose constitutional limits on the powers of the federal government to tax and spend.[20] Some of the common provisions of the proposed amendment would require that: 1. Congress adopt a budget statement in which total outlays are no greater than total receipts; 2. total receipts do not increase by a rate greater than the rate of increase in national income and 3. Congress and the President ensure that actual outlays do not exceed those set forth in the budget statement.[21] None of the proposed amendments have been approved. The economics profession has not been supportive of the idea. In fact, the majority actively opposes it on the grounds that: 1. it is impractical — a statement of outlays and receipts requires making forecasts which may compromise the integrity of the process; 2. it is not easy to implement as it lacks definition of what constitutes receipts and outlays; most importantly, 3. it is ill advised — how is one to hold Congress accountable for failing to balance the budget?

Mancur Olson (1980) best summarizes the issue of reforming the budget in stating that 'one cannot just write a new constitution for the French that would make them behave like the Swiss, or a new constitution for the Swiss that would make them behave like the French. Nor can one write a constitutional amendment for the United States that would make us behave differently from the way we behave now.'[22] Reform, for it to work, requires not only a change in the process but in behavior as well.

APPENDIX

A.I Budget Terminology

Budget authority, obligations, appropriations and outlays

The budget document, *The Budget of the United States Government*, sets forth the President's proposals for the federal government's outlays and budget authority for the ensuing fiscal year. Congress does not vote on outlays directly but rather on budget authority; that is, Congress first enacts legislation that authorizes an agency to carry out a particular program, but does not provide funds for it. This enactment is called authorization. Many programs are authorized for a specific number of years, while others, such as space, defense procurement, or foreign affairs, require annual authorization. The granting of budget authority is usually a separate subsequent action.

Budget authority permits obligations to be incurred by government agencies. Such obligations include liabilities for salaries, interest, supplies, construction, and the like. For most accounts, the amount of the authority is related to the obligations that it is expected will be incurred during this year. Budget authority usually takes the form of appropriations, which permit obligations to be incurred and payments made. Some budget authority takes the form of contract authority, which allows agencies to incur obligations before appropriations but requires subsequent appropriations to liquidate (that is, to pay) these obligations. There is also borrowing authority, which authorizes agencies to use borrowed money to incur obligations and to make payments. Where such authority applies to the use of Treasury borrowing, it is called authority to spend federal debt receipts, and where it applies to agency borrowing, either directly from the public or from government-administered funds, it is called authority to spend agency debt receipts.

Since appropriations are not usually considered until authorizing legislation is passed, many agencies in recent years have received their appropriations late in the congressional session after the new fiscal year has begun. When an agency does not receive its new appropriation before the old one lapses, it operates under a continuing resolution passed by Congress. This continuing resolution allows the agency to spend at the previous year's rate. Appropriations come in several forms, ranging from one-year appropriations, which allow an agency to incur obligations only during one fiscal year (the most common form), to no-year appropriations, which are available until the purpose of the spending is accomplished. Generally, if the obligational authority is not used during the specified period, it lapses and is no longer available to the agency unless Congress specifically passes the appropriation again. Appropriations or reappropriations of this sort are counted as budget authority in the year of the congressional action.

Obligations are liquidated by the issuance of checks. Payments made are called outlays. Outlays out of new budget authority must be obligated within a certain period but need not actually be paid within that period. Even in the case of one-year appropriations, the agency is not required to pay the bills that year (for example, payment need not be made until after deliveries have been made).

Since budget authority may be granted for a period longer than the fiscal year, there is always a substantial carry-over of unobligated authority (called unobligated balances) from prior years. There is also a carry-over of unspent obligations (called obligated balances) from previous years. Thus the outlay totals in a budget year reflect outlays out of uncommitted budget authority, as well as obligated balances carried over from previous years and out of new budget authority requested in the current budget.

Budget resolution
A resolution passed by both Houses of the Congress that does not require the President's signature. It sets forth a congressional budget plan for the upcoming fiscal year.

Reconciliation
A process used by the Congress to ensure that spending and tax legislation conform with the target established in the budget resolution. The budget resolution may contain reconciliation instruction to achieve saving in spending programs or receipts. The reconciliation process affects taxes, entitlement spending, and offsetting receipts.

Sequestration

Sequestration refers to across-the-board cancellation of budgetary resources. These include new budget authority, new loan guarantees, new direct loans, obligation limitations, national defense, unobligated balances, and other spending authority.

A.II Principal Budget Laws

The following are the basic laws governing the federal budget process.

1. Article 1, Section 9, clause of the Constitution, which requires appropriations of funds before money may be spent.
2. Chapter 11 of Title 31, United States Code, which prescribes procedure for submission of the President's budget and information to be contained in it.
3. Congressional Budget and Impoundment Control Act of 1974, as amended.
4. Balanced Budget and Emergency Deficit Control Act of 1985, as amended in 1987. This Act is known as the Gramm-Rudman-Hollings Act (GRH).
5. Budget Enforcement Act of 1990 (BEA), which significantly amended the laws pertaining to the budget process as set by the Congressional Budget Act and the GRH Act.
6. Federal Credit Reform Act of 1990, as part of the BEA, describes the accounting procedures for federal credit programs.
7. Antideficiency Act (Chapters 13 and 15 of Title 31, U.S. Code), which prescribes rules and procedures for budget execution.

A.III The State-Local Budget Process

The state-local budget process is much less complex than that of the federal government. Budget making at the state-local level differs from budgeting for the federal government in two respects: fiscal policy actions are not a matter of concern, hence budget-numbers need not be adjusted for changes in the economic outlook; and, secondly, because the distribution function is mostly a federal function, budgeting for the 'safety net' is not a major decision.

Budgeting practice at the state-local level may be termed 'incremental' budgeting; year-to-year allocations can only affect details but not basic functions. Provision of most state and local services must continue subject to minor modifications.[23]

The process involves the following steps: 1. budget formulation; 2. legislative authorization; and 3. execution. The time period of a budget is governed by the timing of legislative sessions. About one-third of the states have biennial sessions, hence their budgets must be planned for two years.

For the other states and at the local level, the budget is planned annually. The fiscal year, in most cases runs from July 1 to June 30.

The executive preparation of the budget is at variance with that of the federal government; executive recommendations 'may be strong or weak', depending on whether or not agencies and departments are exempt from executive control. For example, departments headed by elected officials are exempt from executive control as they 'receive their mandate' from the electorate. Similarly, budgets of the legislature and the judiciary are exempt on the grounds of separation of powers. Another difference is the constitutional mandate. Most, if not all, states and local governments are required to present a balanced budget. When deficits arise, authorized receipts from loans cover the excess.

The legislative action on the budget takes place upon transmittal of the budget by the executive branch. The legislative branch discusses the budget proposal, modifies and approves it. Following the legislative action, the execution of the budget process begins. A schedule is set for expenditure disbursement to ensure the spending pattern fits the appropriations.

Budget presentations at the state-local level also differ from the federal budget presentation. Many state governments have capital budgets; the federal government does not. Based on a survey of all 50 states concerning state capital budgets which was conducted in 1986, by the U.S. Office of Management and Budget, it was determined that 42 states have capital budgets while 8 did not. Of the 42 states with capital budgets, 37 generally borrow to finance some capital spending.[24] The capital budget process differs among states as follows: in the Governor's budget presentation, 40 states show the capital account in a separate section of the budget or as a separate document. For the other two, California and Mississippi, capital spending data are shown separately with other parts of the budget. In most states with capital budgets, capital spending is shown both as a separate section and as a separate category within agencies or programs.

In the legislature, the capital budget appropriations for most states (34 in number) are presented as a separate bill or a separate section of a larger bill. For the other eight states, capital spending is integrated with non-capital spending in the appropriations bill. Of the 42 states with capital budgets, 25 states have autonomous state authorities with capital spending but are completely outside the budget. Also, in most states, debt service (interest and repayment of principal) is included in the operating budget and not in the capital account. Other states have a separate debt service fund in the operating budget.

NOTES

1. For discussion of motivations, aims and politics of individual agencies see Wildavsky (1974).
2. In recent years, the President's budget has presented two sets of baseline estimates: current services and required by GRH law.

3. Under the conference agreement, Senate Budget Committee meetings are open to the public unless the committee votes for a secret review in circumstance spelled out in the Act.
4. The CBO issues budget score-keeping reports on the status of congressional action on the budget. These reports represent a way of measuring congressional budget action against the budget targets established by Congress in the first concurrent resolution.
5. Because this and subsequent determinations are in the form of concurrent resolutions, they will not have the force of law nor will they directly limit actual outlays.
6. There would be two exemptions from the May 15 deadline for reporting authorization legislation: those dealing with social security programs and entitlement legislation that cannot be considered on the floor until the budget resolution has been cleared.
7. Not all budget authority is approved through the appropriation process. That which is not is called backdoor spending.
8. Congressional Budget Office (1987), ch.1, p.11.
9. Congressional Budget Office (1990), Appendix.
10. The Act gives Congress the power to suspend the deficit reduction targets if either of the two signs of slowing economic growth occur: 1. the Department of Commerce estimates the growth rate of GNP of 1 per cent a year or less for two consecutive calendar quarters; or 2. the CBO or the OMB forecast that the rate of growth will be less than zero for two consecutive quarters within a year of when the forecast was made. For more detail see CBO, *The Economic and Budget Outlook: Fiscal Years 1991—1995* (January 1990), ch. 1, p. 4.
11. Ibid.
12. Doyle and McCaffery (1991), p. 21.
13. Several unanticipated legislative acts and factors were responsible for the rise in deficit in 1990 and projected deficits for 1991, 1992. For details see CBO, *The Economic and Budget Outlook: An Update*, August 1991.
14. Doyle and McCaffery (1991), p. 29.
15. Doyle and McCaffery (1991) provide an excellent review of the Budget Enforcement Act of 1990.
16. See appendix for terminology.
17. See appendix for terminology.
18. Caiden (1991), p.43, attributes this point to Schick (1990).
19. The line item veto would give the President the power to strike an item in a spending or revenue bill that is believed to reflect only narrow interests. See OMB (1992), Part One, p. 410.
20. Several resolutions were introduced to Congress, including H.J. Res. 169, H.J. Res. 350, S.J. Res. 58. These resolutions call for a constitutional amendment to restrain federal deficits and limit growth of federal outlays and receipts. For details see CBO (1982).
21. Ibid.
22. Olson (1980), p. 94.
23. This review is based on the discussion of the budget process given in Maxwell and Aronson (1977), ch. 10.
24. OMB, Preliminary Draft: Tabulation of State Responses to a Survey of State Capital Budgets, July 1986.

REFERENCES

Caiden, N. (1991), 'Do Politicians Listen to Experts? The Budget Enforcement Act of 1990 and the Capacity to Budget', *Public Budgeting and Finance*, **11**, pp. 41—9.

Congressional Budget Office (1982), *Balancing the Federal Budget and Limiting Federal Spending, Constitutional and Statutory Approaches*, September, Washington D.C., U.S. Government Printing Office.

Congressional Budget Office (1987), *The Economic and Budget Outlook: Fiscal Years 1988—1992*, Washington D.C., U.S. Government Printing Office.

Congressional Budget Office (1990), *The Economic and Budget Outlook: Fiscal Years 1991—1995*, January, Washington D.C., U.S. Government Printing Office.

Congressional Budget Office (1991), *The Economic and Budget Outlook: An Update.* August, Washington D.C., U.S. Government Printing Office.

Congressional Budget Office (1992), *The Economic and Budget Outlook: An Update.* August, Washington D.C., U.S. Government Printing Office.

Davis, E. and Keith, R. (1990), *Budget Enforcement Act of 1990: A Legislative History*, Washington D.C., Congressional Research Service, No. 5.

Doyle, R. and McCaffery, J. (1991), 'The Budget Enforcement Act of 1990: The Path to No-fault Budgeting', *Public Budgeting and Finance*, pp. 25—40.

Maxwell, J. and Aronson, R. (1977), *Financing State and Local Governments*, 3rd ed., Washington D.C., The Brookings Institution.

Office of Management and Budget (July 1986), *Tabulation of State Responses to A Survey of State Capital Budgets*, (preliminary draft), Washington D.C.

Office of Management and Budget (1992), *The Budget of The U.S. Government, Fiscal Year 1993*, Washington D.C., Government Printing Office.

Olson, M. (1980), 'Is the Balanced Budget Amendment Another Form of Prohibition?' in Moore, W. and Penner, R. (eds), *The Constitution and the Budget*, Washington D.C., American Enterprise Institute.

Ott, D. and Ott, A. (1977), *Federal Budget Policy*, 3rd ed., Washington D.C., The Brookings Institution.

Rivlin, A. (1976), 'Prepared Statement of Hon. Alice M. Rivlin', in *Five-Year Budget Projections*, Hearings before the Subcommittee on Priorities and Economy in Government of the Joint Economic Committee, 94:1, 18—22, Washington D.C., Government Printing Office.

Rivlin, A. (1986), 'The Need for a Better Budget Process', *Brookings Review*, **4**, pp. 5—6.

Schick, A. (1990), *The Capacity to Budget*, Washington D.C., Urban Institute Press.

Wildavsky, A. (1974), *The Politics of the Budgetary Process*, 2nd ed., Boston, Little, Brown.

Wildavsky, A. (1988), *The New Politics of the Budgetary Process*, Glenview, Scott, Foresman & Company.

5. Federal Budget Trends: The Record

with Kamal Desai

1 INTRODUCTION

The federal budget, just as a family or a business budget, serves many functions: to identify and plan for future government programs; as a medium through which to control government activities, and as a technique for reviewing previous actions. All of these are significant, and any discussion of budgeting must recognize the diverse purposes a budget serves. The U.S. federal budget, especially in the last three decades, has not served these functions well. Part of the difficulty lies in the fragmentation of the budget program; the other is a 'weakened' oversight and control over budget decisions.

This chapter presents background data on the federal budget program as it has evolved over time. The next section reviews the trends in expenditure, receipts, and the budget deficit. In addition to the general trends, the review will examine the degree to which the nation's priorities have changed over time, but especially since the 1960s. Central to the understanding of budget trends is a discussion of causation — whether changes in the national economy and tax changes influence the level of federal expenditure. This issue is explored in Section 3. The chapter closes with a consideration of the controllability of the budget.

2 BUDGET TRENDS

Historical budget data as reported in the National Income and Product Accounts are used to compile budget trends. Trends in federal outlays are presented for the total and by subcategories: spending net of transfers, transfer payments, net interest payments, and grants-in-aid. Trends in budget receipts are calculated for total receipts, income taxes, and contributions for social insurance. Deficit trends are indicated in absolute magnitude and relative to national income. To focus on the sources of the budget gap, transactions in the social security trust funds, receipts and expenditures, are eliminated from budget aggregates in tracing the budget development.

Budget Trends and Issues

The growth of the federal government outlays over the past two centuries is impressive. In 1794, for example, the federal government spent about $7 million; in fiscal year 1993 federal outlays are estimated at over $1,500 billion, an average annual growth rate of 6.3 per cent.

This growth in spending can best be placed in perspective by comparison with growth in other economic magnitudes such as prices, population, and national income. If allowance is made for changes in the general price level and population, the growth in federal spending has been in the order of 3 per cent per annum for 200 years; an impressive growth indeed.[1] Over the 1794—1991 period, the trend of federal outlays is best described as a series of plateaus; wars (the war of 1812, the Civil War, WWI, WWII, the Korean War, and the Vietnam War) have pushed federal spending sharply upwards. Between wars, expenditures have shown long periods of relative stability or slow growth, but when wars or other exogenous shocks came along, expenditures were forced up, eventually levelling off at a higher plateau.[2]

Perhaps the most significant indicator of the growth of government is the ratio of federal spending to national income or gross national product (GNP). Many types of spending, such as on infrastructure can be expected to increase with the growth in national income and urbanization. Of course, there are other influences on spending, such as the influence of the international situation on defense spending and foreign aid and that of the business cycle-recession and inflation on transfer payments and interest payments on the debt.

Comparing federal spending relative to GNP for the past two hundred years, we find the ratio to have risen from five per cent in 1869 to over 20 per cent in recent years (after falling to two per cent in 1912—13). Some light can be shed on the cause of this increase by decomposing federal outlays into 'war-connected' and 'other' spending and comparing how these two items have behaved relative to GNP.[3] War-connected outlays include defense spending, veterans' outlays, and part of the interest on the debt. As might be expected, this spending category rose sharply relative to GNP during WWII, the Korean War, and somewhat during the Vietnam War.

In contrast to the rapid demobilization following WWII, however, war-connected outlays following the Korean War remained at around 12 per cent of GNP throughout the 1960s. In the first half of the 1970s and throughout the 1980s, war-connected outlays fell to less than 10 per cent of GNP. At present, national defense absorbs less than six per cent of GNP (5.4 per cent in 1991). In contrast, 'other' outlays have risen from 3.8 per cent of GNP in 1954 to almost 14 per cent in 1991.

The rising trend in outlays in peacetime is worth examining in somewhat more detail. The trend in outlays can be broken down into three distinct periods: 1960—69, 1970—79, and 1980—91. The last period may be divided into two subperiods: 1980—87 (Reagan years) and 1988—91. Over the entire 1960—91 period, federal outlay growth averaged 9.3 per cent annually, with the highest growth rate in federal spending recorded for the 1970—79 period (10.6 per cent). During the decade of the 1980s, the growth rate of spending was much lower (6.6 per cent) than that for the 1970s or the 1960s. When transfer payments are netted out, the average growth rate for the period fell by about one percentage point (from 9.3 to 8.3 per cent). For the subperiods, netting out transfers produced varying results. In the 1960—69 period, the rate fell by less than 0.3 percentage points, whereas the drop in the rate was much larger (about 1.8 percentage points) during the 1970s. In the last period, the growth rate of spending net of transfers was actually higher than the growth rate of aggregate spending. Decomposing the trends by spending function, we note (Table 5.1) a definite change in budget priorities during the 1960—91 period. Since the 1960s, the growth of federal budget outlays has been caused primarily by the establishment and expansion of federal income assistance programs and the growth of federal aid to state and local governments. Federal assistance programs, i.e. payments to individuals, include such programs as social security, railroad retirement, military and civil retirement, unemployment compensation, and medicaid and medicare benefits, housing assistance, and other types of welfare. Funds for these programs have outpaced those for all other federal activities during the past three decades. Between 1960—91, the average annual growth rate of total spending net of transfers was about 8.4 per cent, while the average annual growth rate of transfer payments was in the order of 11.4 per cent — 135 per cent higher than the growth of funding for all other federal programs.

Federal grants to state and local government have also increased, especially during the 1960s and the 1970s. The growth in federal aid was in line with congressional preference for decentralizing the provision of new programs by relegating them to state and local governments. Between 1960—79, federal grants-in-aid have grown at an average rate of 13 per cent. While this type of spending has increased at a much faster rate than the transfer payments, this category of spending has much less of an impact on the overall size of the budget as it accounts for a smaller percentage of total outlays compared to the ratio of transfer payments to the total.

In the 1960s, payments to individuals accounted for 26 per cent of federal outlays, while federal grants-in-aid accounted for 8.7 per cent. During the 1970—79 period, 38 per cent of budget expenditures were devoted to transfer payments; slightly less than 20 per cent for grants-in-aid. In the 1980—91 period, the transfer payments share increased slightly (to 40 per cent), while the grants-in-aid share in the total fell by 50 per cent, from 20 to slightly over 10 per cent.

The growth of net interest payments has been another important source of increased federal budget expenditures. The average annual growth rate over the entire 1960—91 period was over 12 per cent. The rate of increase

Table 5.1 *Average annual growth rates of major spending categories for 1960—90 and by subperiods (in per cent)*

Description	Average Growth Rate
1960—1991	
Total spending	9.31
Total spending net of transfers to persons	8.35
Transfer payments to persons	11.41
Grants-in-aid	10.26
Net interest	12.38
1960—1969	
Total spending	7.97
Total spending net of transfers to persons	7.61
Transfer payments to persons	9.09
Grants-in-aid	13.10
Net interest	7.50
1970—1979	
Total spending	10.60
Total spending net of transfers to persons	8.85
Transfer payments to persons	13.81
Grants-in-aid	13.31
Net interest	12.88
1980—1991	
Total spending	6.58
Total spending net of transfers to persons	6.73
Transfer payments to persons	6.23
Grants-in-aid	4.79
Net interest	10.25

Source: U.S. Department of Commerce, *Survey of Current Business*, several issues.

in outlays for interest payments was particularly noticeable during the 1970—79 period. The increase in interest outlays in this period, however, was not caused by the rise in the size of debt outstanding. Rather it was mainly due to the 'enormous' increase in interest rates. In 1971, the average interest rate on new issues of three-month U.S. treasury bills was 4.3 per cent; by 1979, the average rate was 10 per cent. As a fraction of the total budget, interest payments have risen from 6.4 per cent during the 1960s to 12 per cent during the 1980s.

Trends in Receipts

The historical trends in federal receipts have not paralleled outlays exactly — the government ran surpluses in some years, deficits in others; the general order of increase has remained the same. Until 1910, customs receipts were overwhelmingly the most important source of revenues, accounting for 90—95 per cent of all receipts. Subsequently, customs receipts were supplemented with excise taxes.[4]

The emergence of excise taxation marked a shift from external to internal revenue. This change gained momentum with the introduction of the individual and corporation income taxes in 1913 and 1909, respectively; by 1929 these two income taxes accounted for more than 75 per cent of all federal receipts. Payroll taxes introduced in the federal tax system by the Social Security Act of 1935 have grown markedly since then from six per cent in 1937 to 42 per cent of tax revenue collected in 1991. Indeed, in recent years, most U.S. citizens have been paying more in social security taxes than they do in income taxes.

During the past three decades (1960—91), the share of the individual income tax in total federal revenue has remained fairly stable at about 42 per cent, while the corporate income tax share has declined substantially from an average of 21 per cent in the 1960—69 period to slightly more than 10 per cent of total tax receipts in the 1980—91 period. In contrast, contributions for social insurance, which averaged some 22 per cent of the total during the 1960s, almost doubled by the 1980s, contributing more than 40 per cent of federal receipts.

Growth rates of total receipts from major sources are reported in Table 5.2 for the entire 1960—91 period and by subperiod. Over the entire 1960—91 period, federal receipts show an average annual growth of about 8.7 per cent. By far the fastest growth was in social security contributions, with the average annual growth rate equal to 11 per cent. By subperiods, except for the 1970—79 period, the growth in total receipts net of social security has averaged about six to seven per cent per annum. During the 1970s all categories of receipts have grown by about 10 per cent per annum, compared to average growth rates of about seven to eight per cent per annum in the 1960s. The reduction in the growth rate of receipts in the 1980s is attributed to tax law changes introduced in the Reagan years which effectively reduced revenue potential of the income and profits taxes. As shown in Table 5.2, the growth rate was cut by about 41 per cent compared to the growth in the 1970s, and by about 20 per cent compared to the average growth rate in the 1960s.

When average annual growth rates of receipts are compared to those of expenditures, we note that the growth in receipts has lagged by less than one percentage point behind that of expenditures over the 1960—91 period. During the subperiods 1960—69 and 1970—79, the difference in the growth rates was quite small — about one-tenth of one percentage point. In the decade of the 1980s, the average annual growth rates of spending and receipts were about equal. When the social security trust fund transactions are removed from the budget totals, the difference between the two growth rates equals 0.8 percentage point for the 1960—91 period. In the first

Table 5.2 *Average annual growth rates of receipts for major sources, 1960—91 and by subperiods (in per cent)*

Description		Average Growth Rate
	1960—1991	
Total receipts		8.66
Total receipts less social security contributions		7.56
Income and profit taxes		7.90
	1960—1969	
Total receipts		7.91
Total receipts less social security contributions		6.96
Income and profit taxes		7.58
	1970—1979	
Total receipts		10.47
Total receipts less social security contributions		9.43
Income and profit taxes		10.21
	1980—1991	
Total receipts		6.61
Total receipts less social security contributions		5.65
Income and profit taxes		6.05

Source: U.S. Department of Commerce, *Survey of Current Business*, several issues.

subperiod, 1960—69, the average annual growth rate of receipts fell short of that of spending by 0.65 percentage points. In the succeeding subperiod, 1970—79 the difference was again small-receipts growth was 0.6 percentage points higher than that for expenditures. In the 1980—91 period, the growth of receipts net of social security contribution was about one percentage point below spending net of social security payments.

The major trends that emerge from this brief consideration of federal expenditures and revenues are: 1. total revenues have grown at just about the same pace as have total outlays; 2. federal revenues growth excluding social security contributions has lagged behind the growth in federal spending after netting out social security payments; the gap equals to 0.8 percentage points per annum in the 1960—91 period; and 3. the growth in social security contributions has outpaced that of the personal income and corporate income taxes.

Deficits and Surpluses

Since 1792 the federal government has run deficits in as many years (100) as it has run surpluses (101). This pattern of deficits and surpluses looks quite different in recent periods. Over the last 31 years (1960—91), the budget was in deficit twenty-eight times. Of the $2,291.2 billion in deficits accumulated over the past thirty-one years, 84 per cent ($1,926 billion) was associated with unbalanced budgets during the period 1981—91.

Federal budget deficits have been growing in absolute size as well as in relation to the nation's income. The growth in deficits and its implications for the federal budget in terms of the budget gap is described in Figures 5.1 to 5.4. A five-year-moving average of the deficit is plotted in Figure 5.1. In Figure 5.2, a moving average of the deficit ratio to GNP is plotted. Year-to-year changes in the deficit/GNP ratio and the budget gap are shown in the last two figures.

From Figure 5.3, it is clear that, except for one or two years, federal spending ratios have consistently outstripped receipts throughout the 1960—91 period. The average size of the gap calculated for the period from 1971—73 was 1.2 per cent of average GNP. Over the period 1974—79, the average shortfall has risen to 1.9 per cent of average GNP. The most dramatic growth in the size of the budget gap relative to GNP has been in the later period — since the beginning of the 1980s. The size of the gap rose to an average of 4.1 per cent of average GNP in 1980—87, falling to 2.7 per cent in the 1988—90 period. When the year 1991 is included, the average size of the budget/GNP gap was equal to 3.1 per cent.

The year-to-year changes in the deficit/GNP path and in the size of the budget gap relative to GNP (Figure 5.4) clearly suggest that a 'fundamental' change in budgeting has taken place since the mid-1970s. Although in each of the subperiods marked by a widening budget gap (see Figure 5.4) the economy was in a state of recession for an average of four quarters, the size of the gap was as much affected by discretionary changes as it was affected by the economy. Over the period 1975—86, five tax reductions were enacted: the Tax Reduction and Revenue Adjustment Act of 1975, the Tax Reduction and Simplification Act of 1977, the Revenue Act of 1978, the Economic Recovery Act of 1981, and the Tax Reform Act of 1986.[5] As mentioned earlier, these tax cuts, especially those enacted in the 1980s are believed to have permanently lowered the revenue-raising potential of the federal budget. In comparison, since the mid-1970s, the growth trend of federal spending fluctuated from period to period and was consistently above the level which could be sustained by the growth in receipts. Projections of the budget path in the early 1980s had consistently pointed to unbalanced budgets for the remainder of the decade. As Musgrave (1983) put it, neither have the 'expected built-in gains' in revenues from the 1981 tax cuts materialized nor has the growth of spending declined, leaving the budget in a state of deficits for years to come.

Figure 5.1 *Budget deficit: 5–year moving average (in billions of dollars)*

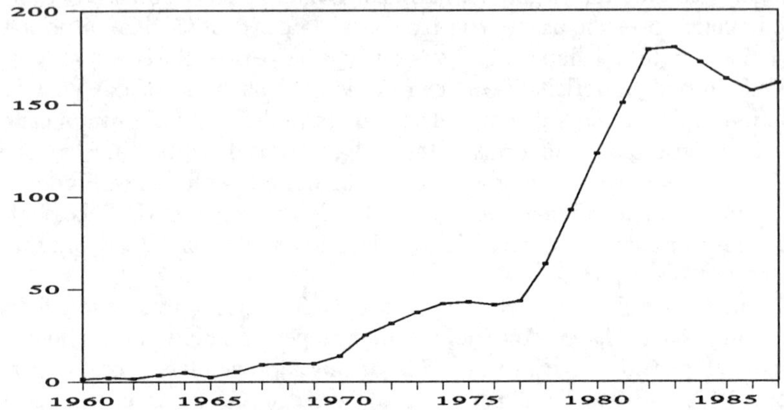

Note: Data based on NIPA quarterly series of the federal sector. U.S. Department of Commerce; *Survey of Current Business,* several issues.

Figure 5.2 *Deficit/GNP ratio: 5–year moving average (in percentages)*

Note: See note to Figure 5.1.

Figure 5.3 ***The budget gap: expenditure and receipts as a percentage of GNP***

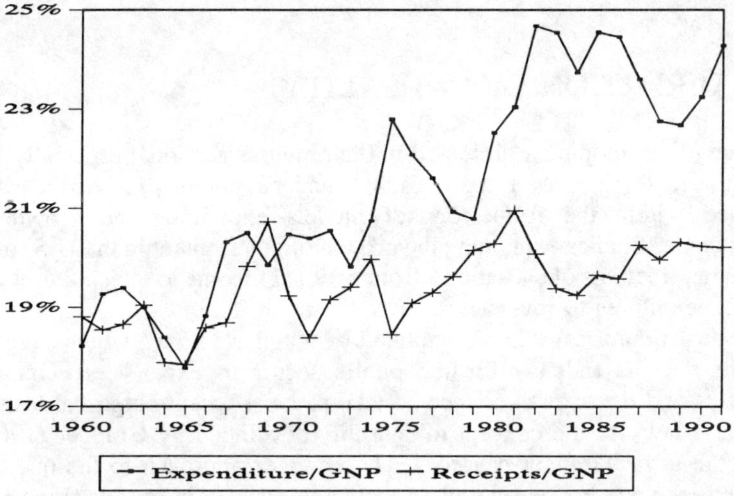

Note: See note to Figure 5.1.

Figure 5.4 ***The development of the budget gap: year–to–year change in growth of spending and receipts as a percentage of GNP***

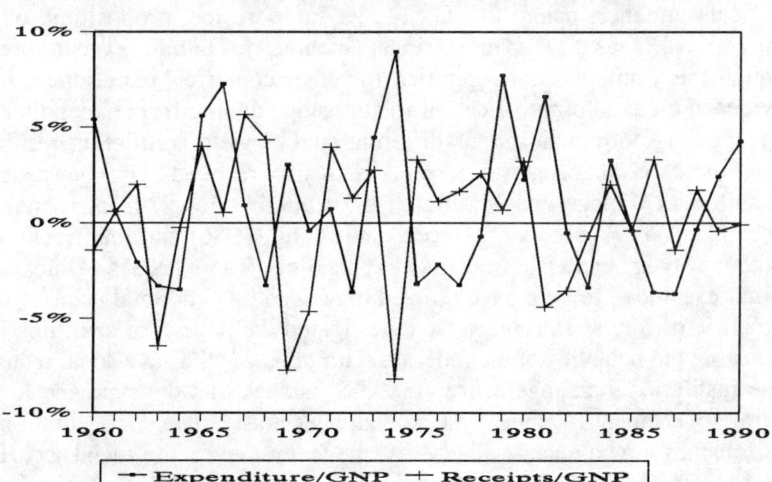

Note: See note to Figure 5.1.

It is worth noting that congressional efforts to control the deficit (like the Gramm-Rudman-Hollings Act) have succeeded in lowering the growth path of the deficit. Unfortunately, the year-to-year fluctuations in the growth rate of the budget deficit were significantly reduced over the period 1985—89, only to rise again in subsequent years.

3 DIRECTION OF CAUSALITY

The budget development discussed in the previous sections, especially that experienced in the past three decades, may be put in perspective when analyzed within the framework of models explaining the growth of government. Studies explaining the growth of government in the U.S. offer two main directions of causation: from national income to expenditures and from expenditures to revenues.[6]

One direction of causality is implied by 'Wagner's Law', which suggests that there is a tendency for the public sector to expand as economic programs and the growth of income take place. Recent empirical tests of Wagner's law use the concept of causality developed by Granger (1969), hence the term 'Granger-caused'. The Granger approach to the question whether income, Y, causes public expenditures, G, is to determine how much of the current G can be explained by past values of G and then to see whether adding lagged values of Y can improve the explanation. Hence, public expenditures, G, are said to be 'Granger-caused' by income, Y, if Y helps in the prediction of G, or equivalently, if the coefficients on the lagged values of Y are statistically significant. Using this method, the empirical evidence using the U.S. data support the proposition of a unidirectional causality from national income to public expenditures, although this finding is not supported for other countries' experiences.[7]

Evidence on an alternative causal relationship running from expenditures to revenues is not conclusive as different studies yield conflicting results: expenditures 'Granger-cause' receipts and also receipts 'Granger-cause' expenditures (Manage and Marlow, 1986); unidirectional, from spending to receipts (Von Furstenberg, Green, and Jeong, 1986) and unidirectional the other way around, from receipts to spending (Ram, 1988). Almost all the studies alluded to here have utilized total spending and total taxes of the federal sector, or, as in Ram, have investigated the pattern of causation by contrasting the behavior of the federal sector *vis-à-vis* the state-local sector.

The institutional arrangement in the U.S. is such that the state and local general government revenues and expenditures must balance (constitutional requirement for a balanced budget). At the federal level, the social security trust fund is also constrained to maintain a trust fund balance (surplus). That is, the social security fund is expenditure-driven; a shortfall in receipts relative to expenditures triggers legislative responses for increasing receipts.

Table 5.3 *Direction of causality : Granger-Causality test results*

Description	Lag structure (Quarters)
1. Unidirectional	
Fed Exp =/=> GNP, but GNP ==> Fed Exp	4,8
Real Fed Exp =/=> Real GNP, but Real GNP ==> Real Fed Exp	8
Real Fed Rev =/=> Real Fed Exp, but Real Fed Exp ==> Real Fed Rev.	4,8
2. Bidirectional	
Nominal Federal Expenditure <==> Nominal Federal Revenue	4,8

Notes: All series were subjected to tests for nonstationarity, or existence of a unit root. The UROOT command (Micro TSP package) runs an augmented Dickey-Fuller (ADF) test for a unit root. A large negative t-statistic indicates rejection of the hypothesis of a unit root, suggesting stationarity of the series. The test showed real expenditures and real revenue to be stationary, while nominal revenue and expenditures to be a random walk.

Source: NIPA quarterly series for GNP, federal expenditures and receipts and the unemployment rates for 1947—91 were used in estimating the VAR model.

No such constraints are imposed on the federal funds transactions. Additional evidence on the causal relationship between federal spending and federal revenues as well as on the growth of federal spending is provided here. The Granger-causality test results based on data for federal expenditures and receipts after netting out social security transactions are summarized in Table 5.3. As indicated in the table, unidirectional causality from national income to expenditure (net of social security) exists, whether the variables are measured in current prices (nominal) or constant prices (real). Unidirectional causality was found from real expenditures (net of social security payments) to real revenues (net of social security contributions). With nominal magnitudes, a bidirectional causality — from revenues to expenditures and from expenditures to revenues-was discovered. This result was less robust than the unidirectional causality; the coefficient on the lagged variable was not significant over different lag structures.

From the unidirectional pattern of causality, one may wish to ascertain whether a one-period shock to national income will affect nominal federal spending and for how long. Vector Auto-Regression (VAR) models are helpful in this regard. The VAR model applied here is spelled out in the appendix. After estimating the VAR model (using quarterly data 1947—91), a shock equal to one standard deviation (of the error term) is given to the endogenous variable in each equation at some time period t. Then the model is simulated to determine the effect on all the model variables in the time interval t to [t+n].

In the simulation, a shock to GNP (equal to one standard deviation of the error term) at time t results in this shock being transferred in the same period t to government spending, G, and taxes, T. In contrast, a shock to government spending G (equal to one standard deviation of the error term) in time period t will affect G and T, but not GNP in the same period. GNP will only be affected from [t+1] on. Similarly, for a shock to T in period t, only T will be affected in the same time period. The time path associated with a one-period shock to GNP is shown in Figure 5.5. The time path associated with a one-period shock to government expenditures (i.e. fiscal stimulus) is indicated in Figure 5.6.

Nominal GNP Shock

An initial one-standard-deviation GNP shock of say $1 billion in quarter one increases to $1.4 billion after five quarters (1.25 years). Subsequently, GNP gradually declines; arriving back at the initial level of the shock after 14 quarters (3.5 years). After six years, nearly 50 per cent of the initial shock is still present in the system. Even after ten years, 16.2 per cent of the original ($1 billion) shock remains, illustrating that GNP shocks can be quite long-lasting. Given the considerable length of time that a shock can persist, the economy will more than likely experience another shock causing GNP to continually increase.

GNP shocks in period t will affect G in the same period, and due to the causal relationship, G will also have a delayed response. After two years from the initial shock (nine quarters), the effect of a $1 billion GNP shock on G will be at its maximum level of nearly $1.45 billion. Just as the GNP path declines gradually over time in response to the shock, so too does G, only the order of effect will be higher than that on GNP. Figure 5.5 shows the delayed response-the GNP path reaches its peak after five quarters, but G reaches its peak a year later (in the ninth quarter).

Nominal G Shock

A (one-standard-deviation) shock of G will initially cause the path of G to decline rapidly for three quarters. This decline is slowed once GNP effects come into play (i.e. high G will increase GNP and later that increase in GNP will impact on G). As shown in Figure 5.6, the first segment of the G path has a very large negative slope, but after the third quarter, it slopes up for one to two quarters (reflecting GNP's impact) then gradually declines. Nearly 60 per cent of the original shock still persists after the first year. After two years, 25 per cent remains, and after three years, less than 12 per cent of the shock is left.

Figure 5.5 *Dynamic response of GNP and G to a shock in nominal GNP*

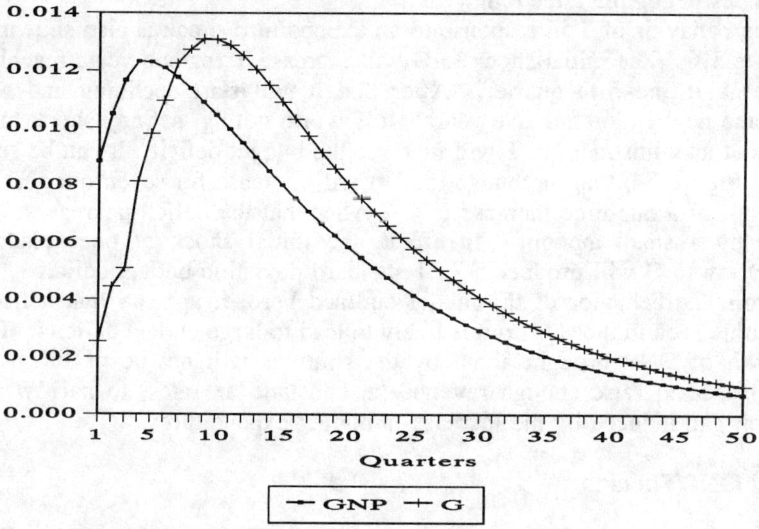

Note: Authors' simulation.

Figure 5.6 *Dynamic response of GNP, G and T to a shock in nominal G*

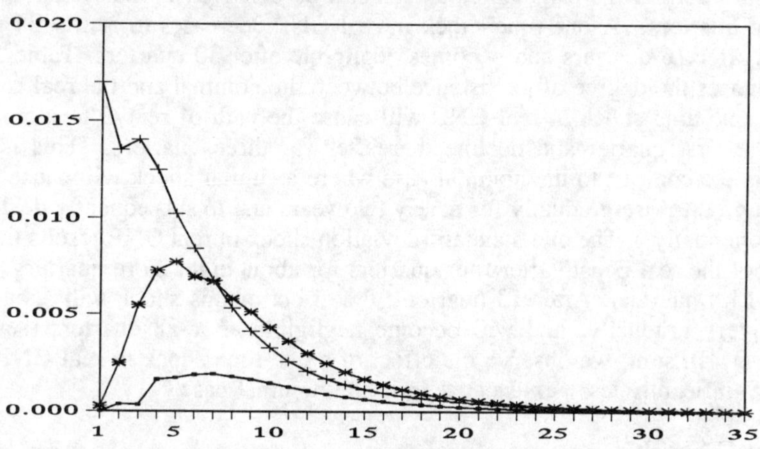

Note: Authors' simulation.

As to the behavior of GNP, the initial shock to G will push GNP up for about seven quarters. The shock effect is very low in the first two quarters, but increases at a fairly high rate for the next two quarters. The GNP path reaches its peak in the seventh quarter, after that it declines very slowly and becomes negligible after four years.

The behavior of T in response to an expenditure shock is also shown in Figure 5.6. The initial shock to G will increase T for one year, reaching its peak in the fifth quarter. After that it will start declining and will become negligible after five years. It is worth noting that any shock to G without an adjustment in T will increase the budget deficit. It can be seen from Figure 5.6 that the budget deficit will increase for seven quarters as a result of a one-time increase in G. After that the deficit decreases, but only by a small amount. In effect, the initial shock of one standard deviation to G will produce a 2.21 standard deviation budget deficit.

From the behavior of the model outlined here, it appears that a fiscal stimulus even in the short run is likely to lead to large budget deficits. The growth of GNP brought about by the stimulus will not be of sufficient magnitude to raise enough revenue (at constant tax rates) to narrow the deficit gap induced by the increase in budget expenditures.

Real GNP Shock

A one-standard-deviation shock given to real GNP in quarter one decreases exponentially. The rate of decline is nearly constant for the entire period (see Figure 5.7). After eight quarters, only 47 per cent of the original shock is left. This is in contrast to a nominal GNP shock, where nearly 128 per cent of the original shock can still be observed in the system after eight quarters. A one-time shock in real GNP decreases to nearly 25 per cent after 16 quarters and becomes negligible after 30 quarters. Table 5.4 compares the degree of persistence between the nominal and the real case.

A one-time shock in real GNP will cause the path of real G to increase in the first quarter and decline thereafter for three quarters. (This is in complete contrast to the nominal case where a similar shock will cause the path of G to rise gradually for nearly two years and to subsequently decline exponentially.) The one-standard-deviation shock in real GNP results in an rise of the real G path after four quarters for about eight more quarters (till the 13th quarter). After 13 quarters, the effect of this shock will subdue, fall very gradually, and will become negligible after 28 quarters (seven years). In sum, we observe the effect of a one-time shock in real GNP to be significantly less persistent than in the nominal case.[8]

Real G Shock

A shock in real G in quarter one will cause the path of G to decline initially, then rise for one to two quarters and finally decline exponentially (see Figure 5.8).

Figure 5.7 *Dynamic response of GNP and G to a shock in REAL GNP*

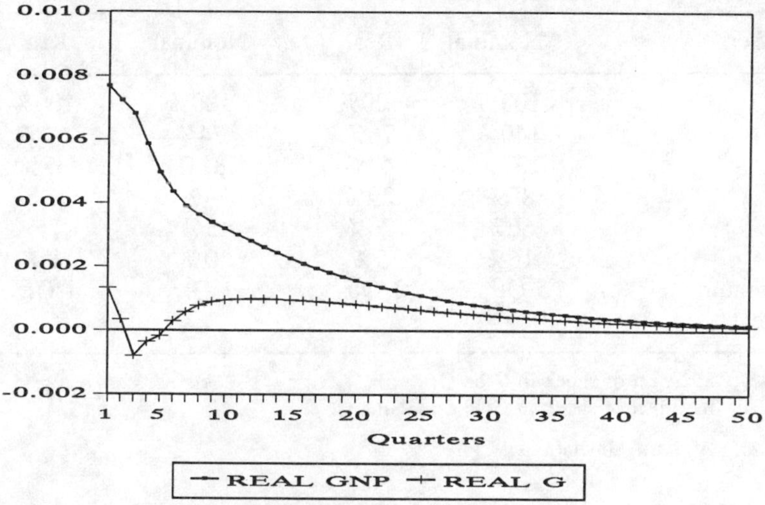

Note: Authors' simulation.

Figure 5.8 *Dynamic response of GNP, G and T to a shock in REAL G*

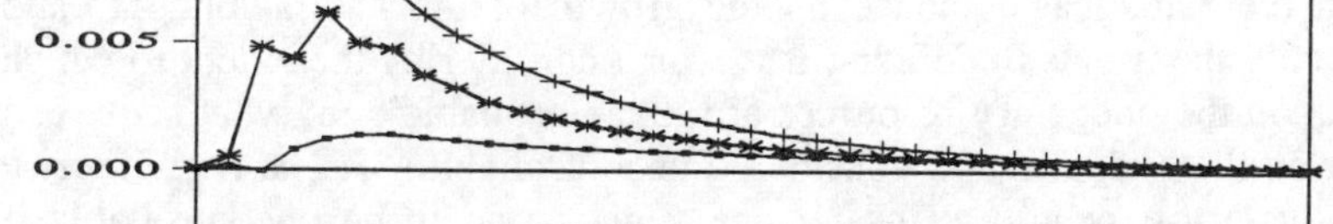

Note: Authors' simulation.

Table 5.4 *Comparison of persistence of a one-time shock between real and nominal data*

	G[a]		GNP[b]	
Quarters	Nominal	Real	Nominal	Real
1	100%	100%	100%	100%
4	140%	76%	74%	64%
8	127%	47%	31%	35%
16	85%	29%	6%	12%
20	66%	20%	3%	7%
40	16%	5%	0%	1%
Maximum effect	5 Qtrs.	1 Qtr.	1 Qtr.	1 Qtr.

Notes: a: Effect of shock in G on G.
b: Effect of shock in GNP on GNP.

Source: Authors' simulations.

Only 32 per cent of the original one-time shock is still observed after eight quarters (two years). A similar shock in nominal G results in nearly 31 per cent of the shock being left after eight quarters. The response of real G to a shock in real G is quite similar to that of the nominal case. Real GNP and real T also respond in a quite similar fashion, yet with less magnitude. Once again, the effect of a one-time shock in real G is temporary.

4 CONTROLLABILITY OF THE BUDGET

Given the statistical evidence on the growth of the federal budget and especially the trends in deficits, it is worth considering the extent to which claims on the budgetary resources are 'uncontrollable'. In what sense is a claim on the budget dollar considered uncontrollable? A claim giving rise to budgetary expenditure in any one year is said to be uncontrollable if satisfying this claim is 'mandated' by an existing law or if it represents a 'contractual' obligation of the government. Take, for instance, social security payments. Under existing laws, current retirees have a claim on the budget dollar. Future retirees' claims are protected by the social contract as the system operates on a pay-as-you-go basis. That is, current retirees' benefits are paid for by current workers; and future generations of workers are expected to finance future retirees (current workers). Another example is interest payments. Interest on the outstanding stock of public

Table 5.5 *Discretionary, entitlements and other mandatory spending as a percentage of total spending*

Fiscal year	Discretionary (Defense & non-defense)	Entitlements & other mandatory	Net interest
1962	76.2	28.7	6.5
1965	70.0	29.4	7.3
1969	67.3	31.9	7.0
1972	58.6	40.8	6.7
1975	51.6	47.1	7.0
1979	50.2	46.5	8.5
1982	45.8	47.7	11.4
1985	45.2	46.2	13.7
1989	43.3	47.6	14.8
1991	40.4	44.9	14.7

Note: Sum may exceed 100% due to offsetting receipts (—) included in total outlays.

Sources: 1962—89 based on data given in CBO, *The Economic and Budget Outlook: Fiscal Years 1991—1995,* Table 5—E, p. 126. For 1991: *The Budget of the United States Government, Fiscal Year 1993*, Part 1, p. 25.

debt represents the liquidation of contractual obligations of the federal government; hence it is uncontrollable. In recognition of these types of claims, the Budget Enforcement Act of 1990 distinguishes these types of federal spending, entitlements, and other mandatory spending from discretionary spending. Discretionary spending is controllable spending. It includes national defense and other non-defense (domestic) expenditures. As a fraction of GNP, discretionary spending accounted for over 40 per cent of total outlays in 1991. On the other hand, entitlements and mandatory spending (including net interest) absorbed about 60 per cent of budget resources (Table 5.5). The best known examples of entitlements, social security and medicare, are the two largest benefit programs run by the federal government. Entitlements also include items such as school lunch programs, student loans and farm subsidies. Other mandatory programs include spending for federal deposit insurance. Entitlements and other mandatory spending have by far been the fastest growing component of the federal spending in the past three decades. Between 1962 and 1991, the average growth rate for this category was 10 per cent per annum. The net interest payments' share of the budget dollar has also risen from 6.5 per cent in 1962 to about 14 per cent in 1991 — a cumulative growth rate of over 200 per cent.

The fact that entitlements and other mandatory spending and net interest payments are classified as 'uncontrollable' does not mean that nothing can be done about their future growth paths. Given that the definition of controllability rests on 'existing legislation' and 'liquidation of contractual obligation', Congress can enact new legislation as well as repeal, modify or terminate outstanding contracts.

Indeed, over the years Congress has revised the underlying social security benefits structure and has revised upward both the tax rate and the wage base for social security contribution. In 1989, Congress repealed the medicare catastrophic coverage which was enacted a year earlier (1988); it became evident to beneficiaries that under the 1988 law, the expansion in coverage would be paid for through higher premiums collected from all beneficiaries in addition to an income tax surcharge that applied to the elderly with high incomes. In short, there is nothing to prevent Congress from acting to reduce the growth in entitlements and mandatory spending. Congress can also cap the growth of future interest payments by exercising 'fiscal' discipline (enact a balanced budget), thereby reducing the need for future borrowing and hence the stock of outstanding debt.

But controllability of outlays is only one part of the equation for controlling the budget. As the discussion above clearly illustrates, the cause of the imbalance lies in the deficiency of budget resources in relation to commitment. To be sure, the imbalance is not to be found in the (social security) trust funds, since these funds have their own earmarked revenue sources. Rather, it is in the federal funds. As pointed out earlier the growth in budget receipts net of social security contribution has consistently lagged behind federal expenditures excluding social security payments. This was particularly evident during the 1980s. The most obvious solution then is to restore a balance to the federal funds accounts. The gap between federal funds receipts and expenditure can be eliminated in one of several ways: first, set the growth rate of federal spending below the growth in receipts and use the excess (in future years) for debt reduction. Second, increase the rate of growth of federal funds receipts enough to pay for some allowable future growth in spending plus a targeted reduction in the deficit. Third, implement a combination of spending reduction and tax increases tied to a targeted reduction in the federal funds deficit.

These, as well as other solutions, are easier to recommend than implement. Back in the early 1980s, Alice Rivlin defined the deficit dilemma by noting that everyone [then] was in agreement 'to reduce the rate of growth of spending . . . We also wanted to reduce the tax burden, not only because people don't like to pay taxes, but because of the feeling that taxes, and corporate taxes particularly, were inhibiting investment and economic growth . . . And everyone also agreed that it would be a good thing to move towards a balanced budget.'[9] There is no shortage of solutions; the problem lies in the inconsistency of objectives.

APPENDIX

The following Vector Auto Regression (VAR) model was used in the estimation of a VAR(2) system:

Endogenous variables: GNP, FEXP (Federal Expenditure), FREV (Federal Revenue).
Exogenous variables: time and UR (unemployment rate).

Equation System

$$GNP_t = c_1 + \alpha_1\, time + \sum_{i=1}^{2} \beta_{1i}\, GNP_{t-i} + \sum_{i=1}^{2} \gamma_{1i}\, FEXP_{t-i} + \sum_{i=1}^{2} \lambda_{1i}\, FREV_{t-i} + \rho_1 UR_{t-1} + \xi_1$$

$$FEXP_t = c_2 + \alpha_2\, time + \sum_{i=1}^{2} \beta_{2i}\, GNP_{t-i} + \sum_{i=1}^{2} \gamma_{2i}\, FEXP_{t-i} + \sum_{i=1}^{2} \lambda_{2i}\, FREV_{t-i} + \rho_2 UR_{t-1} + \xi_2$$

$$FREV_t = c_3 + \alpha_3\, time + \sum_{i=1}^{2} \beta_{3i}\, GNP_{t-i} + \sum_{i=1}^{2} \gamma_{3i}\, FEXP_{t-i} + \sum_{i=1}^{2} \lambda_{3i}\, FREV_{t-i} + \rho_3 UR_{t-1} + \xi_3$$

NOTES

1. A historical record of federal spending is given in Ott and Ott (1977).
2. Ibid., p. 55.
3. The classification of outlays into 'war-related' and 'other' is given in Kendrick (1955). Kendrick includes interest in the war-related spending category because until the recent period, the bulk of outstanding debt was issued to finance wars.
4. For a historical review of trends in receipts, see Ott and Ott (1977), ch. 4.
5. The Tax Equity and Fiscal Responsibilities Act of 1982 scaled back some of the investment incentives of the 1981 Act.
6. A review of models of the growth of government is given in Aronson and Ott (1991).
7. See, for example, Ram (1986) on unidirectional causality. For bidirectional causality see Delorme, Cartwright and Kespohl (1988).
8. This is expected, as nominal GNP and G follow a random walk, and real GNP and G are stationary. Any shock in nominal GNP and G should last forever.
9. Alice Rivlin (1983), pp. 135–6.

REFERENCES

Aronson, J.R. and Ott, A.F. (1991), 'The Growth of the Public Sector', in Greenaway D., Bleaney, M. and Stewart, I. (eds), *Companion to Contemporary Economic Thought*, London and New York, Routledge.

Delorme, C.D., Cartwright, P.A. and Kespohl, E. (1988), 'The Effect of Temporal Aggregation on the Test of Wagner's Law', *Public Finance*, **43**, pp. 373—87.

Granger, C.W.J. (1969), 'Investigating Causal Relations by Econometric Models and Cross-spectral Methods', *Econometrica*, **37**, pp. 409—68.

Kendrick, M.S. (1955), *A Century and a Half of Federal Expenditures*, occasional paper 48 (revised), National Bureau of Economic Research.

Manage, N. and Marlow, M.L. (1986), 'The Causal Relation Between Federal Expenditures-Receipts', *Southern Economic Journal*, **53**, pp. 617—29.

Musgrave, R.A. (1983), 'The Reagan Administration's Fiscal Policy: A Critique' in Stubblebine, Wm.C. and Willett, T.D. (eds), *Reaganomics: A Midterm Report*, San Francisco, Institute for Contemporary Studies Press.

Ott, D.J. and Ott, A.F. (1977), *Federal Budget Policy*, 3rd ed., Washington D.C., The Brookings Institution.

Ram, R. (1986), 'Government Size and Economic Growth: a New Framework and Some Evidence from Cross-section and Time Series Data', *American Economic Review*, **76**, pp. 183—204.

Ram, R. (1988), 'Additional Evidence on Causality Between Government Revenue and Government Expenditure', *Public Finance*, **43**, pp. 261—9.

Rivlin, A. (1983), 'The Deficit Dilemma' in Stubblebine, Wm.C. and Willett, T.D. (eds) *Reaganomics: A Midterm Report*, San Francisco, Institute for Contemporary Studies Press.

U.S. Department of Commerce; Bureau of Economic Analysis: *Survey of Current Business*, Washington D.C., U.S. Government Printing Office.

Von Furstenberg, G.H., Green, R.J. and Jin-Ho Jeong (1986), 'Tax and Spend, or Spend and Tax?', *Review of Economics and Statistics*, **68**, pp. 179—88.

6. Budget Decisions in a Federal System

1 INTRODUCTION

The United States public sector is a federal system comprised of multiple levels of government: federal, state, and local. In a federal system, each level of government has a set of expenditure priorities and taxing powers. The assignment of responsibilities and powers of these strata of government is found in the Constitution.

The focus of this chapter is on how budget decisions are made in a federal fiscal system. How these decisions have shaped the U.S. fiscal system will be taken up in the next chapter. This chapter is divided as follows: the following section sets the framework for the division of powers and responsibilities among the various levels of government. Following this discussion, an economic analysis of budget efficiency in a system of multiple government is given. The chapter concludes with an analysis of intergovernmental grants.

2 THE ECONOMICS OF FEDERALISM

A federal state faces two primary issues of organization: first, which public good should be supplied by which level of government, and secondly, what is the optimal size of the fiscal unit. The first issue addresses the question of the range or nature of benefits, while the second is primarily a matter of scale economies.

The economic analysis of fiscal federalism is rooted in Musgrave's theory of the multi-level public sector. Although Musgrave (1959) warns that 'There is no simple set of principles, nor uniform rules of normative behavior that may be applied to the conduct of public economy',[1] he offers us a useful framework within which one can think about the choices facing the public sector. Musgrave's theory of the public household divides governmental functions into three categories: allocation, distribution and stabilization. The economic analysis of federalism focuses on which level of government is best suited for one or more of these three. Furthermore, the issue of finance in a multiple government setting, especially as it relates to public sector provision of goods and services (the allocation function), has to be addressed. We begin first with the assignment of each of these three functions.

Assignment of Functions

Stabilization

The conventional wisdom holds that spending and taxing decisions intended to affect aggregate economic magnitudes such as the unemployment rate or the inflation rate belong to the national government. The reasoning behind this consensus is simple. Fiscal policies aimed at influencing the rate of growth of the economy and/or the rate of inflation require a coordinated effort of the individual units that is beyond their capacity. No subnational government is large enough to affect the aggregate level of economic activities, and no governmental unit but the national government has authority to change the rate of growth of money.

Bahl (1984), although he does not question this view, makes a case for reassessing the effects of central government stabilization policies on the budgetary decisions of subnational governments. According to Bahl, there is a need to examine first, whether fiscal action by the central government results in unintended spending and/or taxation at the local level, and, secondly, whether local government budget actions complement or offset central government fiscal decisions. Studies by the Advisory Commission on Intergovernmental Relations (ACIR, 1978, 1979), Vogel and Trost (1979), and Reischauer (1978), suggest that in the U.S. the behavioral response of the state-local sector to the federal government's stabilization actions has been 'mildly' countercyclical, hence reinforcing the effort. Other studies (Rafuse, 1965) show that in the post-war period until the early 1960s the revenue and expenditure behavior of the state-local government sector was 'asymmetrical' in its impact during expansion and contraction phases of the business cycle. While revenues were shown to have a stabilizing effect during economic expansion and a destabilizing effect during contraction, the reverse turned out to be the case for expenditures.

Interdependence of the local and national economies is well documented. Indeed recent history provides examples of national governments, as is the case with EC countries, moving towards a coordinated fiscal action to stabilize the 'global' economy. At the same time, there are those governments who prefer to take matters into their own hands — here in the U.S., some state governments frustrated by national government stabilization efforts have been engaged in activities aimed at accelerating the recovery of their local economies.

While it may be the case that during periods of expansion the growth of the national economy most often spills over to benefit the local economy, in periods of recession efforts by the national government to stimulate the national economy may not be sufficient or relevant to the specific needs of the local economy. This asymmetry is not in and of itself a good enough reason for individual governmental units to engage in stabilization. The assignment of the stabilization function to the national level, however, should not preclude a particular unit of government from pursuing independent fiscal action relevant to its own circumstances. But precisely because of the interdependence of fiscal units in a federal system, there is a need for assessing the impact of actions undertaken by one unit on the other units.

Distribution

Assignment of the distributive role is much more controversial than the stabilization function. One can make the argument for a centralized system for redistributing national income or wealth if one views the state of income distribution as a 'national' public good (Thurow, 1971). As a pure public good, the distribution role of government would enter positively, or at least not negatively in the utility functions of all individuals, and, as in the case of such public goods as defense, central provision may be the preferred mode.

Musgrave (1959) and Oates (1972) are strongly in favor of assigning this role to the national government. Their overriding concern is the possibility of misallocation of the population across jurisdictions if redistribution policies were left entirely in the hands of local governments. Because localities differ in terms of income and wealth, if one community were to pursue a more aggressive policy of redistribution than the others, there would be an incentive for the poor to move in and the rich to move out.

Even if all communities were to pursue similar redistribution policies, inequality in the distribution of income across communities, in the presence of such policies at the local level, would give residents incentive to migrate from one locality to another. As Buchanan (1950) has shown, when local governments' tax proceeds are used to provide goods and services to their residents, both these elements must be taken into account in assessing the impact of governmental actions on the individual. The balance between the contribution made by one individual and the value of public services returned to him (fiscal residuum) is the relevant figure that determines whether the individual stays or migrates to another jurisdiction.[2] Only when local governments operate under the benefit principle of taxation, where the individual tax share is equal to the marginal valuation of the public good provided, will the fiscal residuum be zero. Conversely, the more redistributive the fiscal actions of local units, the greater is the difference in fiscal residuum. Since differences between fiscal residuum across jurisdictions arise because of differences in local tax bases, Buchanan suggests that such differences may be reduced through transfers of tax bases among localities. Intergovernmental grants is such a transfer system. Obviously such an action on a nationwide base can only be effected by the national government.

Pauly (1973) offers some reservations concerning the assignment of the redistributive role to the national government. Recognizing interdependence of utilities (altruism) among residents of a community and assuming that transfers of income from the rich to the poor are in the nature of a pure 'local' public good, Pauly suggests that the utility of such transfers is inversely related to distance. That is, the altruistic motive is strongest the closer the ties between donor and recipient. Benefits from redistribution are likely to decrease with distance, either because the perception of who the poor are is reduced and/or the disadvantages (negative externalities) associated with poverty decrease as the separation between the rich and poor increases. If one accepts Pauly's proposition that redistribution is more in the nature of a 'local' than a 'national' public good, differences in tastes and income across communities may require different levels of redistribution. Decentralization rather than centralized provision may then be called for.

The inability to reach some kind of consensus about redistribution policies is believed by many to be a source of tension and frustration in the U.S. fiscal relations. The challenge before policy makers in a federal fiscal system is to come up with policy options for redistributing national income that displease the smallest group of the population and impose the least amount of distortion to the economy. Obviously, that level of government that can secure such an outcome is the appropriate level for the provision.

Allocation

Unlike the stabilization and the distribution functions, allocation is the classical function of government. The government's primary task is to allocate society's scarce resources between private and public uses in the most efficient fashion. In a federal system, some of the allocative functions are assigned to lower levels of government; others are reserved for the national government. In such an assignment, the first decision rule follows from a consideration of the benefit derived principle. Clearly the national government would assume responsibility for the provision of those goods and services whose benefits are national in character, while local governments would be assigned the task of providing those goods and services whose benefits accrue only to their constituents. Aside from providing for national defense, the conduct of foreign policy, and the protection and enforcement of property rights, it would appear that all other goods provision would be carried out at the local level. This is not always the case, however. Most often national governments have taken on responsibilities for the provision of goods and services whose benefits are 'local' in character, in addition to public provision of pure private goods.

The economic literature offers guidelines as to the assignment of the allocative role in a system of multiple government: efficiency of provision and, secondly, meeting preferences of a diverse population. A good is said to be provided efficiently when it is produced at the lowest average cost or, alternatively, when the maximum amount is attained from a given total outlay. When scale economies are present, and assuming no congestion, centralized provision would minimize the cost. When congestion costs are present, i.e. when the size of the population exceeds that which is compatible with minimum cost of provision, then more than one unit of government may be needed to provide the good or service. Decentralized provision also is called for when individuals' preferences for both the level and type of the public good to be provided are not uniformly distributed across the population.

Breton (1965) offers an 'optimal constitution' for the mapping of the allocation function in a federal system based on the number of users of the public good. He argues for assigning the responsibility of provision of the public good to that level of government representing *only* those affected. Although this 'constitution' guarantees that each local public good provided corresponds to local preferences, it may not satisfy the efficiency criterion. If this principle were adhered to in the presence of very diverse preferences, the number of jurisdictions may be too large, and the number of users too small for exploiting economies of scale in production. Obviously, one way of overcoming this source of inefficiency would be for smaller communities to 'bond together' and offer the service to their combined residents. This consolidation, however, may only be possible in the case of one or a few goods where local preferences are similar and tax bases are not too unequal.

Scale economies, congestion costs and diversity of preferences are concerns that are addressed in models of spatial allocation of resources. In Section 3 of this chapter, the efficiency conditions for spatial allocation of resources are discussed within the Tiebout model framework.

The Division of Revenue-Raising Responsibilities

The separation of revenue sources principle, i.e. the notion that each level of government should employ revenue bases not utilized by other levels, is perhaps the oldest prescription in the literature of fiscal federalism. The principle's main appeal is that it allows each level of government to build its tax system on the idea of comparative advantage. In this approach, each unit of government would levy those taxes which it can effectively administer and no others. A level of government with absolute advantage in certain tax sources would limit its tax raising activities to such sources. A level of government with no absolute advantage with respect to any tax source would rely on those levies with the least comparative disadvantage. According to the separation of sources principle, the national government would reserve for itself the income tax source; for the states the sales tax base, and the property tax base for local government, even though the national government may have absolute advantage in raising taxes from any one of these revenue sources.

With few exceptions, the separation of revenue sources is not perfect in any country. Tax overlapping is common. In the U.S., tax overlapping — the use of the same tax source by two or more levels of government — has steadily been on the rise. The federal and state governments utilize the income tax base, the sales and wealth transfer tax bases and both charge for the provision of certain services (user charges). The separation of revenue sources approach to taxation has had 'a bad name in public finance literature' on the grounds that its use has given rise to fiscal imbalance. Fiscal imbalance is defined as the ratio of tax capacity relative to needs,[3] the presumption being that the national government not only has absolute advantage in tax sources *vis-à-vis* subnational governments but also lower demand for its services relative to the demand for services of local governments. Netzer (1974) offers three reasons for supporting the separation principle: 1. unequal distribution of tax paying capacity among levels of governments; 2. differences in administrative efficiency; and 3. tax-induced locational decisions.

A worse-case scenario — unequal tax capacity and differences in administrative efficiency among levels of government — argues for the assignment of the tax power to the national government, coupled with a system of tax sharing among the different levels of government. This method, even though efficient as it utilizes scale economies in raising the tax dollar, may not be desirable on other grounds. Subnational governments may not want to surrender their power over tax bases to the national government.

Differences in taxable resources among local units of government are more difficult to address and, indeed, are a source of continuous friction in the U.S. fiscal system. Communities with smaller tax bases must raise tax efforts (higher tax rates) to maintain a standard level of service. Evidence from the U.S. federal system suggests that needs for public services are inversely related to taxable capacity.[4] Within metropolitan areas, low property values per capita are usually found in jurisdictions with a larger concentration of the disadvantaged population. At the same time, smaller variations in per capita local expenditures were evident between jurisdictions with different levels of tax capacity. This, in effect, has meant that effective tax rates per unit of service are much higher in poorer jurisdictions. With perfect mobility among jurisdictions, differential tax treatment of tax bases will likely influence the allocation of resources. In some cases, tax differentials may be too small to have an impact on locational choice, but along with other economic factors may at the margin be critical to the choice. Fearing the loss of tax bases, jurisdictions engage in tax-base competition. Competition for tax bases by jurisdictions is said to have given rise to efficiency loss in the U.S. federal system.

To the extent that high tax efforts are associated with low taxable capacity, a strong argument can be made for intergovernmental grants. Also, where fiscal imbalance exists between the subnational governments and the national government, some form of tax-sharing arrangement may be called for. Indeed both of these conditions are said to exist in the U.S. fiscal structure and, as discussed in Chapter 7, are used as the basis for establishing a system of intergovernmental transfers.

3 OPTIMAL PROVISION OF PUBLIC GOODS

The allocative role of government involves two budgetary decisions: first, the total size of the allocation budget and secondly, the allocation of the sum total among competing demands. In the case of a single government providing one public good, budget choice is much simplified. The only relevant information for a non-zero level of provision is that the public good provided enters positively (non-negatively) in the utility function of the community. The optimal level of provision is reached when the residents' marginal valuation of the public good is equal to the marginal cost of provision. More formally, an efficient budget size for allocation is one that equates society's marginal rate of product transformation and the total sum of individuals' marginal benefits. Samuelson (1954) describes this condition as follows:

$$\Sigma(g_y^i/g_x^i) = f_y/f_x \qquad i=1,\ldots,n \tag{6.1}$$

where n refers to the number of individuals in society, x is the private good and y is the public good. It follows from equation (6.1) that if the sum of the individual marginal rates of substitution exceeds the rate of product transformation, a larger allocation budget is called for. A smaller budget is needed when the cost of provision exceeds society's valuation.

Since f_y/f_x measures society's marginal cost of producing y in terms of x (ratio of marginal cost) and g_y^i/g_x^i measures for every individual what he is willing to give up in terms of utility of x to secure y, budgetary efficiency will be attained only when for each individual his marginal benefit is equal to his marginal cost. This means that each individual pays a marginal tax price (f_y^i/f_x^i), so that

$$g_y^i/g_x^i = f_y^i/f_x^i \tag{6.2}$$

where f_y^i/f_x^i is individual i's share in the marginal cost of producing y and x. Assuming all members of society are taxpayers, then $f_y^i = (1/n)\, f_y$. When the number of taxpayers falls short of total population, then $f_y^i = (1/(n-k))f_y$, with k = the number of non-taxpayers.

When public provision involves more than one good or service, i.e. y contains m elements, efficient allocation between budget categories (j,l) is given by:

$$f_y^j/f_y^1 = d_y^1/d_y^j \qquad j=1,\ldots,m \tag{6.3}$$

Under constant cost, tax collections will equal the cost of providing for public goods. Under either decreasing or increasing cost conditions, and when the tax price is set to equal individuals' marginal valuation, the allocation budget either will be in deficit or in surplus. Tax collections will fall short of the cost of provision under decreasing costs, while they exceed the cost of provision when average and marginal costs are increasing.

The equality of the marginal rate of transformation and the sum of the individual marginal rates of substitution assumes that the social cost of raising an extra dollar in taxes is equal to the private marginal utility of that dollar. This is only valid in the case of lump sum taxation. The social cost of raising one dollar may be greater than the private marginal utility due to the presence of excess burden associated with taxation.

The efficiency conditions stated above (equations (6.1) and (6.2)) also do not hold where public provision takes the form of intermediate (input) rather than final goods — assuming that firms producing the private good x utilize, in addition to private factors, the services of some public good y. In this case, rather than adding marginal valuations of consumers for the public consumption, efficiency of public good provision requires the addition of firms' marginal valuation of the public input. But since the use of the public input by firms is non-rival, a decentralized pricing in regards to public input cannot be relied on. Financing of the public good input must be provided from other revenue sources. Kaizuka (1965) gives the necessary conditions for Pareto efficiency when the public good is an input and when public provision involves the supply of final as well as intermediate goods. In this case, market failure is said to be 'more complete' in that not only can we not rely on decentralized pricing in regards to inputs of public goods to attain the efficiency condition but also, the necessary conditions depend on how the values of constraints are specified.

The efficiency conditions for public goods provision stated above imply, of course, that the means of raising the required revenue is known by each individual. In making a choice between public and private goods and between levels of expenditures on two or more public goods, it is assumed that the individual knows his tax share and every combination of expenditures and taxes that is feasible. This assumption is not objectionable when the budget choice is made at the local level. In the U.S. municipal government finance, revenues are largely raised by taxing real property. The tax rate is known, and the individual (property owner/tax payer) is usually informed about the implication of this type of finance on his 'own' tax share. At the state or the federal level of government, this assumption may not be valid. The U.S. government makes decisions about tax sources based on considerations other than pure allocation. For many fiscal structures, taxes serve functions other than the financing of public provision, i.e. redistribution of income and stabilization. Accordingly, individuals are likely to face taxing schemes designed to gain the support of the majority, rather than tailored to meet their individual preferences for public goods.

Where the community is sufficiently small, one may view the decisions of local governments in the same way as one views decisions reached in a 'club' setting. As Buchanan (1968) points out, club choices are optimal so long as individuals belonging to a given club have the opportunity to exit from it, and provided that there exists a large number of different clubs to choose from. By analogy, fiscal choices of local governments are said to be efficient as long as individuals residing in a local governmental unit have the opportunity to migrate to another locality and that at least one other locality offers a preferred tax-expenditure package to them. Mobility of individuals across communities supplying different mixes of public goods and tax rates guarantees that community size is optimal and that budgetary decisions approximate the wishes of resident voters. This conclusion is the well-known Tiebout efficiency of local public good provision (Tiebout, 1956). With perfect mobility, people will sort themselves out among local units to the point where no further gain from migration is feasible.[5]

Optimal Spatial Allocation of Resources: The Tiebout Model

If we drop the assumption of unitary government and consider budgetary actions in a federal system where free mobility of households and tax bases among communities are feasible, the public goods model described above requires several modifications. One basic ingredient to a model of spatial allocation of resources stems from the interdependence between the level of provision and the optimal size of the community. The first issue to be considered is the potential for congestion or 'crowding out'.

Congestion and community size

Consider first a community of size N_o providing G_o level of public goods to its residents. Assume the level G and the tax scheme had been approved by residents through referendum or some other system. Under equal tax sharing, the cost of provision to the community member is equal to total community expenditures on G divided by the number of residents, i.e. E_o/N_o where $E_o = C_r G_o$, and C_r is the resource cost per unit of provision, assumed to be constant for all levels of G. If the size of the community was to expand by the addition of one extra member ($N_1 = N_o + 1$), the resident tax share will be equal to E_1/N_1, $E_1 \geq E_o$. In the absence of congestion cost (no 'crowding out' of use of the public good), the addition of the extra member would leave unaffected the level of benefit derived by all community members, old and new. With each expansion in community size the tax share facing each community member is reduced. The efficient or optimal community size in the absence of congestion is that which encompasses the entire population. In most instances, this scenario is not realistic. Most local public goods are characterized by crowding out in consumption. The benefit each individual derives from the use of the public good depends upon the number of users. The crowding out or congestion property of local public goods implies that, as more members are added to the community, the benefits that previous users (original members) obtain from a given supply is decreased. This reduction in per-member benefits may offset the scale economies generated from the addition of extra tax bases. The existence of congestion costs associated with a given level of provision will have a bearing on the optimal size of the community. These two offsetting elements — reduction in tax share and lower levels of benefits — set the conditions for the optimal community size. Studies by Buchanan (1965), Oakland (1972), and Sandmo (1972) provide the theoretical framework for analyzing optimal provision of congested public goods.

Consider the Samuelson efficiency condition given by equation (6.1). This condition determines the optimal level of provision, given the number of individuals in the community. Once congestion is considered, we need to add to the Samuelson condition the relevant condition for determining the optimal size of the community. Congestion cost may be represented in either of two ways: first, as the difference between each member's marginal valuation of benefits before and after congestion (≤ 0), or secondly, as the members share the extra cost of addition to capacity to secure an unchanging benefit level for all users (≥ 0).

Following Oakland (1972), congestion is modelled to depend on usage and capacity. Let:

$$C = C(k,x) \tag{6.4}$$

where: x = local public good, or capacity
k = congestion or average utilization rate with

$$k = \sum_{j=1}^{N} \frac{x_j}{x} \qquad j = 1,\ldots,n;$$

and:

$$\delta C/\delta x = C_x \geq, < 0;$$
$$\delta C/\delta k = C_k \geq 0;$$
$$dC/dx = C_x - (k/x)\, C_k \leq 0.$$

When congestion is present, Pareto optimality requires that

$$S^i = S^j = -(C_k/x) \textstyle\sum_j S_c^j \tag{6.5}$$

where S^i is the marginal rate of substitution between public and private good, and S^j and S_c^j are the marginal valuations in terms of private goods of individual j of one unit of public good and one more unit of congestion.

Equation (6.5) states the condition that the marginal benefits from one more unit of public good consumption must just offset the congestion cost of this extra consumption. Since each individual's consumption imposes the same congestion cost, individuals' marginal valuations must be equal. In other words, individuals solving their budget problems will equate marginal valuation of the public good with the price. The price must equal the congestion damage caused by sharing the good.

Free mobility and efficiency

The next issue to be considered is the efficiency of resource allocation in a decentralized system of provision. This was first explored by Tiebout (1956). Tiebout's model is derived from a simple premise: households' locational choice is governed by their preferences for local public goods. Individuals who are dissatisfied with the fiscal package offered by their community would vote 'with their feet'. A federal system of government consisting of a large number of communities, each offering a mix of local public goods and local taxes corresponding to residents' wishes, not only would guarantee an optimal level of 'local' public goods provision in each locality but also the efficient allocation of residents among communities. Communities that offer the fiscal package individuals like will gain residents; communities that fail to do so will lose residents. The political process will respond to these signals in the same way firms in the private economy respond to market signals. Essential to this efficient outcome implied by the Tiebout adjustment process is that residents are free to move among communities, that information and mobility are costless, and that the number of communities is large enough to allow variations in the tax-expenditure package offered to residents.

Tiebout's model has been subjected to a great deal of criticism at the theoretical level and through empirical testing. Besides the restrictive assumptions the model requires for the validity of its hypothesis, several qualifications have been stated. Sources of inefficiency in a Tiebout-like adjustment process are: spillovers or externalities associated with local goods; location inefficiency and inequality across communities.[6]

Empirical tests of Tiebout's hypothesis basically fall into one of three categories: Oates' (1969) findings showed that a community that has a low tax rate relative to its public goods supply, will have this favorable fiscal surplus capitalized into its housing values. Based on these 'capitalization' finding, Oates concludes that a 'Tiebout-like' equilibrium exists. Oates' findings have, however, been disputed, for instance by Edel and Sclar (1974) and Hamilton (1976) who have shown that for a Tiebout equilibrium to exist, there should be no capitalization.

The second category of evidence is supplied by Reschovsky (1979) and Twoomey (1987) among others. Their studies showed local mobility patterns to be influenced by fiscal variables. A third type of model, e.g.

Gramlick and Rubenfeld (1982), undertakes a comparison of local public spending within communities and across communities. Their findings lend some support to the Tiebout hypothesis. Shadbegian and Ott (1992), using disaggregated data for the U.S., examined county-to-county migration flows in response to fiscal surpluses. The study provides evidence that individuals do sort themselves by fiscal surplus.

Efficiency Loss in a System of Multiple Government

In a fiscal system with multiple governments and free mobility of households, budgetary actions of government will impact on those of the others. Because of this interrelationship, efficiency losses may be introduced. Three sources of inefficiency need to be considered: fiscal externalities or spillovers; interregional competition for tax bases; and fiscal imbalance.

Fiscal externalities or spillovers

In a system of multiple governments, the main beneficiaries of a local public good are the local residents. In many cases of local provision, services provided by one community to its residents may confer benefits or impose costs on neighboring communities. Services with major geographic spillovers include public health services, education, and specialized hospitals.

Intergovernmental spillovers are considered to be the most significant source of budgetary inefficiencies. Budgetary decisions about the level of goods provision within any locality are based on a comparison of the cost (tax shares) and benefits of the goods to the community's own residents. If some of the benefits are transferred to other localities, the local budget decision will not be optimal. This may be illustrated by the case of two localities, each producing one public good. Locality A offers its residents free access to higher educational institutions (E); locality B offers its residents free access to long-term care hospital facilities (H). If each locality acts efficiently, then

$$\Sigma\, g_E^{iA} = MC_E^A \qquad i = 1,\ldots n$$

and

$$\Sigma\, g_H^{jB} = MC_H^B \qquad j = 1,\ldots m \tag{6.6}$$

where $\Sigma\, g_E^{iA}$ is the sum of marginal valuation of residents in community A for the good E and MC_E^A is the marginal cost of provision in A. $\Sigma\, g_H^{jB}$ is the sum of marginal valuation of residents in community B and MC_H^B is the marginal cost of provision in B.

Now consider spillover effects on the efficient levels of provision. In the case of one-way spillovers or externalities, the public service in A benefits residents of community B, but the reverse is not true (no spillouts from B to A). The efficient level of output in localities A and B, after allowing for spillovers is given by:

$$\Sigma\, g_E^{iA} + \Sigma\, g_E^{jB} = MC_E^{A}$$

and (6.7)

$$\Sigma\, g_H^{jB} = MC_H^{B}$$

That is, in the presence of spillovers, a budget size that was efficient (without spillovers) no longer is. In this example, community A needs to expand its provision beyond the locally efficient level.

Since the 'extra' provision of good E in community A can only be achieved either by raising taxes on community A's residents or reducing the supply of other public services, community A's residents are worse off than they were in the absence of spillovers. If community A continued to supply the same level of the good, 'crowding out' would disturb the equality between marginal valuation and marginal cost of the good for the residents of the community. The efficient level of provision, clearly would require not only the restoration of equality between marginal benefits and marginal costs, but also an expanded level of provision.

As suggested by Olson (1965) and Williams (1966), when geographic externalities exist, efficient provision can be achieved by the use of compensating grants or taxation. In the case of positive externalities — those yielding benefits to outside communities — the national government may be called upon to provide compensating grants. Without such grants, the level of local services will be less than optimal. If on the other hand, spillovers are negative (impose cost on other communities), the national government may impose taxes on the community responsible for the externality. Taxes raise the cost of provision, hence a lower level will be demanded. Alternatively, the national government could provide the affected community with funds to mitigate the negative effects of the spillovers for a given level of provision.

Another source of spillovers is a phenomenon known as 'tax exporting'. A local governmental unit is said to export its taxes when a part of its tax incidence is borne by non-residents. Tax exporting activity is commonly associated with local sales and corporation income taxes and local property taxes. When tax exporting takes place, the marginal cost to residents from expanding local provision falls short of the marginal benefit, since part of the cost is borne by non-residents. In such a case, the tax-exporting community may over-expand its public sector, as the effective tax price for its provision has been reduced. With multiple jurisdictions, tax exporting will be prevalent. Each jurisdiction will be exporting some of its taxes as well as receiving fallout from other jurisdictions. The net effect is that all jurisdictions will have an incentive to expand their public sectors beyond the optimum.

Interregional competition for tax bases

A prominent feature of federalism is intergovernmental competition for tax bases. In the simple framework for determining the optimal size of the community described earlier, tax shares for a given level of service are reduced as the community size is increased. This conclusion is derived from the fact that a newcomer enhances the community fiscal capacity and, with noncongested provision, the residents of the community benefit with each expansion in the size of the community. When congestion is allowed for, the cost to the community from adding an extra member has to be at least equal to the benefit accruing to the community through the expansion of the tax base. As long as scale economies exist, community size will not remain static.

As with any system of exchange where sellers compete for buyers, local units of governments compete among themselves to attract individuals and businesses to their jurisdictions. The behavior of local governmental units may be described by the Marshallian offer curve, where each point on the curve represents a package of tax concessions and a specified level of public services offered in exchange for units of tax bases. With free mobility guaranteed among jurisdictions, communities offering the lowest tax rates associated with a standard level of service, or higher levels of service per dollar of tax base, will attract residents (tax bases); those with unfavorable fiscal climate lose residents (tax bases). The threat of losing tax bases inhibits a local government from raising its own tax rates above those of its neighbors. The net result is that tax rates at the local level are much lower than they would be in the absence of tax competition.

Intergovernmental competition for tax bases has been blamed for the fiscal crisis of the largest cities in the U.S. and for tension in intergovernmental relations.[7] Critics of tax competition seem to repudiate the benefits of competitive pricing in the choice of residence, on the grounds that by keeping tax rates low, tax competition will result in lower levels of public goods being provided. Interestingly enough, Tiebout's seminal paper extols the virtues of interregional competition. As explained above, since preferences are not uniform among individuals, competition among jurisdictions for residents would lead to local public goods provision which approximates those preferences. As with a club setting, there will be some jointly efficient combination of population size and budget size for any given jurisdiction, depending on the level of income, cost of provision and individual preferences for the goods supplied.

The general finding with regard to tax base competition is that such activities are far less 'disastrous' in terms of their impact on local governments than often claimed. Studies of state-local tax influences on location of industry in the U.S. have shown such influences to be much smaller in magnitude than differences in economic conditions or location-specific amenities. And when such influences exist, they reinforce rather than offset other influences on location decisions.

Fiscal imbalance

In addition to spillovers and tax-base competition, the organization of the public sector in a federal system is said to be characterized by fiscal imbalance among the different levels of government (vertical imbalance). This may be thought of as reflecting different sets of budget constraints defined in terms of needs relative to capacity. If, for example, the national government's capacity to raise taxes exceeds those of subnational governments but citizens' preferences call for local public goods provision, the federal fiscal structure could lead to fiscal imbalance. Fiscal imbalance also may occur among subnational governments. This phenomenon is referred to as horizontal imbalance.

In the U.S. federal system, states vary in their assignment of responsibility for the financing and provision of public services. In some states, city governments are responsible for providing education, health and welfare services whereas in other states such functions are reserved for other units of governments. Determining the fiscal need of a city or township government requires that differences in responsibilities be taken into account.[8] Even if city governments were to provide the same package of public services, fiscal need is likely to differ among them. Differences in service needs are determined by three factors: 1. assignment of responsibility, 2. location-specific social and economic conditions and 3. cost factors.

Assignment of responsibilities to local units rests with state governments. As 'creatures' of the state, a local government cannot alter the scope of its responsibilities. Differences in service need among cities, for example, most often reflect differences in the characteristics of the residential population, the environment and settlement patterns. Cost differences reflect the cost of inputs in different locations. Since public services are labor intensive, it is not surprising to find the cost of providing 'standard' levels of services varies across communities simply because of differences in labor market conditions.

High service needs in one locality *vis-à-vis* another should not be viewed as an indication of fiscal imbalance. The second part to the equation is fiscal capacity and effort. Fiscal capacity refers to resources (tax bases) that can be tapped to fund local services; tax effort refers to the local unit's willingness to tax its residents to fund public services.

High service needs are not a problem if a local government has both high fiscal capacity and sufficient ability to raise needed revenues through own tax effort. Fiscal imbalance arises when the ratio of service needs to fiscal capacity (with the same level of tax effort) in one community exceeds those of others. Without compensating transfers, a fiscally needy community must tax its residents at relatively high rates merely to provide a standard level of public service.

The premise that fiscal imbalance is a feature of federalism argues for tax sharing among levels of government. In the U.S., the national government is said to be most efficient in raising revenues whereas geographical diversity in taste and need for public goods calls for provision at subnational levels. As suggested earlier, to exploit scale economies in the production of tax yields, the national government would be assigned the tasks of raising revenue and sharing the tax yield with subnational governments. In this context, federal grants to state and local governments are viewed as a way of addressing the fiscal imbalance in the U.S. federal system.

Many question the above premise, however. Break (1980) and Wagner (1971) argue that fiscal imbalance between levels of governments should not be taken as a 'permanent' fixture of the federal fiscal system. According to Wagner, fiscal imbalance can persist only 'if there is significant imperfection in the operation of our fiscal democracy'.[9] Wagner believes that, if these imperfections do not exist, political competition will produce changes in the national and the state-local tax rates that would correct the fiscal imbalance. This correction comes about in two ways: first as the demand for local public services increases (reflecting citizens' preferences for decentralized provision), there will be an offsetting reduction in the demand for national public goods, thus reducing the need to raise revenues at the national level. Secondly, if political competition operates efficiently, the shift in the demand for public goods will be accommodated by an increase in the local taxes and reduction in taxes at the national level.

Horizontal fiscal disparities are not as easy to correct. State and local governments with low fiscal abilities relative to the need of their residents cannot count on offsetting transactions at the national level. Inequality in the distribution of tax capacities among local governments has been and still is a source of tension in the U.S. federal fiscal system. It is often asked: why should citizens of wealthy communities be able to purchase (consume) a high quality 'public' good at a lower tax price than citizens of poor communities?[10]

The Serrano v. Priest, and San Antonio Independent School District v. Rodriguez court cases attacking the equity of school finance in the U.S. brought this question to public attention and demonstrated the need to address horizontal fiscal disparities among local communities. One suggested solution is the aggressive use of intergovernmental grants to bring about equalization in the level and quality of local services. This of course would involve an income redistribution program at both the federal and state levels. But, this solution is not easy to implement. Moreover, the argument has been made that in an efficient market, fiscal disparities between communities cannot be maintained for long.

Locational decisions are not made solely on the basis of local public goods prices. In choosing a community in which to reside, the 'rational' resident-consumer is likely to base that decision on the relative prices of 'comparable' packages containing both private goods and public goods. As we saw earlier, in a community with both public and private provision of goods, efficiency requires that resources be allocated so as to maximize the 'total' value of output from both private and public goods. A community-specific improvement in public goods provision and/or reduction in the tax share, with unchanged private goods provision, might invite immigration and vice versa. With free mobility and when exclusion is not possible, the necessary conditions for efficiency will be satisfied. That is, the optimal distribution of residents among communities requires that, for each person and for each pair of locational alternatives, the equality of marginal private good value plus the marginal public good value holds for all persons and for all alternatives. Following Buchanan-Goetz (1972), for each person i and for each pair of communities A,B, the necessary condition is:

$$MVP_{iA} + MVG_{iA} = MVP_{iB} + MVG_{iB} \tag{6.8}$$

where MVP_{iA} represents the marginal utility of private output of the ith individual in community A and MVG_{iA} represents the marginal utility of public output in community A. These efficiency conditions assume no congestion and no spillovers of benefits or costs.

As pointed out earlier, precisely because of congestion, spillovers, cost of mobility and in addition the possibility of exclusion (e.g. rich communities' ability to exclude the poor through zoning laws), efficiency limits of fiscal mobility could be very significant.

4 THE ROLE OF INTERGOVERNMENTAL GRANTS

In a federal system, intergovernmental transfers are a natural if not an essential feature of the system. Transfers take the form of tax sharing with or without strings attached and grants-in-aid. Tax sharing is a tax transfer scheme. Essentially it involves the performance of two functions: raising taxes from the national population from designated sources in the most efficient manner and sharing all or part of the yield among all levels of government. Empirical evidence on the cost of raising a dollar in taxes suggests that the national government has a comparative advantage for raising taxes over subnational governments. How revenues thus raised are to be distributed clearly is a function of the national government's objectives and/or the negotiation powers of subnational units, who not only have to share the tax dollar with the national government, but also among themselves.

Grants-in-aid refers to the transfer of money from one level of government (national) to another (state and local). This sharing of resources may or may not be a part of a tax-sharing arrangement. That is, the national government may wish to share its tax revenues with subnational governments without designating a specific revenue source or the prior arrangement with other levels of government.

While grants-in-aid can be found at all levels of government, federal grants-in-aid are by far the most important feature of fiscal federalism in the U.S. Grants-in-aid are of two types: special purpose and general purpose grants. There is a great variety in the characteristics of U.S. grants-in-aid programs including eligibility requirements, uses of funds, distributional mechanisms and cost-sharing or 'matching'.[11]

Types and Uses of Grants

Grants-in-aid is a fiscal instrument for effecting a redistribution of national resources for the use of various levels of government. A system of grants, whether between the national or subnational units or from state governments to local governments, is likely to be shaped by the grantor's objectives. As shown earlier in the chapter, intergovernmental transfers may be needed to offset inter-jurisdiction spillovers, equalize fiscal capacities and/or guarantee a minimum standard of public services. Transfers, especially from the national government to subnational governments, may be made to promote national goals (e.g. the Anti-recession Fiscal Assistance Program initiated in 1976 as part of the U.S. federal government policy to stimulate growth and combat recession). Thus, a useful way to discuss goals and instruments is to link grant types to uses of grant monies. Grants-in-aid are classified into three basic types: categorical grants, general purpose (unconditional) grants and block grants.

Categorical or functional grants (as they are called sometimes) are given to meet specific needs. They are designed to provide funding for a 'narrow' range of activities, on a project-by-project basis. Specific purpose grants permit the grantor to tailor its assistance to those activities that give rise to spillover effects such as urban mass transportation. The grant rate would be determined in such cases by the degree of spillover or by a standard minimum of provision after allowing for the externality. The grant rate may be fixed as the ratio of spillovers to the sum of spillovers (externality) and internal benefits. A matching requirement may be mandated. For example, the grantor may require the recipient to spend a specified amount for each unit of grant it receives. Whether special purpose grants are for spillovers or to fund specific services, this type of grant requires the functions aided to be identified. The problem this requirement poses is quite complex: from assessing the degree and extent of spillovers to the ranking of interest (especially national interest) in different program areas.

In some cases, matching may be required for receiving categorical grants. Recipients' matching, when required, may be on an open-ended basis or restricted to a fixed amount of grantor funds (closed-end basis). Also, grant funds designed to aid specific functions may be targeted (formula grants) to benefit certain groups of the population. Formula grants typically involve a clear definition of the eligible population. If matching requirements are used with formula grants, some measure for matching is usually spelled out by statutes.

The second category, unconditional or general purpose grants, provide unrestricted aid to recipient governments. This type of grant is usually given to jurisdictions to equalize their fiscal capacity in relation to needs. The problem here is to identify a set of measures for determining fiscal capacity and tax efforts of the different jurisdictions as well as measures of fiscal needs. Also relevant to the grant design is the degree of equalization desired and the control to be exercised by the grantor. Revenue sharing is the most widely known form of general purpose grants.

Revenue sharing as a system of intergovernmental transfers is identified best with the U.S. General Revenue System enacted in 1972 (the State and Local Fiscal Assistance Act). The Act provides for transfers of funds from the federal government to the state and local governments. These transfers were authorized for a 5-year period, ending in 1977. The revenue-sharing program was extended three times in 1977, 1980 and 1983 terminating in 1987. Until the 1980 extension, the federal program provided aid to both state and local governments, but in 1980, the aid was limited to local governments. Transfers from the federal to state and local governments have taken place according to formula (3-factor and 5-factor formula). In addition to the allotment formula, certain stipulations were made (maximum and minimum rules) fixing the relative size of grant received by one unit of government v. all others or guaranteeing a minimum level of grant. Both of these limits have been criticized as restrictive or undesirable on efficiency grounds.

In the U.S. federal system, tax sharing also takes place at the state level. Most state governments designate one or more taxes for partial or full sharing among local governments. The state government decides on the tax base to be shared, on the tax rate as well as on the allocation formula. Tax revenues are often returned to the communities where they were collected although other forms of distribution have been used.

The third category, block grants, occupy the middle position in the federal grants-in-aid spectrum.[12] These are much broader in scope than categorical grants, allowing recipients greater discretion over the funds within a functional classification (i.e. education or community development), but unlike general purpose grants, block grant programs have specific goals and objectives that have to be met. In the U.S., block grant funds are usually distributed according to formula.

Theories for Intergovernmental Grants

Assuming that the intergovernmental grant system is and will continue to be a feature of fiscal federalism, one may want to ask: Does it make a difference if national government aid to subnational governments takes the form of direct transfers to the residents or in the form of grants to governments themselves? Competing models in the literature give different answers.

According to George Break, an intergovernmental transfer system may be viewed as representing some form of 'fiscal partnerships' between levels of government.[13] Looking at it in such a way would make it easier to understand the exchange. Public choice models offer one way of analyzing this exchange. The predictions of these models suggest that either form of transfer would have the same effect on the recipient. Voters-taxpayers are assumed to choose that level of transfer which maximizes their utility; their choice reflects the same calculus as that involved in the choice of other public goods provision and private goods provision. The voter-taxpayer will treat grants received by him in the same manner as grants received by local government, both types reducing his tax share for the given provision (grants to the government) or increase his consumption for the public good (as well as private goods) by raising his income (direct transfers). Moreover, to the extent that the grant reduces the cost of provision (the tax share for a given level of provision), it is immaterial whether the grant comes from the national or subnational government.

This conclusion is disputed. It is argued that bureaucratic behavior makes a difference as to how the outside money is used. The resident and the local government maximize different utility functions. Bureaucratic models predict that whereas transfers of lump-sum amounts to residents would have little effect on local government taxes and spending, restricted government grants would alter significantly public expenditures with little effect on private spending. This is the so called 'fly paper' effect of grants suggesting that the money sticks where it hits. This conclusion is derived from the model assumption that government officials pursue self-interest and exhibit behavior designed to maximize agency budgets.[14]

Whether the voter-taxpayer models or bureaucratic models predictions are the correct ones, it is evident that many factors come to play in the grantor's choice of the form of aid to be given. The political process and governmental structure may impose constraints that are not part of the economists' constraint.

5 CONCLUSION

Budget allocation in a federal system is as much a matter of history as of choice. The organization of the public sector — whether to rely on a centralized or decentralized form of government — once established determines the allocation of functions and assignment of revenue sources among the different levels of government.

The focus in this chapter is on issues relating to the federal form of government. These issues were discussed with reference to the U.S. federal system. Here we identify the issues surrounding the allocation of budget expenditures among the national and subnational governments. Interdependence between the various units of government in a federal fiscal system raises problems for the efficient delivery of services. Spillover effects, competition for tax bases, and fiscal imbalance are sources that give rise to inefficiencies. A system of grants-in-aid is viewed not only as a means for addressing these externalities, but also as a means for guaranteeing 'equitable' if not efficient provision of public goods.

NOTES

1. Musgrave (1959), p. 5.
2. Buchanan (1950), p. 588.
3. Netzer (1974), p. 387.
4. Break (1980), pp. 134—5.
5. This efficient outcome may not be certain. As has been argued in studies by Buchanan and Goetz (1972), Stiglitz (1977) and Wildasian (1980) among others, the free mobility of individuals among communities may generate negative externalities which result in inefficient outcomes.
6. For a review of inefficiency in Tiebout-type models see Atkinson and Stiglitz (1980).
7. Break (1980), p. 90.
8. For a discussion of fiscal capacity and needs see ACIR (1971).
9. Wagner (1971), p. 89.
10. Break (1980), p. 90.
11. For a clear description of the U.S. grants-in-aid programs see Rich (1993), ch. 2.
12. Ibid., p. 3.
13. Break (1980), p. 87.
14. The 'fly paper' term was first used by Arthur Okun. For a discussion of the model see Gramlick, (1977).

REFERENCES

Advisory Commission on Intergovernmental Relations (ACIR) (1971), *Measuring the Fiscal Capacity and Effort of State and Local Areas*, Washington D.C., Government Printing Office.

Advisory Commission on Intergovernmental Relations (1978), *Countercyclical Aid and Economic Stabilization*, Washington D.C., Government Printing Office.

Advisory Commission on Intergovernmental Relations (1979), *State-local Finances in Recession and Inflation*, Washington D.C., Government Printing Office.

Atkinson, A. and Stiglitz, J. (1980), *Lectures in Public Economics*, New York, McGraw-Hill.

Bahl, R. (1984), *Financing State and Local Government in the 1980's*, New York, Oxford University Press.

Break, G. (1980), *Financing Government in a Fiscal System*, Washington D.C., The Brookings Institution.

Breton, A. (1965), 'A Theory of Government Grants', *Canadian Journal of Economics and Political Science*, **31**, pp. 175—87.

Breton, A. and Scott, A. (1968), *The Economic Constitution of Federal States*, Toronto, University of Toronto Press.

Buchanan, J.M. (1950), 'Federalism and Fiscal Equity', *American Economic Review*, **40**, (September), pp. 583–9.

Buchanan, J.M. (1965), 'An Economic Theory of Clubs', *Economica*, **32**, pp. 1–14.

Buchanan, J.M. (1968), *The Demand and Supply of Public Goods*, Chicago, Rand Co.

Buchanan, J.M. and Goetz, C.J. (1972), 'Efficiency Limits of Fiscal Mobility: An Assessment of the Tiebout Model', *Public Economics*, **1**, pp. 25–43.

Buchanan, J.M. and Wagner, R. (1970), 'An Efficiency Basis for Federal Fiscal Equalization', in Margolis, J. (ed.), *The Analysis of Public Output*, New York, Columbia University Press.

Edel, M. and Sclar, E. (1974), 'Taxes, Spending and Property Values: Supply Adjustment in the Tiebout-Oates Model', *Journal of Political Economy*, **82**, pp. 941–54.

Gramlick, E. (1977), 'Intergovernmental Grants: A Review of the Empirical Literature', in Oates, W.E. (ed.), *The Political Economy of Fiscal Federalism*, Lexington, Lexington Books.

Gramlick, E. and Rubenfeld D.L. (1982), 'Microestimates of Public Spending Demand Functions and Test of the Tiebout and Median Voter Hypothesis', *Journal of Political Economy*, **90**, pp. 536–60.

Hamilton, B. (1976), 'The Effects of Property Taxes and Local Public Spending on Property Value: A Theoretical Comment', *Journal of Political Economy*, **84**, pp. 647–50.

Kaizuka, K. (1965), 'Public Goods and Decentralization of Production', *Review of Economics and Statistics*, **48**, pp. 118–20.

Maxwell, J. (1965), *Financing State and Local Governments*, Washington D.C., The Brookings Institution.

McLure, C.E. (1967), 'The Interstate Exporting of State and Local Taxes: Estimates of 1962', *National Tax Journal*, **20** (March), pp. 49–77.

Musgrave, R. (1959), *The Theory of Public Finance*, New York, McGraw-Hill Co. Inc.

Netzer, D. (1974), 'State-Local Finance and Intergovernmental Fiscal Relations', in Blinder, A., et al. (eds), *The Economics of Public Finance*, Washington D.C., The Brookings Institution.

Niskanen, W. (1971), *Bureaucracy and Representative Government*, Chicago, Aldine-Atherton.

Oakland, W.H. (1972), 'Congestion, Public Goods, and Welfare', *Journal of Public Economics*, **1**, pp. 339–58.

Oates, W. (1968), 'The Theory of Public Finance in a Federal System', *Canadian Journal of Economics*, **1** (February), pp. 37–54.

Oates, W. (1969), 'The Effects of Property Taxes and Local Spending on Property Values: An Empirical Study of Tax Capitalization and the Tiebout Hypothesis', Journal of Political Economy, **77**, pp. 957–71.

Oates, W. (1972), *Fiscal Federalism*, New York, Harcourt, Brace, Jovanovich.

Olson, M. (1965), *The Logic of Collective Action*, Cambridge, Mass., Harvard University Press.

Pauly, M. (1973), 'Income Redistribution as a Pure Public Good', *Journal of Public Economics*, **2** (February), pp. 35–58.

Rafuse, R. (1965), 'Cyclical Behavior of State and Local Government Finances', in Musgrave, R. (ed.), *Essays in Fiscal Federalism*, Washington D.C., The Brookings Institution.

Reischauer, R. (1978), 'The Economy, the Federal Budget and the Prospects for Federal Aid', in Bahl, R., (ed.), *The Fiscal Outlook for Cities*, Syracuse, Syracuse University Press.

Reschovsky, A. (1979), 'Residential Choice and the Local Public Sector: An Alternative Test of the Tiebout Hypothesis', *Journal of Urban Economics*, **6**, pp. 501—20.

Rich, M. (1993), *National Goals and Local Choices: Distributing Federal Aid to the Poor*, Princeton, Princeton University Press.

Samuelson, P.A. (1954), 'The Theory of Public Expenditure', *Review of Economics and Statistics*, **36** (November), pp. 387—9.

Sandmo, A. (1972), 'Optimality Rules for the Provision of Collective Factors of Production', *Journal of Public Economics*, **1**, pp. 149—57.

Shadbegian, R. and Ott, A.F. (1992), 'Is Migration Fiscally Induced?: An Empirical Assessment of the Buchanan-Goetz Model', Worcester, Clark University, processed.

Stiglitz, J. (1977), 'The Theory of Local Public Goods' in Feldstein, M. and Inman, R. (eds), *The Economics of Public Services*, London, Macmillan, pp. 274—333.

Thurow, L.C. (1971), 'The Income Distribution as a Pure Public Good', *Quarterly Journal of Economics*, (May), pp. 327—36.

Tiebout, C.M. (1956), 'A Pure Theory of Local Expenditures', *Journal of Political Economy*, **64**, pp. 416—24.

Twoomey, T. (1987), 'Local Authority Fiscal Stance and the Patterns of Residential Migration in the Northwest of England', *Applied Economics*, **24**(4), pp. 1391—94.

Vogel, R. and Trost, R. (1979), 'The Response of State Government Receipts to Economic Fluctuations and the Allocation of Countercyclical Revenue Sharing Grants', *Review of Economics and Statistics*, **61**, p. 389—400.

Wagner, R.E. (1971), *The Fiscal Organization of American Federalism*, Chicago, Markham Publishing Co.

Wagner, R.E. (1973), *The Public Economy*, Chicago, Markham Publishing Co.

Wildasian, D. (1980), 'Locational Efficiency in a Federal System', *Regional Science and Urban Economics*, **10** (4), pp. 453—71.

Williams, A. (1966), 'The Optimal Provision of Public Goods in a System of Local Government', *Journal of Political Economy*, **74** (February), pp. 18—33.

7. The Fiscal Structure of the United States

with Ronald Shadbegian

1 INTRODUCTION

Governments perform many functions. Government spending and taxes are used to stabilize the national economy: when private demand is weak, taxes may be adjusted downward (or transfer payments upwards) or expenditures increased or both. Even if stabilization goals were satisfied, government spending would continue to take place to fulfil other roles in the economy. These roles manifest themselves in the provision of certain goods and services to society at large or to specific individuals. Given the multiplicity of roles the public sector performs in the economy, how is one to judge the allocation or assignment of these roles in a system of multiple governments? In other words, how can one decide what the national government should do in each of these areas? And how is one to judge the government's actual performance?

In the previous chapter (Chapter 6) the economic rationale for the assignment of powers and responsibilities in a multiple government setting was presented. In the context of country experiences, this assignment may be shaped by the existing set of fiscal institutions. Hence, an understanding of what a particular level of government should or should not do requires the study of the existing fiscal structure.

The fiscal structure of the United States is the subject of this chapter. The chapter begins with a brief history of the U.S. federal system. This is followed by an overview of the fiscal organization of the public sector. Purposes of government spending and sources of funding are discussed in the following two sections. The chapter concludes with an analysis of the role of intergovernmental grants in the U.S. federal system.

2 FEDERAL VERSUS STATE AND LOCAL RESPONSIBILITY: A BRIEF HISTORY

The U.S. is a federal system with three levels of government: federal, state, and local. The legal division of responsibility among the various levels of government is found in the Constitution and in court interpretations of the Constitution. The Constitution assigns powers to the individual levels of government: those of the national government are specified in Article 1, Section 8, while those of the states and their subdivisions are residual. The Tenth Amendment reserves for the states all powers not granted to the national government or prohibited to the states. The federal government, through Congress, was given the power to levy and collect taxes, duties, imposts and excise, to pay the debts and provide for the common defense and general welfare of the Unites States, a provision which was intended to restrict the scope of federal activity.[1] There is no specific mention of spending on education, health, highways, and the like in Article 1 or anywhere else in the Constitution, and since the Tenth Amendment does not deny these powers to the states, they are presumed to be residual powers of the states. Interpretation of what expenditure functions would fall under the term 'general welfare' was left to the Courts.

Until the 1930s the Courts were reluctant to allow the national government to assume powers beyond those necessary to provide for national defense and to regulate interstate trade and commerce, and the Congress was generally reluctant to seek new responsibilities. As a result, in 1927 the federal government accounted for less than one-fifth of total government expenditures for civilian purposes (some 17 per cent).[2]

However, during the 1930s, amidst the problems and pressures of the greatest economic depression in United States history, there developed a shift in social philosophy and judicial thinking. The judicial interpretation of the Constitution that emerged in the 1930s, 'accepted a reading of the general welfare clause that placed no discernible judicial limits on the amounts or purposes of federal spending....'.[3] During this period, federal government expenditures helped pay for public works and various other projects providing direct benefits to states and localities. Federal spending also provided relief for unemployed persons, thereby relieving strains on state and local finances. The Social Security Act of 1935 established programs benefiting the needy, especially the aged population. By 1938, the federal share of civilian expenditures had risen to more than 45 per cent. At present (1991), the federal share of the total civilian expenditures is around 65 per cent. In short, the powers and responsibilities of the national government have come to be interpreted broadly indeed and now cover many areas formerly reserved for state and local governments.

State-Local Responsibility

As mentioned above, the Tenth Amendment to the Constitution reserves to the states all powers not granted to the federal government or prohibited to the states. The states can decide on the level of spending and taxes, but their authorities are limited in certain activities. Article 1, Section 10 of the Constitution prohibits the states from levying any excise on imports or exports; Article 1, Section 8, gives the federal government exclusive control over customs and concurrent jurisdiction with the states in all areas of taxation. Other constitutional provisions, however, set limits on the taxing power of the federal government over the states and their corresponding local governments, and on the taxing power of subnational units over the federal government. The 'immunity' doctrine forbids federal taxation of state and local instrumentalities and disallows states from taxing instrumentalities of the federal government. The states are also prohibited by the 'equal protection' clause of the Fourteenth Amendment from discriminating against out-of-state citizens. The Amendment holds that a state must not 'deny to any person within its jurisdiction the equal protection of the laws'.

The fiscal relationship between state and local governments is found in legal provisions. The doctrine of state supremacy over subgovernmental units gives the legislature and the courts authority to issue directives to local governments. This power is affirmed by the Courts. In 1868, the Court held that: 'municipal corporations owe their origin to, and derive their powers and rights wholly from, the (state) legislature. It breathes into them the breath of life, without which they cannot exist.'[4] Again in 1923, the U.S. Supreme Court in the case of Trenton v. New Jersey, refused to recognize the right of local self-government.[5] Accordingly, state governments have the power to dictate and/or modify both the spending and taxing power of their local governments. That is, if a state so desires, it can create or eliminate local units, for there are no constitutional prohibitions against it; the only constraints are the limits of political feasibility.

In the United States the degree of state control over local governments varies from state to state such that a great deal of diversity exists in state-local relations. For example, some states (so-called home-rule states) grant local governments certain powers that they may use without any direct control by the grantor state, while others give such powers only to their larger cities. Some states have developed methods for sharing own revenues with their local governments, and some are more active in developing revenue sources beside the property tax for their localities. Moreover, some states have opted for 'passing through' federal aid to local governments, while other states have retained for themselves the function for which federal aid was given.

During the more than 200 years since the nation was formed, federal, state and state-local relations have not remained static. The power of the states *vis-à-vis* the national government has 'waxed and waned' as the federal structure adjusted with the changes in social and political philosophy and the environment.[6] The politics and economics of budgeting have shaped the roles of government in the U.S. beyond the legal assignment of powers and responsibilities. Over the past decades, a whole host of programs were assigned to state-local governments with partial or total funding from the federal government. With the exception of key functions (such as defense and police protection), there are generally no precise legal boundaries to the areas of responsibility of the various levels of government. In the next section we present an overview of the fiscal organization of the U.S. public sector.

3 THE ORGANIZATION OF THE PUBLIC SECTOR

The organization of the U.S. public sector, as of 1987, is given in Figure 7.1. In addition to the federal government and the 50 states, there were 83,186 units of local governments. Of these, 38,933 are general-purpose local governments — 3,042 units represent counties, 19,200 municipalities, and 16,691 township governments. The remainder are limited-purpose local governments consisting of 14,721 school district governments and 29,532 special district governments.[7]

Since 1952, there has been little change in the number of general-purpose governments, although limited-purpose governments have experienced dramatic changes. School districts have declined in number from 67,355 units in 1952 to 14,721 in 1987. On the other hand, special district governments increased from 12,340 units in 1952 to 29,532 units in 1987. The form of government varies by type of unit; almost all are run by elected officials. The specific form of representative government is identified in the figure.

The Fiscal Structure

The fiscal structure of the U.S. for 1986—87 is given in Table 7.1 and Figure 7.2. In the table, which includes public expenditures and revenues, data are presented in two ways: in lines 1 and 4 of the table, the total includes intergovernmental grants at the level of origin; the alternative reports totals net of intergovernmental transfers. Direct expenditures correspond to transactions with the public only, and general revenues after netting transfers are referred to as revenues from the public.

We begin with the entire public sector in which all levels of governments are included. As shown in the table, total public expenditures amounted to $2,070 billion in 1987. After netting out intergovernmental expenditures ($258 billion), expenditures to the public were $1,812 billion or 87.5 per cent of the total. Total public sector revenues amounted to $1,941 billion, of which some $261 billion were in the form of intergovernmental revenues. Excluding these transactions, total revenues from the public amounted to $1,680 billion, or 86.5 per cent of the total. The overall deficit, i.e. the difference between total expenditures and total revenues,

Figure 7.1: Organization of the U.S. public sector, 1987

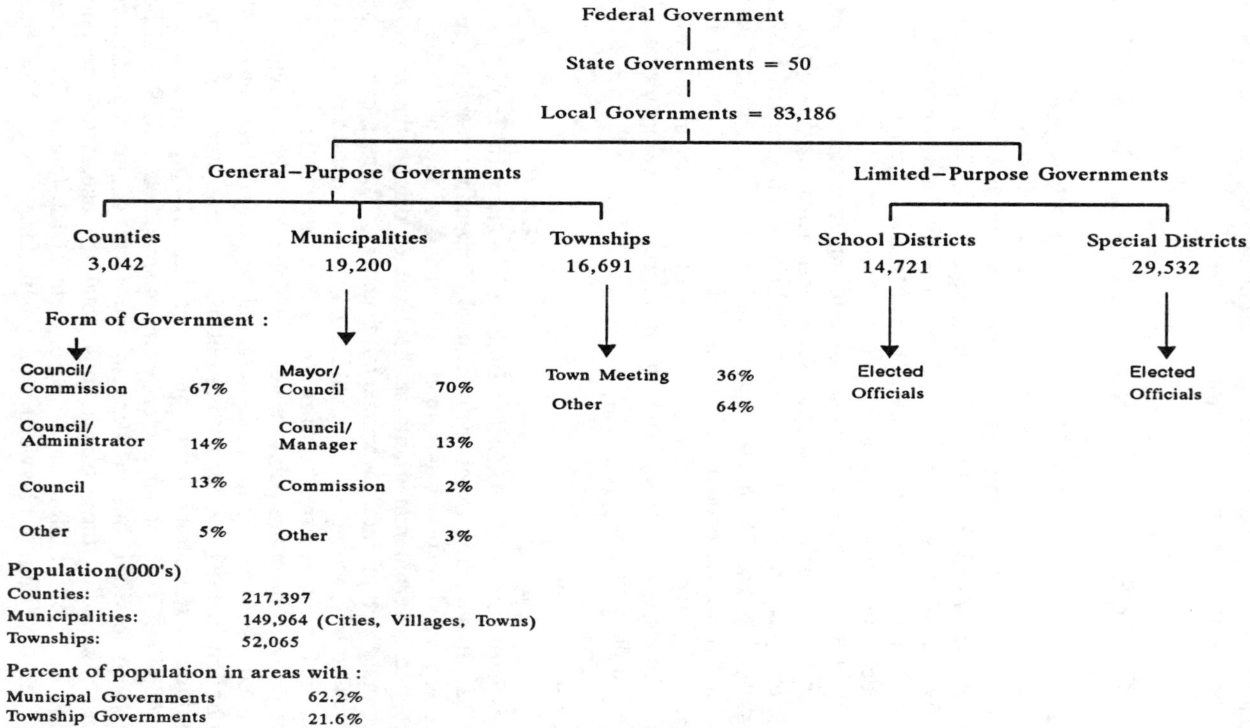

Note : Details do not add up due to nonresponse.
Source: 1987 Census of Governments, U.S. Department of Commerce, Bureau of the Census.

Figure 7.2 *U.S. fiscal structure, 1986–1987*

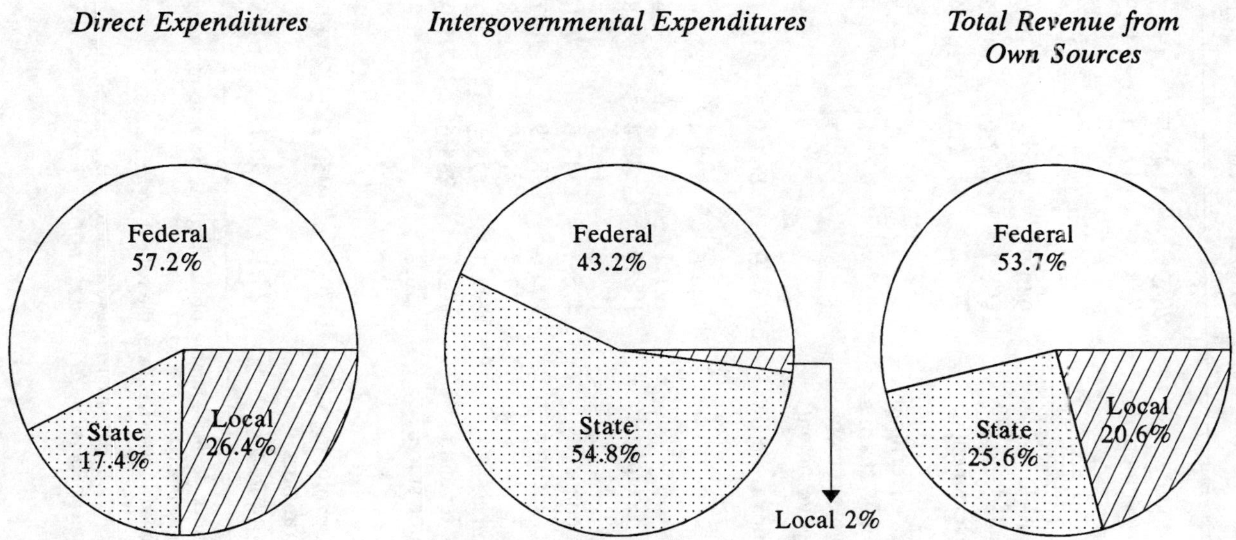

Table 7.1 *Expenditures, revenues and deficit totals by level of government 1986—1987 (in billions of dollars)*

ITEM	Total	Federal	State	Local
Expenditures, total[a]	2069.8	1148.7	455.7	465.4
less intergovernmental expenditures	258.1	111.5	141.3	5.3
Direct expenditures	1811.7	1037.1	314.4	460.2
Revenues, total[a]	1940.7	952.6	517.2	470.9
General Revenue	1498.1	667.0	419.5	411.6
less intergovernmental revenues	261.2	2.5	102.4	156.3
from federal government			95.5	19.4
general revenue sharing				2.5[b]
from state government		2.5		136.9
from local governments			6.9	
General revenues from own sources	1236.9	664.5	317.1	255.3
taxes, total	944.6	539.4	246.9	158.3
property	121.1		4.6	116.5
sales, gross receipts & customs	193.0	48.4	119.8	24.7
individual income	476.2	392.6	76.0	7.7
corporate net income	106.6	83.9	20.7	2.0
other	47.7	14.5	25.8	7.4
charges & misc.	292.3	125.1	70.2	97.0
Insurance trust revenue	392.5	285.6	91.9	14.9
Utility and liquor stores revenues	50.2		5.8	44.4
Total revenues excluding intergovt'al transfers	1679.6	950.1	414.8	314.6
Deficit (+) or Surplus (—)	129.1	196.1	—61.5	—5.5

Notes: a: Includes double counting of transactions because of intergovernmental disbursements.
b: Included in transfers from the federal government.

Source: Based on U.S. Department of Commerce, Bureau of the Census (1987), *Government Finances, 1987 Census of Government*.

was equal to $129 billion, a shortfall equal to six per cent of aggregate expenditures. The way in which total direct expenditures and own revenues are divided among the three levels of government is depicted in Figure 7.2 in terms of percentage shares (dollar amounts are given in the table). On the expenditure side, we note that the federal government's expenditure share was the largest, accounting for 57.2 per cent of the total expenditures to the public. The share of local governments in total direct expenditures ranked second with 25.4 per cent of the total. State governments accounted for only 17.4 per cent of direct expenditures. The distribution of (total) revenue from own sources shows the federal government's share in the total to have been almost as large as its expenditure share (53.7 per cent). The states' share of total revenues from own sources was the second largest with 25.6 per cent; local governments' share in the total was slightly less than 20.7 per cent.

To transfer these highly decentralized decisions into a coherent review, budget expenditures for the three levels of government are regrouped to correspond to the familiar 'Musgravian' functions: allocation (i.e. the provision of public goods), redistribution and merit goods. The first functional category, public goods, consists of those activities leading to non-market supply of goods and services. The second category, redistribution, includes those activities which redistribute private incomes, while the third, merit goods, combines those government activities which modify, through relative price effects, private supply of goods and services. The non-market supply category includes expenditures on national defense, international affairs, general science, space and technology, energy, national resources and the environment, administration of justice and government administration. Budget spending in the category of redistribution consists of pension and disability payments, unemployment compensation and welfare payments. Government activities that modify private supply (provision of merit goods) include spending on education and training, health, agriculture, housing and transportation. How the division of these functions has evolved over time in the U.S. federal system, will be discussed with reference to data reported in Tables 7.2 to 7.4.

It is worth emphasizing from the outset that in grouping public sector expenditures to fit the above three classifications, several heroic assumptions are made. For example, budget expenditures on housing have both an income and a price effect, spending on education also alters both the price structure of education facing consumers and their lifetime income. Here both housing expenditures and spending on education are listed as merit goods.

Distribution of Expenditure Functions

Looking first at the distribution of aggregate public sector spending across the three spending categories (Table 7.2), we find spending for public goods

Table 7.2 *Classification of direct government expenditures, all levels, 1986—1987 (in millions of dollars)*

Expenditure categories	Total	Federal	State	Local
I NON—MARKET SUPPLY (public goods)				
National defense & int'l relations	319,084	319,084	—	—
Space research & technology	7,450	7,450	—	—
Transportation				
Highways	52,978	623	31,488	20,867
Air transportation	8,737	3,823	476	4,438
Water transportation and terminals	3,722	1,971	535	1,216
Other transportation	1,002	—	105	898
Public safety	61,210	4,960	17,293	38,958
Environment				
Natural resources	93,006	83,063	7,354	2,588
Parks and recreation	12,521	1,503	1,876	9,142
Sanitation				
Sewerage	15,148	—	406	14,742
Sanitation other than sewerage	6,499	—	—	6,499
Government administration	44,136	9,230	13,339	21,566
TOTAL	625,493	431,707	72,872	120,914
TOTAL excluding national defense and space	298,959	105,173	72,872	120,914
II DISTRIBUTIVE				
Social service & income maintenance				
Public welfare	106,407	26,187	61,270	18,950
Social insurance administration	6,775	4,023	2,741	11
Federal social security	282,212	282,212	—	—
Unemployment compensation	15,412	164	15,174	74
Employee retirement	55,594	25,991	22,189	7,414
Other insurance trust expenditures	14,040	8,087	5,953	—
TOTAL	480,440	346,664	107,327	26,449

Table 7.2 continued

Expenditure categories	Total	Federal	State	Local
III MODIFYING MARKET SUPPLY (merit goods)				
Postal service	32,243	32,243	—	—
Education services	244,308	14,393	61,935	167,980
Hospitals	47,970	7,786	17,995	22,189
Health	24,634	7,731	9,207	7,696
Housing & community development	21,308	9,538	1,308	10,462
Veterans' services[a]	17,217	17,088	129	—
Utility and liquor store expenditure	68,642	—	8,441	60,201
TOTAL	456,322	88,779	99,015	268,528
GRAND TOTAL excluding national defense & space	1,235,721	540,616	279,214	415,891
GRAND TOTAL	1,562,255	867,150	279,214	415,891

Notes: Total expenditures classified in this table differ from direct expenditures in Table 7.1 because of unclassified expenditures. Unclassified expenditures include interest on the debt and other expenditures not specified.
a: Public provision of other private services to veterans.

Source: See Table 7.1.

to have been the largest category absorbing \$625 billion out of \$1,562 billion or 40 per cent of total direct expenditures.[8] The remaining 60 per cent was split almost evenly between the other two categories; \$480 billion for redistribution and \$456 billion for merit goods. After netting spending on national defense and space exploration out of the total, spending for redistribution occupied the top spot with almost 39 per cent of the total net of these expenditures. Spending for merit goods came next with 37 per cent, while spending for public goods accounted for only 24 per cent of this total.

The percentage distribution of spending among the three spending categories, as one would expect, differed between the various levels of government. After netting out spending on defense and space exploration, we find the distributive function to have dominated spending at the federal level, accounting for 64 per cent of its total. This is followed by spending for the purpose of public goods provision (19.5 per cent). The remaining

16.5 per cent were spent on merit goods. Expenditure allocation at the state level showed a somewhat more equal distribution among the three functional categories: 26.1 per cent for public goods, 38.4 per cent for distribution and 35.5 per cent for merit goods. At the local level, spending on merit goods came first with 64.6 per cent, followed by 29.0 per cent for spending on local public goods and 6.4 per cent for distribution.

Turning now to the distribution of each expenditure function among the federal, state, and local governments as shown in Table 7.3, we find the following: the provision of merit goods was concentrated at the local level with 59 per cent of the total spending in this category, redistribution at the federal level with 72 per cent of the total. The provision of public goods (excluding defense and space) was divided between the three levels of government with almost 40 per cent of the total supplied at the local level.

Disaggregating these three expenditure categories by major function, one can clearly identify those goods whose benefits are local in nature and those whose benefits cut across governmental units. As shown in the table, local provision is the preferred mode for sanitation and sewage treatment, education, parks and recreation, and public safety while the development of national resources and the provision of social insurance are assigned to the federal government. State governments' spending functions are those which are characterized both by spillover of benefits across jurisdictions such as highways, health and hospitals, as well those where there is a greater need for centralized provision to ensure minimum standards of services (welfare). A further breakdown of spending functions among local units of government is given in Table 7.4. This breakdown is quite useful in that it conveys the degree of decentralization in service provision at the local level. As shown in the table, except for educational services, the provision of most local goods is carried out by municipal governments. County governments are assigned a few services such as correction services (prisons), public health and welfare. Education is the primary responsibility of school districts (single-function government), while special district governments are assigned specific functions such as water transport, and the development and conservation of natural resources.

Revenue Sources

Federal, state and local governments finance their activities from two main sources: from the public (own sources) and from intergovernmental grants. Revenues from own sources consist of two components: general revenues and insurance trust revenues. Almost all of federal revenues are raised directly from the public. As shown later on, intergovernmental transfers are an important source of revenue for some local units, such as school districts whose revenues are more than 50 per cent in the form of grants. County and township governments also receive a significant amount of their revenues, about one-third, through intergovernmental transfers.

Table 7.3 *Expenditure shares by category and by level of government 1986—1987 (in per cent)*

Expenditure categories	Total	Federal	State	Local
I NON-MARKET SUPPLY (public goods)				
including defense and space	100.0	69.0	11.7	19.3
excluding defense and space	100.0	35.2	24.3	40.4
National defense	100.0	100.0	—	—
Space research	100.0	100.0	—	—
Transportation				
Highways	100.0	1.2	59.4	39.4
Airports	100.0	43.8	5.4	50.8
Water transports and terminals	100.0	53.0	14.4	32.7
Other	100.0	—	10.5	89.5
Public safety	100.0	8.1	28.3	63.6
Environment				
Natural resources	100.0	89.3	7.9	2.8
Parks and recreation	100.0	12.0	15.0	73.0
Sanitation				
Sewerage	100.0	—	2.7	97.3
Other	100.0	—	—	100.0
Current administration	100.0	20.9	30.2	48.8
II DISTRIBUTIVE	100.0	72.1	22.3	5.5
Public welfare	100.0	59.4	40.5	—
Social insurance administration	100.0	59.4	40.5	—
Federal social security	100.0	100.0	—	—
Unemployment compensation	100.0	1.1	98.5	0.4
Employee retirement	100.0	46.8	39.9	13.3
Other insurance expense	100.0	57.6	42.4	—
III MODIFYING MARKET SUPPLY (merit goods)	100.0	19.4	21.7	58.8
Postal service	100.0	100.0	—	—
Education services	100.0	5.9	25.4	68.7
Hospitals	100.0	16.2	37.5	46.3
Health	100.0	31.4	37.4	31.2
Housing and community development	100.0	44.8	6.1	49.1
Veterans' services	100.0	99.3	0.7	—
Utility and liquor stores	100.0	—	12.2	87.8

Source: Calculated from data in Table 7.2.

Table 7.4 *Percentage distribution of expenditures by function and by type of local government, 1986—1987*

Function	County	Munici-pality	Township	School Districts	Special Districts
I.					
1. Transportation					
Highways	38.6	48.3	10.4	—	2.6
Airports	21.7	49.7	0.3	—	8.5
Water transport	6.8	36.0	0.3	—	56.9
2. Public Safety					
Police protection	24.9	69.8	5.3	—	—
Fire protection	10.4	75.4	6.3	—	7.9
Correction	77.9	22.1	—	—	—
3. Environment					
Natural resources	45.7	3.4	1.3	—	49.6
Parks and recreation	18.8	65.0	4.3	—	12.0
4. Sanitation					
Sewerage	12.1	59.2	4.5	—	24.3
Sanitation other than sewerage	20.1	68.1	7.8	—	3.3
II.					
Welfare	71.9	27.3	0.8	—	—
III.					
1. Education services					
Education	8.0	8.0	2.1	81.8	0.1
Libraries	26.4	53.1	6.4	—	14.0
2. Hospitals	42.9	24.6	0.3	—	32.2
3. Health	71.7	24.5	1.3	—	2.5
4. Housing & community development	7.4	53.3	0.8	—	38.5

Source: U.S Department of Commerce, Bureau of the Census (1987), *Compendium of Government Finances (12-47), 1987 Census of Government.*

Own revenue sources: general revenues

Looking at the general revenue structure of the U.S. public sector (Table 7.1), we find that taxes (property, sales and income) accounted for the bulk of receipts at all levels of government: 81 per cent at the federal level, 77 per cent at the state level and 62 per cent at the local level. User charges for public services came next accounting for 38 per cent of general revenue at the local level, 22 per cent at the state level and 19 per cent at the federal level.

The distribution of tax receipts by type of tax was not uniform among the three levels of government. The federal government generated the bulk (72 per cent) of its tax revenues from taxes on income (individuals and corporate), with lesser amounts from taxes levied on specific commodities, estates and gifts. At the state level, tax revenues were derived mainly from two sources: income (31 per cent) and sales (38 per cent), while local governments relied heavily on property taxes, raising 46 per cent from this source alone. The sharply differing distribution of revenue sources by level of government is to be expected in a federal system. The U.S. fiscal system is organized — although not perfectly — around the principle of separation of tax sources among the three levels of government: the income tax base for the federal government; the sales tax for the state government, and the property tax base for local governments. However, as the data in the table show, multiple use of the same tax source is not uncommon in the U.S. federal system — both the federal and state governments levy taxes on the income base, and all three levels tax sales.

Own revenue sources: trust fund revenues

The federal, state and local governments also receive income from the public in the form of contributions to social insurance. These receipts are 'earmarked' for pension payments. Federal social security contributions (OASDHI) constituted by far the largest program accounting for 70 per cent of the total trust funds receipts at all levels of government. At the state level, trust fund receipts for employee retirement were equal to 20 per cent of the total, while unemployment insurance accounted for 4.8 per cent of total trust fund revenues.

Intergovernmental transfers

As noted earlier, intergovernmental transfers appear both on the expenditure side and on the revenue side. The federal government makes a substantial transfer to state governments with little direct transfers to local governments. State governments make transfers to local units out of own revenue sources as well as 'pass-through' some of the grants they receive from the federal government.

Intergovernmental transfers received by local governments are not uniformly distributed among them. In 1986—87, 35 per cent of county government revenues were in the form of grants; 30.4 per cent from the states and 3.4 per cent from the federal government and 1.4 per cent from local government. Most of these funds were used by county governments to fund welfare (10.6 per cent); education (6.8 per cent); highways (3.6 per cent) and health and hospitals (three per cent). Grants received by municipal governments accounted for about 22 per cent of their total revenue, most of which was in the form of state grants. Out of these transfers, 4.2 per cent was for education finance, 3.1 per cent for public welfare, and 2.7 per cent for highways.

Townships received about 27 per cent of their revenues in the form of intergovernmental grants, of which eight per cent funded education. School districts, as indicated earlier, rely heavily on intergovernmental grants for funding their expenditures. Fifty-five per cent of their revenues stemmed from this source. As a single-function government, school districts used all grants received for educational purposes.

4 DECENTRALIZATION OF SPENDING

Data analysis reported in the previous sections showed which level of government in the U.S. is primarily responsible for which expenditure function. We now turn to the distribution of functions among local units. From the percentage distribution of local government spending among local units (Table 7.4), we note that county government spending is concentrated in three major areas: welfare, health and hospitals. Municipal government spending priorities are public safety, sanitation, and parks and recreation. The five top-ranked spending priorities by type of local government are shown in Table 7.5. Education does not appear among the top five as it is provided mainly by school districts.

The effect of decentralization on the level of provision is measured by per capita spending on local services. Table 7.6 gives mean values of per capita spending for eight spending functions for county and municipal governments. A few interesting findings emerge. First, the mean value of per capita spending by municipalities is more than twice that of county governments. Second, by category of spending, municipal governments' spending per capita is a multiple of county expenditures per capita on such services as sanitation (eight times), parks and recreation (seven times), housing (five times) and police protection (five times). For those functions where county governments spend the most (as a percentage of the total), per capita spending on those functions at the county level does not differ significantly from per capita spending of municipalities. For example, county government spending on health and welfare is about 71 per cent of total local governments spending on these two functions but on a per capita basis the mean ratios of county government spending relative to municipality is only 1.1 for welfare and 1.7 for health.

Variance Between Community Service Provisions

Summary statistics regarding the level of provision by expenditure function and type of local government are reported in Tables 7A.2 and 7A.3. Based

Table 7.5 *Five top-ranked spending functions by type of local government, 1987*

Function	County government Per cent spending	Rank	Municipal government Per cent spending	Rank
Health	71.1	(2)		
Welfare	71.9	(1)		
Hospital	42.9	(3)		
Transportation (highways & airports)	35.6	(4)	48.5	(5)
Public safety	32.1	(5)	68.0	(1)
Parks and recreation			65.0	(2)
Sanitation			61.9	(3)
Housing			53.3	(4)

Note: a: Ranking is based on the percentage distribution of total local government spending on each function by type of unit.

Source: Based on U.S. Department of Commerce, Bureau of the Census (1987), *Government Finances, 1987 Census of Government*.

on the per capita level of spending, one notes a great deal of variation in the level of services provided by local governments across the U.S. Across units of governments (counties or municipalities), many localities (between 50 to 70 per cent) fail to provide the U.S. average of services while others spend as much as 100 times the average level of service. For example, whereas 75 per cent of all county governments spent less than the average $73 per capita on health, Elliot County, KY, spent about $2,500 per capita at the municipal level. While mean spending on sanitation by municipal governments was about $100, Orlando, FL, spent about $712 per capita or seven times as much as the average in 1986—87. Variation in per capita spending is most noticeable in the case of education. In 1986—87, some school districts in the U.S. spent about $1,000 per capita or about one-fourth of the mean per capita spending, while other school districts, notably in Alaska, spent about $22,571 or five times the nation's average.

The same diversity is also evident when the data are disaggregated by region. In Tables 7.7 and 7.8, the four U.S. regions: Northeast (NE); Midwest (MW); the South (SO); and the West (WST) are ranked according to the mean ratio of per capita spending on local public goods. As evident from the data, the Western counties lead the regions in the country in almost all categories of spending: their per capita spending on public safety, airports, and welfare was almost twice as high as the national average. Next

Table 7.6 *Mean per capita spending on local public goods by type of local government*

Function	Counties' mean value (1)	Municipalities' mean value (2)	Mean value (2)/(1)
Education	$181.1	$451.8	2.49
Health	73.4	43.9	0.60
Welfare	43.3	38.5	0.89
Hospital	12.8	18.4	1.44
Housing and community development	7.3	39.1	5.36
Highways	86.7	67.8	0.78
Airports	7.4	33.8	4.60
Sanitation	12.2	98.6	8.10
Natural resources	6.8	5.4	0.79
Parks and recreation	6.4	47.2	7.38
Public safety	33.2	172.4	5.19
Total spending	$453.9	$1,043.9	2.30

Source: Based on U.S. Department of Commerce, Bureau of the Census (1987), *Government Finances, 1987 Census of Government*.

is the Midwest, with the mean ratio of spending per capita being highest for spending on natural resources (1.39), welfare (1.35) and highways (1.23). The Northeast leads all other regions in only two categories: welfare (3.79) and sanitation (1.72). This poor showing may in part be attributed to the fact that in New England most public goods are provided by municipalities as opposed to counties. The Southern region has the highest mean ratio for only one category of spending, education, where the ratio is 1.78 times the average for the nation.

A different pattern is found for municipal governments. The ranking reported in Table 7.8 shows the Northeast with the highest mean ratio for total spending, and for spending on education, health and housing. Municipalities in the South have higher mean ratios of per capita spending on welfare, hospital, sanitation and natural resources, while municipalities in the West have higher mean ratios for spending on airports, parks, highways and public safety. The Midwest trails in all categories of spending. It is to be emphasized that regional variations between and within local units may be due to institutional arrangements (assignment of expenditure functions) in addition to other factors such as tastes and income.

Table 7.7 Ranking by mean ratio of county governments' per capita spending on local public goods by region

Function	NE[a] Ratio	NE[a] Rank	MW Ratio	MW Rank	SO Ratio	SO Rank	WST Ratio	WST Rank
Education	0.11		0.03		1.78	(1)	1.64	(2)
Health	0.47		1.20	(1)	0.91		1.07	(2)
Welfare	3.79	(1)	1.35	(3)	0.27		1.79	(2)
Hospital	0.86		1.09	(1)	0.83		0.93	
Housing & community development	0.90		0.44		1.09	(2)	1.61	(1)
Highways	0.39		1.23	(2)	0.73		1.42	(1)
Airports	0.62		0.49		0.85		1.96	(1)
Sanitation	1.72	(1)	0.66		1.08	(3)	1.11	(2)
Natural resources	0.41		1.39	(2)	0.59		1.62	(1)
Parks	0.71		0.77		0.97		1.61	(1)
Public safety	0.39		0.86		0.92		1.82	(1)
Total spending	0.73		0.86		0.99		1.54	(1)

Note: a: Mean values of county governments in the Northeast reflect the level of provision in New England where most public goods are provided by municipalities.

Source: Based on U.S. Department of Commerce, Bureau of the Census (1987), *Government Finances, 1987 Census of Government*.

Given the institutional setting, differences in spending across jurisdictions may be attributed to two factors: differences in preferences (tastes) for public goods, and/or differences in capacity (income) to allow for a 'standard' level of provision. Both these explanations are said to apply to the U.S. setting. Therefore, to the extent that variability in per capita spending reflects differences in 'ability to spend' (deficiency in fiscal capacity), a standard level of provision can only be attained with help from the national government. The relationship between fiscal capacity and community needs are examined below.

Fiscal Capacity and Fiscal Effort

A community's fiscal capacity may be defined as the sum of the total per capita income earned plus the total value of its property per capita. A community's fiscal effort refers to the ratio of its own tax sources to its fiscal capacity. Based on these definitions, one would expect to find an

Table 7.8 *Ranking by mean ratio of municipal governments' per capita spending on local public goods by region*

Function	NE[a]		MW		SO		WST	
	Ratio	Rank	Ratio	Rank	Ratio	Rank	Ratio	Rank
Education	1.35	(1)	0.03		0.81		0.34	
Health	1.66	(1)	1.00	(3)	1.18	(2)	0.72	
Welfare	1.13	(2)	0.22		1.31	(1)	0.92	
Hospital	0.49		1.16	(2)	1.33	(1)	1.15	(3)
Housing & community development	1.32	(1)	0.85		0.95		0.94	
Highways	0.75		1.09	(2)	0.94		1.16	(1)
Airports	0.33		1.18	(2)	0.89		1.31	(1)
Sanitation	0.87		0.96		1.21	(1)	0.91	
Natural resources	0.52		1.42	(2)	1.50	(1)	0.71	
Parks	0.59		0.78		1.19	(2)	1.28	(1)
Public safety	1.09	(2)	0.90		0.92		1.10	(1)
Total spending	1.25	(1)	0.75		1.19	(2)	0.86	

Source: Based on U.S. Department of Commerce, Bureau of the Census (1987), *Government Finances, 1987 Census of Government.*

inverse relationship between the level of a community's fiscal capacity (tax base) and fiscal effort (average rate), because communities with higher capacity do not need to raise the same amount of revenue per capita as communities with low fiscal capacity. Also to be expected is a negative relationship between a community's fiscal capacity for a given tax effort and federal intergovernmental grants — the reason being that communities with higher fiscal capacity are more capable of raising revenues from their own tax base and can, therefore, be expected to pay for more of their own public goods and services. But since community needs also vary across jurisdictions, the two sides of the equation — capacity and needs, given the level of effort — are likely to influence the level of intergovernmental transfers.

Municipalities in the U.S. exhibit variability in their fiscal capacity as well as tax effort. In 1981, the average fiscal capacity for all municipal units was estimated to be around $7,700; this value had risen to $11,300 by 1985. Compared to the national average, municipalities in the West exhibited the highest average value, the Northeast the lowest (Table 7.9). Given the disparities in fiscal capacity, the expectation is that a community with low fiscal capacity will have to tax its citizens at a much higher rate

Table 7.9 *Fiscal capacity, tax effort and intergovernmental grants per capita: municipalities, total and by region (amount in dollars, rate in per cent)*

Description	All	NE	MW	SO	WST
Capacity 81	7,712.4	6,800.5	7,857.6	7,368.2	8,587.8
Capacity 85	11,292.4	10,654.3	11,202.0	10,903.6	12,219.9
Tax effort 81	2.8	5.4[a]	1.9	2.6[a]	1.9[a]
Tax effort 85	2.3	4.0	1.6	2.4	2.0
Revenues 81	580.9	829.0	505.0	590.2	455.8
Revenues 85	730.3	1008.9	598.2	747.5	624.6
Intergovt'al grants 81	203.0	337.7	186.7	194.9	127.1
Intergovt'al grants 85	212.0	405.3	162.3	187.3	140.0
No. of municipalities	342	70	85	92	95

Note: a: Tax effort for 1979.

Source: Based on U.S. Department of Commerce, Bureau of the Census (1987), *Government Finances, 1987 Census of Government*.

than those with higher fiscal capacity to meet the community needs. This turned out to be the case. Municipalities in the Northeast and the South of the U.S. showed much higher levels of tax effort in both 1981 and 1985 than the municipalities in the Midwest and the Western regions.

Community Needs

To put these concepts, capacity and effort, in the same perspective, information about local demand for services which justifies the taxing away of private resources in the first place, is needed. Local demand for services is said to reflect need. But community need is a very general concept; it is somewhat difficult to define and hard to measure. A congressional study of city needs identified three main facets of community need: social, economic and fiscal.[9] According to the study, a community may be said to have excessive social need if a large proportion of its population faces any or all of the following problems: low income, high unemployment rate, low level of education, high crime rate, and poor infrastructure. A community is said to have high economic need if it has a hard time attracting new businesses and/or retaining its old businesses (i.e. creating new jobs or sustaining the old jobs). A community has high fiscal need if it faces either or both of the following problems: a short-term financial crisis (current expenditures are greater than current tax revenues) and a long-term financial crisis (loss of tax bases).

These three aspects of need are highly interdependent. As discussed in the previous chapter, an individual's choice of residence is influenced by a number of factors not least of which are spending on local public schools, the crime rate, and incidence of poverty. If a community has a high crime rate (social need), it will attract less households and businesses and, therefore, will have low job creation (economic need). The fewer jobs there are in an area, the lower will be the tax base (fiscal need). Moreover, the lower the tax base, the lower will be public spending, including spending on public schools (economic need), and the less public spending on public schools, the less educated will be the local population. High skill (high wage) jobs will not be created, and the cycle of need starts all over again. Several communities in the U.S. face all three types of problems. This phenomenon is often referred to as 'urban plight'.

Variation Among Communities in Fiscal Capacity Relative to Need

A community's need and a community's fiscal capacity often do not correspond. In other words, a community with high need (be it social, fiscal, or economic) often has very low fiscal capacity. For example, a community which is losing business (and therefore has a higher unemployment rate) will be considered a community with high economic need. At the same time as it is losing jobs, it will be losing fiscal capacity as well (due to falling incomes and falling property values). This community then is said to have both increasing levels of economic need and decreasing levels of fiscal capacity. However, there are other communities with low need (high employment, low crime etc.) and high fiscal capacity (growing job base and property values). Given this fiscal imbalance, the expectation is that the federal government would provide more funds (in the way of grants) to the former communities. This expectation is borne out by the data analysis provided in the next section.

5 INTERGOVERNMENTAL GRANTS IN RELATION TO NEEDS

The provision of federal grants-in-aid to the state-local sector was quite extensive during the 1960s ($10.9 billion in 1965). According to the Advisory Commission on Intergovernmental Relations (ACIR), there were 370 grants-in-aid programs as of 1967, yet municipalities' needs were not being met. Faced with inattention to their needs in their state capitals, mayors turned to Washington for assistance. Washington responded 'with a cornucopia of programs', many of them under the umbrella of President Johnson's 'war on poverty'.[10] By 1967, nearly one in five federal programs provided direct assistance to local government. According to Rich (1993), mayors of major U.S. cities soon discovered that there was no system to the federal grant programs in force. Few mayors had any idea how much money their cities were eligible for compared to what was actually coming.

In an attempt to address this problem, Richard Nixon's New Federalism brought forth three major sets of legislation: General Revenue Sharing (GRS) enacted in 1972, the Comprehensive Employment and Training Act (CETA) in 1973 and the Community Development Block Grants (CDBG) in 1974. By 1976, federal grants-in-aid had risen from $24.1 billion in 1970 to $59.1 billion. Federal assistance continued its ascendancy during the Carter years; funding for old programs expanded, new programs were created. By 1980, federal grants-in-aid reached $91.5 billion or 15.5 per cent of total federal expenditures for that year and 26 per cent of total state and local expenditures. The growth of federal assistance to state-local governments was reduced during the Reagan years. Reagan's New Federalism was intended to fulfil a Reagan campaign pledge to 'get the government off the backs of the American people'.[11] By the end of his term, federal grants-in-aid had increased from $91.5 billion to $108 billion, an average annual rate of increase of two per cent. Although federal assistance during the Bush administration increased somewhat, city governments are more than willing to renew their demand for higher federal support from the incoming administration. Whether federal assistance is needed and to what end are important questions for budget makers in a federal system. As we saw earlier, communities across the U.S. do indeed differ in terms of need and the resources at hand to address those needs. We also noted that total federal grants-in-aid were not insubstantial.

On a per capita basis, the average (federal and state) aid received by municipalities in 1986—87 was around $212 or 20 per cent of per capita spending by municipal governments on municipal services. With this amount of aid going to municipalities, the question that needs to be answered is whether or not federal aid was distributed according to needs. Put differently: Do cities that rank highest according to the various measures of need also rank highest on the list of federal intergovernmental transfer recipients? Below we offer some empirical evidence concerning this relationship.

To answer this question, U.S. cities were ranked in terms of both their needs and the amount of federal aid received, and the Spearman rank correlations were calculated. The methodology and empirical results are given in the appendix. A positive correlation (relationship) between city need and the level of federal intergovernmental transfers would be indicative of a federal response to local problems. This turned out to be the case. First, the calculation shows a significant positive relationship to exist between the city social index (the first measure of need) and the level of federal intergovernmental transfers for both 1981 and 1985 (0.33 for 1981; 0.25 in 1985).

Second, whether or not the federal government responded to economic need may be ascertained from the correlation between growth in commerce (shipment and sales), and federal intergovernmental transfers. If the federal government responded to cities in economic need, one would expect to find a negative correlation between growth in commerce (shipment and sales) and federal aid. In other words, cities with higher growth rates in their private sector activity are more able to pay for their own public services and, therefore, would receive less aid from the federal government. In all cases the data show a significant negative correlation between growth in shipment and federal aid (—0.29 in 1981 and —0.31 in 1985), and between growth of sales and federal aid (—0.30 in 1981 and —0.29 in 1985).[12]

Lastly, the relationship between fiscal need and federal support is captured by the correlation between the fiscal need measures and federal aid. If the federal government responded to such need, we would expect a positive relationship between both measures of fiscal need and federal assistance. In other words, cities with higher (lower) short-term deficits and long-term debt will receive more (less) aid from the federal government. As it turned out, there is a significant positive relationship between both measures of fiscal need and federal government assistance. In the short term, the correlation coefficient between fiscal need and federal aid is equal to 0.85 for 1981 and 0.77 in 1985. In the long term the correlation coefficient is equal to 0.52 in 1981 and 0.19 in 1985.

The empirical results presented above suggest that in the U.S. federal structure, the federal government did indeed respond to the needs of the cities, no matter how the term need is defined. What could not be answered from the data however, is how effective federal assistance was in addressing the so-called 'fiscal crisis' of U.S. cities.

6 CONCLUSION

This review of the U.S. fiscal structure suggests that budget making in a federal system is a highly complex process. Many functions, from allocation to redistribution, are carried out by more than one level of government, and tax powers, although unequally distributed, are to some extent shared by all, by virtue of the system of intergovernmental grants.

Communities across the U.S. exhibit a great deal of variation in the provision of essential public services such as sanitation, public health and public safety. They also differ in the level of provision for such meritorious goods as education and affordable housing. Differences in the level of services provided by counties and municipal governments reflect both differences in tastes and ability to fund local services. When imbalances exist between the demand for services relative to the availability of resources, the national government is called upon to supplement local resources or to take over the provision of certain services. In the U.S. federal system, federal grants-in-aid have played a significant role in mitigating this problem.

APPENDIX

Measures of Community Needs

Three measures are used to estimate community or city needs: social need, economic need and fiscal need.

City social need index
Following Nathan and Adams (1976), six indicators were used to construct a measure of social need. The indicators are: unemployment rate, average income, percentage poor dependency ratio, educational deficiency and overcrowded housing condition.

The social index (SI) is calculated as follows:

$$SI = 1/n\Sigma X_i \tag{7A.1}$$

where: n = the number of indicators, and

$$X_i = (Y_i - Y_a)/(Y_b - Y_a) \tag{7A.2}$$

with: Y_i = value on a measure of city need for each city
Y_a = value of Y least in need
Y_b = value of Y most in need

In the calculation of the index, a score of 100 was assigned to the most needy city and a score of zero to the least needy city.

Economic need
Two indicators of economic need are used: the percentage growth rate of manufacturing total value of shipments (TVS), between 1977 and 1982; and the growth rate of retail sales (SALES), between 1977 and 1982.

Fiscal need
Short-term fiscal need is defined as the difference between current expenditures and revenue per capita for 1981 and 1985. Long-term fiscal need is defined as the ratio of total outstanding debt to total current own tax

revenues for 1981 and 1985.

Federal response

As a measure of federal response the level of federal intergovernmental transfers per capita in 1981 and 1985 is used.

Table 7A.1 *Structure of government finance: percentage shares of revenue sources by selected functions, 1986—1987*

	Total revenues	*Education*	*Public welfare*	*Health & hospitals*	*Highways*	*Housing & community development*
Total	100.0	100.0	100.0	100.0	100.0	100.0
Federal	4.1	0.3	0.3	0.1	0.1	1.5
State	29.1	18.7	18.7	0.8	1.4	—
Own sources	66.8	81.0	81.0	99.1	98.5	98.5
Counties						
Total	100.0	100.0	100.0	100.0	100.0	100.0
Federal	3.4	0.1	0.1	0.1	0.1	0.7
State	30.4	6.6	10.5	2.9	3.4	—
Local	1.4	0.1	—	0.1	0.2	—
Own sources	64.8	93.2	89.4	96.9	96.3	99.3
Municipalities						
Total	100.0	100.0	100.0	100.0	100.0	100.0
Federal	4.9	0.1	0.2	0.1	0.1	1.9
State	15.5	3.9	2.7	0.4	1.5	—
Local	1.7	0.2	—	—	0.1	—
Own sources	77.8	95.8	97.1	99.5	98.3	98.1
Townships						
Total	100.0	100.0	100.0	100.0	100.0	100.0
Federal	3.2	0.2	—	—	—	0.2
State	21.3	7.6	0.1	0.1	2.5	—
Local	2.0	0.1	—	—	0.3	—
Own sources	73.6	92.1	99.9	99.9	97.2	99.8
School districts						
Total	100.0	100.0	100.0	100.0	100.0	100.0
Federal	0.8	0.8	—	—	—	—
State	52.5	52.5	—	—	—	—
Local	1.6	1.6	—	—	—	—
Own sources	45.0	45.0	—	—	—	—
Special districts						
Total	100.0	100.0	100.0	100.0	100.0	100.0
Federal	11.4	—	—	0.2	—	6.1
State	3.9	—	—	0.2	0.1	—
Local	6.1	0.5	—	0.2	—	—
Own sources	78.7	99.5	100.0	96.4	99.9	93.9

Note: a: Percentage allocation of intergovernmental revenue may not add up to total because of others and unallowable.

Table 7A.2 *Per capita spending on local goods by county governments: summary statistics (amounts in dollars)*

Category	# of counties[a]	Mean	Std. Dev.	Minimum	Maximum	% below the mean	Max county[b]
Education	1192	181.40	303.91	0.01	3628.59	50	North West Artic Borough, AK
Health	2848	73.40	128.58	0.02	2490.15	75	Elliot County, KY
Welfare	2582	43.27	69.54	0.01	479.38	75	St. Louis County, MN
Hospital	447	12.78	24.62	0.01	288.37	75	Mills County, IA
Housing & community development	700	7.25	16.26	0.01	314.04	75	North Slope Borough, AK
Highways	2804	86.66	91.97	0.02	1752.36	50	North Slope Borough, AK
Airport	778	7.44	25.39	0.01	401.91	75	North Slope Borough, AK
Sanitation	1774	12.18	22.22	0.02	257.20	50	North Slope Borough, AK
Natural resources	2710	6.82	12.47	0.02	266.10	70	North Slope Borough, AK
Parks / Recreation	2131	6.42	13.36	0.01	304.07	75	Kaweenaw County, MI
Public safety	1582	33.18	39.74	0.06	550.17	70	North Slope Borough, AK
Total expenditure	3040	453.91	405.57	2.50	6373.77		
Total revenue	3040	462.49	406.11	2.66	6323.63		

Notes: Total number of counties is 3040.
a: Number reporting provision of the service.
b: Max county: counties with maximum expenditure.

Source: Based on U.S. Department of Commerce, Bureau of the Census (1987), *Government Finances, 1987 Census of Governments.*

Table 7A.3 *Per capita spending on local goods by municipal governments: summary statistics (amounts in dollars)*

Category	# of municipalities [a]	Mean	Std.Dev.	Minimum	Maximum	% below the mean	Max city[b]
Education	89	451.84	283.50	0.01	1155.84	25—50	Anchorage, AK
Health	248	44.80	118.03	0.03	887.02	75—80	Owensboro, KY
Welfare	137	38.63	102.07	0.01	894.59	75—80	Washington, DC
Hospital	18	18.35	28.34	0.47	105.23	50—75	Washington, DC
Housing & community development	321	39.20	42.18	0.40	317.68	50—75	Washington, DC
Highways	342	68.17	40.25	3.24	337.32	50	Anchorage, AK
Airport	128	33.85	52.08	0.01	363.10	75	Denver, CO
Sanitation	284	99.24	67.84	13.35	712.71	50—75	Orlando, FL
Natural resources	52	5.42	8.33	0.01	43.48	75	Tampa, FL
Parks / Recreation	336	48.70	38.47	0.01	423.97	50-75	Mountain, CA
Public safety	331	171.80	54.83	67.70	534.04	50	Washington, DC
Total expenditure	342	1055.52	671.41	225.83	5853.04	50—75	Washington, DC
Total revenue	342	1029.73	617.62	241.75	5480.12	50—75	Washington, DC

Notes: Total number of municipalities is equal to 342.
a: Number of municipalities reporting provision of the service.
b: Max city : cities with maximum expenditure.

Table 7A.4 *City needs: summary statistics (amounts in dollars)*

	Mean	Std. Dev.	Min	Max
Inter 81	202.98	178.98	9.20	1200.40
Inter 85	212.22	219.21	8.95	1650.90
Social need	0.31	0.08	0.06	0.61
Growth shipment	0.43	0.41	–1.30	2.04
Growth sales	0.37	0.18	–0.27	1.44
S-T deficit 81	188.80	180.90	–100.00	1079.00
S-T deficit 85	190.00	228.90	–216.20	1565.70
L-T debt 81	41.41	38.24	0.00	230.00
L-T debt 85	87.72	91.80	0.00	683.20

Notes: Inter 81: intergovernmental grants per capita in 1981.
Inter 85: intergovernmental transfers in 1985.
Growth shipment: growth rate of manufacturing shipments from 1977 to 1982.
Growth sales: growth rate of retail sales from 1977 to 1982.
S-T deficit: current expenditures minus current revenues (per capita) for 1981 & 1985 respectively.
L-T debt: outstanding debt relative to the tax base for 1981 & 1985 respectively.

Table 7A.5 *Correlations between city needs and federal intergovernmental transfers (1981—1985)*

	Social need [a]	Growth TVS	Growth sales	S-T deficit	L-T debt
Inter 81	0.33	–0.29	–0.30	0.85	0.52
	(.0001)	(.0011)	(.0001)	(.0001)	(.0001)
Inter 85	0.25	–0.31	–0.29	0.77	0.19
	(.0001)	(.0001)	(.0001)	(.0001)	(.0010)

Notes: Number of observations = 342.
p—values in parentheses.
a: Social need: Index of social need.

NOTES

1. Maxwell and Aronson (1977), p. 12.
2. Ibid., p. 16.
3. Advisory Commission on Intergovernmental Relations (1955), p. 29.
4. City of Clinton v. Cedar Rapids and Missouri Railroad Company, 24 Iowa 455 (1868).
5. Maxwell (1965), p. 31.
6. Maxwell (1965), p. 11.
7. Special district governments are independent units which exist as separate entities with substantial administrative and fiscal independence from general purpose governments. Most special districts are established to perform a single function such as flood control, soil and water conservation, and fire protection.
8. Only direct expenditures are classified in the tables as these reflect expenditures to the public (total net of intergovernmental transfers).
9. The terminology and the methods used to estimate city needs are based on a study by the Committee on Banking Finance and Urban Affairs, Subcommittee on the City, *City Needs and Responsiveness of Federal Grants Programs* (August 1978).
10. Rich (1993), ch. 2. See also Advisory Committee on Intergovernmental Relations (1977 and 1981).
11. Rich (1993), ch. 2.
12. All of the following results are qualitatively the same if we add in state intergovernmental transfers with federal transfers.

REFERENCES

Advisory Commission on Intergovernmental Relations (ACIR) (1955), *A Report to the President*, Washington D.C., U.S. Government Printing Office.

Advisory Commission on Intergovernmental Relations (ACIR) (1971), *Measuring the Fiscal Capacity and Effect of State and Local Areas*, Report M-58, Washington D.C., U.S. Government Printing Office.

Advisory Commission on Intergovernmental Relations (ACIR) (1977), *Federal Grants: Their Effects on State-Local Expenditures, Employment Levels, and Wage Rates*, Washington D.C., U.S. Government Printing Office.

Advisory Commission on Intergovernmental Relations (ACIR) (1981), *Significant Features of Fiscal Federalism*, Washington D.C., U.S. Government Printing Office.

Anton, T. (1976), 'General Revenue Sharing and State-Local Government Structure', in Juster, T. (ed.), *The Economic and Political Impact of General Revenue Sharing*, U.S. Government Printing Office, pp. 131—42.

Bahl, Roy (1984), *Financing State and Local Government in the 1980's*, New York, Oxford University Press.

Break, George F. (1980), *Financing Government in a Federal System*, Washington D.C., The Brookings Institution.

Committee on Banking Finance and Urban Affairs, Subcommittee on the City (1978), *City Needs and the Responsiveness of Federal Grants Programs*, Washington D.C., U.S. Government Printing Office.

Fiscal Relations in the American Fiscal System (1975), Hearings before a Subcommittee of the Committee on Government Operations, House of Representatives, Washington, D.C., U.S. Government Printing Office.

Maxwell, J.A. (1965), *Financing State and Local Governments*, Washington D.C., The Brookings Institution.

Maxwell, J.A. and Aronson, R. (1977), *Financing State and Local Governments*, Washington, D.C., The Brookings Institution.

Nathan, R. and Adams, C. (1976), 'Understanding Central City Hardship', *Political Science Quarterly*, **91**(1), pp. 47—62.

Netzer, D. (1974), *State-Local Finance and Intergovernmental Fiscal Relations*, Washington, D.C., The Brookings Institution.

Ott, D., Ott, A.F., Maxwell, J.A. and Aronson, R. (1975), *State and Local Finance in the Last Half of the 1970's*, Washington D.C., The American Enterprise Institute.

Reischauer, R. (1974), *Rich Governments — Poor Governments: Determining the Fiscal Capacity and Revenue Requirements of State and Local Government*, Washington D.C., The Brookings Institution.

Rich, M. (1993), *National Goals and Local Choices: Distributing Federal Aid to the Poor,* Princeton University Press.

U.S. Department of Commerce, Bureau of the Census (1987a), *Census of the Government, Government Finances*, Washington D.C, U.S. Government Printing Office.

U.S. Department of Commerce, Bureau of the Census (1987b), *Census of the Government, Government Organization*, Washington D.C., U.S. Government Printing Office.

U.S. Department of Commerce, Bureau of the Census (1987c), *Census of the Government, Compendium of Government Finances*, Washington D.C, U.S. Government Printing Office.

PART TWO

Comparative Budgeting: Case Studies

8. Public Sector Service Provision and the Form of Government

The search for a 'second best' size of government is an ongoing process. Back at the time of Adam Smith, when the role of government was well defined and quite limited in scope, people did not much worry about the size of government or about implications of its actions for the long-run potential of the economy.

Two hundred or so years later these are the issues that concern all societies. Referring to the growth of government in Western industrialized countries, Friedman asks: Can we halt Leviathan? Basic to our understanding of the growth of government is not only a knowledge of what governments do, but also at what levels of decision making these decisions are made.

In democratic societies, the government is a political institution to which the public has assigned the task and the power of defining and protecting the property rights and, when necessary for the enhancement of the general welfare, the redistribution of these property rights. Charged with this responsibility, an efficient organization — whether it be public or private — would act to maximize the public's interest and/or minimize the costs of its actions for any given assignment.

In a private economy, the efficiency criterion is easier to achieve than is the case in the public economy. In the private economy, the market system in most cases (in the absence of externalities and imperfections) guarantees efficient use of resources by providing incentives for appropriate behavior. In the public economy, the political system replaces the market system. To ensure efficiency in the public economies, incentives have to be put in place to induce governments to behave appropriately.

Which form of government is likely to provide 'sufficient incentives' for efficient fiscal action? The debate over centralized versus decentralized forms of government, in essence, aims at this puzzle. At one level, the debate is about the fiscal framework — a choice between a unitary government or a federation. At another level is the 'degree' of centralization in the provision of public services.

In this volume issues pertaining to both decisions — the form of government and degree of centralization — are addressed. In Part One, Chapters 6 and 7, the debate about the federal form of government and about the decentralization of provision of services was explored in the U.S.

context. In this part of the volume, Part Two, we offer a comparative study of fiscal arrangements in Canada (Chapter 9) and in the German Federal Republic (Chapter 10), both of which are organized as federations, and the U.K. (Chapter 11), which represents a unitary form of government.

The theoretical framework provided earlier in the volume (Chapter 6) defining the issues underlying the choice among the forms of government and the degree of centralization of provision forms the basis for evaluating countries' experiences. In such an evaluation, the following points should be highlighted:

1. How have fiscal arrangements evolved over time in a unitary system compared to a federated system?
2. Is the government's response to fiscal needs in relation to capacity a function of the form of government?
3. What patterns of provision of services have emerged in the alternative form of government? In other words, does the de facto assignment of functions reflect an 'efficient' structure of provision stated by the theoretical model assignment?
4. Within a federated system, are existing jurisdictions efficient — is community size optimal?
5. Does the form and degree of centralization of the public sector make a difference to the Leviathan proposition — growth of government?

Discussion in Chapters 9, 10, and 11 will shed light on these factors. Chapter 12 offers a survey of the literature about the Leviathan question and provides empirical evidence derived from data analysis of the countries studied.

9. The Budget Process and Fiscal Federalism in Canada

Gladstone Hutchinson

1 INTRODUCTION

Public sector budgeting in a federal system is a complex process. This is particularly so in a country like Canada because of its diverse linguistic, cultural, ethnic and spatial realities. Hence the dominant institutional imperative for public budgeting in Canada is the proper organization and management of intergovernmental budgeting, or *fiscal federalism*. This chapter will discuss the issues pertinent to fiscal federalism in Canada.

Because of Canada's large geographic size and low population density, its government has historically played a vital role in the provision and preservation of its social and economic infrastructure. Canada has one federal government, ten provincial governments, and over 5,000 local government units.[1] Three basic characteristics combine to create the need for intergovernmental budgeting in Canada. They are: 1. the existence of open regional economies within Canada; 2. the presence of areas of joint expenditure responsibilities; and 3. the need for different levels of government to share the same tax source.[2] Open regional economies create the possibility of budgetary action taken within a province spilling over into another province. Interdependency between the levels of government in the provision of joint expenditure programs is routine and must be accommodated under fiscal federalism. Lastly, the need to preserve the common tax base shared by different levels of government points to the necessity for tax harmonization and the coordination of public sector policies.[3]

This chapter is organized as follows. The next section provides an overview of the political aspects of budgeting and lays out the institutional framework within which conflicting purposes of budgeting are resolved. Section 3 discusses the assignment of powers and responsibilities to the three levels of government. The following two sections use current budgetary data to review the fiscal structure (i.e. the actual distribution of expenditure and taxing powers) within Canada's multi-level public sector and to examine the fiscal relations between the different levels of government. Special attention is paid to the efficiency and equity implications of the budgetary choices and the interdependency of public budgeting at the three levels of government. Section 6 concludes.

2 BUDGETING AND THE INSTITUTIONAL SETTING

Government budget decision making in Canada is best represented as a hierarchy of responsibilities. At the upper levels, decisions are made about the direction and policies of the government which are then implemented at the lower levels of government. The federal and provincial levels of government each have an elected legislature and an executive branch, headed by a Prime Minister or Premier, and a Cabinet made up of members of the political party in power. The Cabinet collectively establishes priorities, defines objectives, and outlines policies. All levels of government are tied together in fiscal arrangements that govern tax revenue collection and the system of expenditure disbursement.[4]

Institutional Accountability

The financial structure and accountability framework of the government at the federal level has its origins in the British North America Act of 1867 (Constitution Act, 1867). By this Act, Parliament, the elected body, has supreme authority over the public purse. It has jurisdiction over reviewing and approving government expenditures and tax policies. Hence, Parliament must grant spending authority before disbursements can be made from the Consolidated Revenue Fund (CRF), in which all receipts of the federal government must be deposited. Before granting disbursement of federal funds, Parliament first receives for review documents containing information pertinent to the control of the public purse from the three key federal departments: the Department of Finance, the Treasury Board, and the Supply and Services Canada (SSC).

The Department of Finance submits the Budget Papers which relate the government's financial plan for the economy. The Treasury Department submits the Estimates document which acts as the government's formal request for spending authority, and the Supply and Services Canada submits the Public Accounts which show actual spending versus amount authorized and the overall financial position of the government. These financial relationships between the federal departments and Parliament are all spelled out in and governed by the Financial Administration Act, the Auditor General Act, and the Government Reorganization Act.[5]

The Treasury Board — a committee of the Cabinet composed of the President of the Treasury Board, the Minister of Finance, and four other Cabinet ministers — is responsible for the detailed annual review and analysis of departmental financial expenditures prior to their parliamentary submission and for the overall financial management within the government. The Board has two agencies — the Secretariat and the Office of the Comptroller General. The Secretariat implements the policies set by the Board and has the responsibility for the management of human and material resources which covers personnel policy, collective bargaining in the public sector and the enhancement of the efficiency of government operations. The Office of the Comptroller General is responsible for establishing and maintaining the Board's policies and practices in financial management, program evaluation, and internal audit.

Another important office involved in the budget process is the Office of the Auditor General. The Auditor General reports directly to the legislature and is charged with providing independent audits of government financial expenditure policies. The Auditor General's Annual Report, together with the Public Accounts of Canada, is reviewed by the House of Commons Standing Committee on Public Accounts. Under the House of Commons rules, the government must respond within 120 days to any recommendations made by a Committee of the House.

Premchand (1990) demonstrates the effectiveness of the 'watch-dog role' played by the Auditor General: in the 1975 and 1976 Auditor General's reports the assessment was made that the departmental systems and procedures for financial management and control were seriously inadequate. Several initiatives aimed at improving accountability and control were subsequently adopted:[6]

1978 Office of the Comptroller General established and issued standards governing internal financial audits.
1979 Policy and Expenditure Management System (PEMS), a new budgetary system, was introduced.
1981 Program evaluation guidelines were published, and the reform of Estimates was upgraded.
1985 Policies governing cash management and directives were issued.
1986 A program to Increase Ministerial Authority and Accountability (IMAA) was introduced.
1989 Cabinet Committees were restructured and the overall resource allocation process was revised to help control spending and reduce the debt and deficit.

Summary of Budget Formulation

Apart from the major policy decisions whose formulation was previously discussed, most decisions on government activity are made during the formulation of the government budget. The budget document reflects decisions made during this phase of budgeting. It details the government's expected revenues and planned expenditures. More specifically, it is the government's plan of operation as prepared by the executive or Cabinet for approval by the legislature or the House of Commons and shows the government's objectives, programs and activities, and purchases for the coming fiscal year. Hence, it serves the executive as a plan of action; it

Table 9.1 *Budgetary cycle: Expenditures for the fiscal year April 1989 — March 1990*

Steps	Time period
Priorities determined by Cabinet Committee on Priorities and Planning (CCPP)	Oct—Nov 1987
Treasury Board (TB) calls for Program Forecast	Dec 1987
Departments prepare Program Forecast	Jan—Feb 1988
TB Secretariat reviews Program Forecast	Mar—May 1988
TB, CCPP and Cabinet review Program Forecast and establish expenditure guidelines	June—Aug 1988
Departments prepare Main Estimates	Sept—Oct 1988
TB Secretariat reviews Main Estimates	Oct—Nov 1988
TB and Cabinet approve Main Estimates	Dec 1988
Main Estimates tabled in Parliament and referred to House Committees	Feb 1989
House Committees review Main Estimates	Feb—May 1989
Vote of Interim Supply	Mar 1989
Parliament debates and passes Appropriation Acts	May—June 1989
Supplementary estimates prepared, reviewed and appropriated	Sept—Dec 1989
Final supplementaries prepared, reviewed and appropriated	Jan—Mar 1990
Post expenditure audit by Auditor General	April—Nov 1990
Public Account's and Auditor General's Report tabled in Parliament and referred to Public Accounts Committee	Nov 1990
Public Accounts Committee examines Public Accounts and Auditor General's Report and reports to the House	Dec 1990—1991

Source: Adapted from Strick (1978), p. 33.

serves the legislature as a means of control over the executive; and it serves administrators in the internal management of their respective departments. Table 9.1 uses the 1989—90 fiscal year to provide a chronological summary of the steps taken during the executive formulation of the budget.

Budgeting at the Subnational Level

Much of the powers and responsibilities governing the budgetary and financial practices at the provincial level of government were assigned under the British North America Act (Constitution Act of 1867) and subsequently refined and revised. As with the federal government, the Cabinet at the provincial level receives expenditure estimates and program proposals from the various departments of the provincial government and must in turn seek authorization from the elected legislature. Many provinces have a central financial screening agency similar to the Treasury Board at the federal level. Pre-audit and post-audit functions are carried out by the offices of the Auditor General (Comptroller General in some cases), and public accounts are normally subject to committee reviews and audit reports.

At the municipal or local level of government, budgeting varies depending on the operational type of organization and authority. Governments in cities, towns, villages and townships, counties and special service areas can reasonably be considered as municipalities because of their separate responsibilities for the provision of government functions (police, roads, tax collection, sewers, garbage collection etc.). Government authority at this level usually consists of an elected council, committees, a treasurer, departments of government and municipal boards. Expenditure estimates from the various departments and boards are submitted yearly to the Treasurer and the council where they are reviewed and revised if necessary (in limited cases). Some Canadian cities have a city manager who reviews estimates instead of the Treasurer. Generally, municipalities distinguish between current and capital budgets for purposes of finance, with capital budgets subject to review and approval by the provincial government.

3 THE ROLE OF GOVERNMENT IN CANADA'S FEDERAL SYSTEM

Efficiency and equity objectives often conflict within a federal fiscal system, for example, by calling for differing degrees of decentralization. Equity considerations typically call for a greater degree of centralization while efficiency (economies of scale) considerations may dictate centralized public sector provision. Indeed, the trade-off among these two underlies the debate over centralization versus decentralization with much of the recent literature favoring efficiency over equity. A decentralized government would more than likely be smaller and more efficient and be able to respond better to local preferences than a central government would.[7] Thus, the de facto division of power in Canada between the various levels of government clearly reflects the body politic's judgements about efficiency versus equity considerations. To better understand federalism in the Canadian context, we begin with an overview of the assignment of powers and responsibilities to the three levels of government. The criteria of efficiency and equity will be discussed in conjunction with these assignments.

Efficiency is better understood within a unitary state than within a federal state. Within a unitary state, efficiency is focused on fully exploiting all possible gains from trade. Hence, in an economy producing only private goods, economic efficiency is achieved when the conditions necessary for efficiency in production and exchange and overall efficiency are satisfied. In this setting, government intervenes only when the market fails. In a federal system of government with spatial, jurisdictional and political distinctions, additional efficiency considerations arise because of spillovers and externalities, differences in fiscal and economic capacities and differences in local service costs.[8] As to be discussed below, these considerations have to some extent shaped the expenditure assignments in Canada.

The assignment of expenditure functions in the Canadian system is not unlike that in most federations. The federal government is assigned the task of providing for the national defense, international affairs and the conduct of foreign trade and interprovincial commerce. Provincial government functions are those usually associated with local-type benefits with spillovers and/or those whose performance is subject to economies of scale. These functions include maintaining law and order, the jurisdiction of civil rights, the provision of education and welfare. Local governments are assigned the task of providing those goods whose benefits are local in character such as fire protection, police, sewer and water and the like.

In a federal system, equity considerations are undertaken in a two-stage process. First, society must decide on its equity obligations and desired level of distribution; and, secondly, it must decide on the level of government (federal, provincial, local) that should be primarily responsible for implementing the redistribution that would achieve society's objective. Within the Canadian context, all the redistributive programs — with the exception of unemployment insurance and the sharing of public pension between the federal and provincial government — are the legislative responsibility of the provinces.

Discussions concerning the assignment of equity responsibilities have been important in the debate over centralization versus decentralization of the public sector and over possible amendments to the Canadian Constitution. The 1982 Constitutional Act made explicit that the redistributive responsibility was to be jointly shared by the federal and provincial governments with the provinces having the responsibility to pursue redistributive policies within their own jurisdiction and the federal government having the overriding responsibility for national equalization.[9]

In short, the assignment issue boils down to that of matching different governmental responsibilities with the appropriate level of government. The next step is determining how each level of government can finance its expenditures. These two — assignment of functions and designation of financing sources — can be done independently with federal/provincial transfers being used to reconcile aggregate differences. Hence intergovernmental transfers play a crucial role in a federal system. For example, if on efficiency grounds a local unit were assigned a particular function but that unit's ability to fund it is limited, then the needed funding may be provided by the national or the provincial government. In the Canadian system, transfers have been implemented to address the equity issue.

One of several equalization schemes is a system of transfers which is funded from the federal government's general revenues with the proceeds allocated as unconditional grants to provinces with low tax capacity. The main purpose of these grants is to bring revenue per capita of the low tax capacity provinces up to par with the average revenue per capita of five representative provinces: Ontario, Quebec, Manitoba, Saskatchewan and British Columbia. Raising per capita revenue to some national average allows the poorer provinces to provide their citizens with comparable levels of public services at comparable tax rates.

Another scheme is the so-called Established Program Financing (EPF). The EPF is a system of block grants whose funds are financed from federal general revenue and allocated by formula. It was established in 1977 (EPF Act) to assist provincial governments in the provision of health care and post-secondary education programs. Prior to the Act, federal funds for these programs were related to the overall provincial expenditures on these programs. EPF changed the cost-sharing basis for funding these programs, replacing it with the block-funding system and thereby eliminating the need to tie the level of transfers to the level of expenditures. EPF, in effect, is a system for sharing federal revenue (vertically) between the federal and provincial governments. In addition to these two transfer systems, the federal government administers a large number of grants to the provinces that are tied to specific uses and which may or may not be matching. Grants provided under the Canada Assistance Plan Act of 1966 (CAP) are the most significant. These grants require matching for eligibility. Under CAP requirements, the federal government transfers to each province one half of the costs of eligible programs such as social assistance and social services expenditures, with the provincial governments meeting the other half of the cost.

Tax sources are shared among the three levels of government under the provisions of the Tax Collection Agreement. The agreement spells out certain conditions for participation: the federal government collects the personal and/or the corporate income taxes on behalf of the provinces. The provinces must accept the same tax base as the federal government, but are free to set their own tax rates and establish their own systems of non-discriminatory credits. In essence, the provincial tax base is co-occupied by the federal and provincial governments; the total tax rate applied to this common base and the revenue derived from it are divided between them.[10] Clearly, the higher the federal tax rate, the less room there is for the province to extract revenue from that base. Hence, the relative amount of funds available to the federal and provincial governments is partly determined by the division of the income tax bases.

Given this brief overview of the assignment of expenditure functions and taxing powers, we now turn to a quantitative review of the fiscal structure.

4 THE MULTI-LEVEL PUBLIC SECTOR IN CANADA

The assignments of expenditure and taxing powers in the Canadian system are highlighted in the data reported in this section. Our discussion of the data will have two main focuses: first, we will look at how the various public sector functions are divided among Canada's multi-level government compared to the distribution of revenue sources. Secondly, we will discuss the financial arrangements among them that make functional this fiscal structure.

Expenditures and Revenue Structure

Summary information on the structure of revenues and expenditures for the federal, provincial, and local governments for the 1989 fiscal year is given in Table 9.2. Public sector budget expenditures have been grouped into the three functional categories: expenditures on public goods, (re)distributive expenditures, and spending on merit goods. This breakdown emphasizes not only the public sector's role in addressing problems arising from market failure, but also its involvement in the supply and/or consumption of private goods. The public sector accomplishes this latter task through price changes.

The public good category consists of those activities leading to the non-market supply of goods and services. These are expenditures on foreign affairs and international assistance, research, transportation and communication, protection of personal property, protection of the environment, recreation and culture, and on general services (administration). The distributive goods category consists of expenditures on social services, manpower, and immigration with the purpose of redistributing private income. Merit goods refer to those public expenditures undertaken by the public sector to influence the outcome in the private market. This category includes expenditures on education, health, housing, regional development planning, resource conservation, and industrial development. As pointed out in Chapter 7, the classification of

Table 9.2 Financial balance sheet 1989: financial management systems (in millions of Canadian dollars)

Categories	Consolidated government	Federal government	Provincial government	Local government
Expenditure categories				
Public goods	57,069	27,147	14,222	15,702
Distributive goods	62,133	39,575	20,211	2,348
Merit goods	106,437	13,982	60,377	32,079
Unclassified goods	63,275	40,965	17,453	4,862
TOTAL	288,914	121,669	112,263	54,990
Revenue sources				
Income taxes	110,706	69,766	40,940	—
Property and related taxes	21,156	—	849	20,307
Consumption taxes	54,630	28,760	25,799	71
Health & social insurance levies	20,396	10,646	9,720	30
Transfers	870	−26,026	2,589	24,307
Other revenue sources	47,452	10,255	27,705	9,492
TOTAL	255,210	93,401	107,602	54,207
Surplus (Deficit)	(33,704)	(28,268)	(4,660)	(783)

Notes: Numbers may not add up due to rounding errors.

a: Unclassified goods include — General purpose transfers (to other levels of government and to own enterprises); Debt charges and Other expenditures.

b: Revenue transfers refer to other levels of government and to own enterprises.

c: Other revenue sources include — Petroleum and natural gas tax; National resources revenue; Privileges license and permits; return on investment; Other revenues from own sources.

Source: Calculated from data reported in Statistics Canada, *Public Finance Historical Data.*

public sector expenditures in these three categories is tenuous at best. They are carried out here to match the role assigned to governments with the actual provision.

Data in Table 9.2 show that spending on merit goods (47.2 per cent) was the largest component of classified expenditures at the consolidated level of government. This is followed by spending for distribution (27.5 per cent), and the remainder was for public goods (25.3 per cent). However, this spending pattern was not consistent across all levels of government. Merit goods accounted for the smallest percentage of spending at the federal level (17.3 per cent) but dominated spending of the provinces (63.7 per cent) and local governments (64 per cent). Expenditure on redistribution was dominant at the federal government level (49 per cent) but insignificant at the local level (4.7 per cent). Spending on public goods did not dominate expenditures at any government level. Altogether it accounted for one-third of classified expenditures at the provincial (33.6 per cent) and at the local level (31.3 per cent).

The revenue structure shown in Table 9.2 lists the various revenue sources used by the different levels of government. As shown in the table, in addition to intergovernmental transfers, there are four major sources of tax revenue: income taxes, consumption taxes, property taxes and insurance levies. As mentioned earlier, most tax sources are shared among the three levels of government, the exception being income taxes and insurance levies which are not shared by local governments and the property tax base which is not shared by the federal government. The relative importance of the various expenditure functions and revenue sources for each level of government is discussed below.

Expenditure Distribution

Disaggregated data on expenditure categories by service function for the three levels of government are given in Table 9.3. As evident from the expenditure pattern shown, the provincial governments are dominant in the provision of merit goods due primarily to their being responsible for health expenditures. Provincial governments contributed 89 per cent of total expenditures on health. The provision of education services was met largely at the local level (62 per cent) with the provincial governments accounting for 34 per cent of total consolidated government expenditures on education. The other items showed no dominance at any level of government.

In the distributive goods category, the federal dominance came from social service expenditures (63 per cent). The provincial governments accounted for 33 per cent of the total, with minimal contribution to the total (four per cent) made by local governments. This pattern of expenditure distribution was similar for spending on labor, employment and immigration. In the public goods category, federal government spending topped all others especially for spending on the protection of personal property (61 per cent).

Revenue Sources

The distribution of major revenue sources among the federal, provincial, and local governments may be ascertained from data provided in Table 9.2.

As might be expected, the great majority (roughly 63 per cent) of the federal government's tax revenues are obtained from taxes on income; 26 per cent of revenue is collected from taxes on consumption. Levies for health and social insurance account for roughly 10 per cent of total federal tax receipts. At the provincial level, income taxes contribute 39 per cent to total receipts from own sources with consumption taxes accounting for 25 per cent. Intergovernmental transfers (mainly from the federal government) make up only a small percentage of total provincial government receipts (2.4 per cent). Local governments relied mainly on transfers from both federal and provincial governments with transfers amounting to 45 per cent of total revenues. Revenue from own sources is dominated by taxes on property (68 per cent, leaving 32 per cent for receipts from other sources).

5 FISCAL FEDERAL RELATIONS

In the previous sections, we presented an overview of the structure and rationale for the activities of the Canadian public sector. This section is devoted to examining the fiscal relations between the different levels of government. An important point to emphasize at the outset is that federal-provincial fiscal arrangements have helped shape the Canadian economic environment and are the key to understanding the financial relations between the three levels of government. These arrangements include tax harmonization and expenditure harmonization.

Tax harmonization in Canada takes the form of a single tax collection administration for most provinces with a common base and rate structure for both personal and corporate taxes. The provinces retain the right to set their own tax rates and to implement non-discriminatory credit, but the federal government has the sole authority to set the base and rate structure. This system offers Canada the following advantages: it reduces 1. the cost of tax collection and compliance; 2. the possibility of double or non-taxation for inter-provincial firms; 3. tax avoidance and evasion; and 4. inter-jurisdictional tax competition.

Expenditure harmonization is needed to increase the efficiency of provision of certain public services. For example, disparities between provinces in health insurance, welfare, or public pension provision may encourage inefficient inter-provincial migration. Similarly, provincial differences in expenditures on programs like education, which are characterized by spillover effects, also require central coordination of provision to achieve efficiency. To realize these goals of harmonization, the Canadian system relies on many schemes: equalization payments, regional development programs, cost-sharing etc. The effectiveness of these programs in eliminating disparities in fiscal capacity and economic needs is ascertained with reference to data reported below.

Table 9.3 *Government expenditures 1989: financial management systems (in millions of Canadian dollars)*

Categories	Consolidated government	Federal government	Provincial government	Local government
PUBLIC GOODS				
Foreign affairs & international assistance	4,420.0	4,120.0	—	—
Research establishments	1,549.0	1,276.0	273.0	—
Protection of personal property	22,344.0	13,694.0	4,179.7	4,470.3
Environment	6,311.0	601.0	737.4	4,972.7
Recreation & culture	6,006.0	1,111.0	1,509.8	3,385.2
General services	16,739.0	6,343.0	7,522.1	2,874.0
SUBTOTAL	57,069.0	27,147.0	14,221.9	15,702.1
Per cent of expenditure[a]	100.0	47.6	24.9	27.5
Per cent of spending[b]	19.8	22.3	12.7	28.6
DISTRIBUTIVE				
Social services	59,664.0	37,604.0	19,712.5	2,347.5
Labor employment	2,469.0	1,971.0	498.0	—
SUBTOTAL	62,133.0	45,210.0	21,589.1	2,347.5
Per cent of expenditure[a]	100.0	63.7	32.5	3.8
Per cent of spending[b]	21.5	32.5	18.0	4.3
MERIT GOODS				
Education	35,091.0	1,296.0	11,919.3	21,875.6
Health	39,228.0	1,057.0	35,066.6	3,104.4
Housing	2,885.0	1,736.0	935.8	213.2
Transportation & communication	14,430.0	3,436.0	5,228.3	5,765.7
Regional planning & development	1,584.0	463.0	608.7	512.3
Resource conservation & industrial development	13,219.0	5,994.0	6,617.7	607.4
SUBTOTAL	106,437.0	13,982.0	60,376.4	32,078.6
Per cent of expenditure[a]	100.0	13.1	56.7	30.1
Per cent of spending[b]	36.8	11.5	53.8	58.3

Table 9.3 continued

Categories	Consolidated government	Federal government	Provincial government	Local government
TRANSFERS				
General purpose transfers to other levels of govt	—	—	—	—
Transfers to own enterprise	4,880.0	2,251.0	1,616.1	1,012.9
Debt charges	57,982.0	38,694.0	15,755.1	3,532.9
Other expenditures	413.0	20.0	81.6	316.4
SUBTOTAL	63,275.0	40,965.0	17,452.8	4,862.2
Per cent expenditure[a]	100.0	64.7	27.6	7.6
Per cent spending[b]	21.9	33.6	15.5	8.8
TOTAL[c]	288,914.0	121,660.0	112,263.7	54,990.4

Notes: Numbers may not add up due to rounding errors.
a: Fraction of expenditure by levels of government.
b: Fraction of expenditure by the category of spending.
c: Grand total of all expenditures by levels of government.

Source: Calculated from data reported in Statistics Canada, *Public Finance Historical Data.*

Disparities in Income and Capacity Among Provinces

Data in Table 9.4 show per capita income in the provinces calculated in relation to the national (five provinces) average. Earned income is used as a measure of self-sufficiency of the residents of a province. After-tax personal income captures disposable income. Much of the income disparity between the provinces shown in the table can be traced to the differences in their economic structure. The Atlantic provinces, for example, are particularly disadvantaged because of a relatively heavy dependency on a primary sector compared to the other provinces and the resulting susceptibility to revenue and income volatility.[11] The variations between the economies of Ontario, Quebec, and the Western provinces (Manitoba, British Columbia, Alberta and Saskatchewan) are not as severe; yet disparities in earned income do exist. Quebec and Ontario have similar sectoral dependence (goods and services), although residents of Ontario have higher incomes and generate larger per capita output. Primary industries have greater relative importance for the economies of the Western provinces (less so in Manitoba and British Columbia). Alberta benefits greatly from its rich oil and gas sector, while Saskatchewan — despite its

Table 9.4 *Provincial indexes of per capita income, 1989 (five-province average = 100)*

Provinces	Earned Income[a]	Personal income Before tax[b]	Personal income After tax[b]	Change in earned income (1970—1989)	Change in before-tax income (1970—1989)	Change in after-tax income (1970—1989)
Newfoundland	60	69	74	5	8	9
Prince Edward Island	64	71	74	6	7	5
Nova Scotia	76	79	82	5	6	8
New Brunswick	69	74	77	3	5	6
Quebec	88	91	89	2	4	1
Ontario	115	111	111	1	—4	—2
Manitoba	80	85	89	—8	—4	—1
Saskatchewan	70	79	83	4	4	11
Alberta	96	98	99	1	—6	5
British Columbia	96	98	100	—7	8	—4
Yukon & Northwest Territories	127	111	113	11	8	13

Notes: a: Wages, salaries and supplementary income plus unincorporated business income.
b: Personal taxes.

Source: Ip (1991), p. 158.

productive oil and gas sector — is somewhat handicapped by the volatility associated with its dependence on a large agricultural sector. Disparities in the distribution of per capita earned income across provinces are mitigated by the equalization transfers.

The data reported in Tables 9.4 to 9.6 bear this out. Two types of information are given in Table 9.4: earned income and personal income data are given before and after payments of personal taxes. The difference between earned income and personal income before taxes reflects transfer payments. In 1990, of the ten Canadian provinces and the two territories, Ontario and the Yukon & Northwest Territories show earned income per capita in excess of 100 per cent of the average, while in four other provinces — Newfoundland, Prince Edward Island, New Brunswick and Saskatchewan — earned income per capita was 30 to 40 per cent below the average. After transfers but before tax payments, Ontario and Yukon were 'equalized' in that personal income per capita in each was set at 111 per cent of the national average. Personal income in the four poorest provinces was raised somewhat so that they were within 20 to 31 per cent of the average. After tax payments, the disparities between the provinces named were reduced further. After-tax personal income in Newfoundland, the poorest of the provinces, was raised to 74 per cent of the national average compared to earned income which averaged 60 per cent. In the richest area, Yukon & Northwest Territories, after-tax personal income was 'levelled' from an index of 127 per cent for earned income to an index for per capita personal income after taxes of 113 per cent.

Additional information about fiscal capacity of the provinces may be gathered from data in Table 9.5A and Table 9.5B. From the distribution of revenue by source, the Canadian government's efforts towards equalization of provincial governments' fiscal capacity are noted. The poorest Canadian provinces — Newfoundland, New Brunswick, Prince Edward Island and Saskatchewan — received significant amounts of transfers from the federal government, averaging between almost 43 per cent of total revenue for Prince Edward Island to 17.5 per cent for Saskatchewan.

Table 9.6 offers information on the relative contribution of federal transfers to the fiscal capacity of the different provinces. As is evident from the data, the three wealthy provinces — British Columbia, Alberta and Ontario — had negative transfers reducing their fiscal capacity by about seven to eight per cent, whereas Newfoundland, Prince Edward Island, and New Brunswick received additional capacity through taxes in the range of 20—29 per cent in fiscal year 1989—90.

Transfer Patterns

In fiscal year 1989—90, the federal government in Canada provided transfers in one form or another to the provincial, territorial and local

Table 9.5A *Consolidated provincial, territorial and local revenue per capita, 1989 (in Canadian dollars)*

Revenue source	NFL	PEI	NS	NB	QUEB	ONT	MANIT	SASKAT	ALB	BC
Total revenue	5,664	5,469	5,231	5,516	6,032	5,778	6,280	6,737	6,676	5,535
Current revenue	5,403	5,177	4,985	5,200	5,774	5,539	6,012	6,394	6,276	5,294
Capital revenue (CCA)	261	292	246	316	258	239	268	343	401	241
Own source current revenue	3,011	2,846	3,183	3,179	4,724	4,949	4,488	5,214	5,470	4,560
Taxation	2,583	2,415	2,799	2,762	4,230	4,551	3,593	3,324	3,176	3,675
Indirect taxes	1,641	1,454	1,651	1,640	1,981	2,521	2,315	2,125	1,577	2,106
Direct taxes on persons	793	800	965	932	2,032	1,479	1,021	999	1,055	1,140
Direct taxes on corporations & busin.	107	123	131	146	87	284	200	126	371	176
Other transfers from persons	42	38	52	45	130	267	56	73	173	2,531
Investment income	427	431	384	417	494	398	896	1,891	2,294	885
Transfers from federal government	2,392	2,331	1802	2,021	1,050	591	1,524	1,180	806	734

Source: Calculated from data reported in Ip (1991).

Table 9.5B *Consolidated provincial, territorial and local revenue per capita: percentage distribution by major source*

Provinces	Total Current /Total Prov.	Current Revenue Own Sources /Total Prov.	Intergovt.T. /Total Prov.	CCA /Total Prov.
Newfoundland	95.39	53.16	42.23	4.61
Prince Edward I.	94.66	52.04	42.62	5.34
Nova Scotia	95.29	60.85	34.45	4.70
New Brunswick	94.27	57.63	36.64	5.73
Quebec	95.72	78.32	17.41	4.28
Ontario	95.86	85.65	10.23	4.14
Manitoba	95.73	71.46	24.27	4.27
Saskatchewan	94.91	77.39	17.52	5.09
Alberta	94.00	81.94	12.07	6.00
British Columbia	95.65	82.38	13.26	4.35

Source: Calculated from data reported in Table 9.5A.

Table 9.6 *The fiscal capacity of the provinces, fiscal year 1989—90 (all Canada average = 100)*

Provinces	Fiscal capacity from: Own source revenue	Own source revenue + equalization	Difference
Newfoundland	62.7	91.5	28.8
Prince Edward Island	64.4	91.5	27.1
New Brunswick	71.1	91.5	20.4
Nova Scotia	74.9	91.5	16.6
Manitoba	79.1	91.5	12.4
Saskatchewan	83.8	91.5	7.7
Quebec	86.0	91.5	5.5
Ontario	111.2	104.3	—6.9
British Columbia	106.5	98.5	—8.0
Alberta	130.5	122.3	—8.2

Note: Fiscal capacity is calculated by applying the average Canadian tax rate to standardized bases of each revenue source included in the equalization formula.

Source: Calculated from data reported in Ip (1991), p. 295.

Table 9.7 *Major transfers from the federal government to the provinces, territories & municipalities, fiscal year 1989—90 (amount in millions of Canadian dollars)*

Type of transfer	Amount	Percentage
General purpose transfers	8,842	36.8
Fiscal equalization	7,295	32.3
Territorial financial agreements	916	3.8
Miscellaneous	631	2.7
Established Programs Financing	9,142	38.0
Health	6,871	28.6
Post-secondary education	2,271	9.4
Special purpose transfers	6,075	25.2
Canada Assistance Plan	4,779	19.9
Other health & welfare	164	0.6
Miscellaneous	1,132	4.7
TOTAL	24,059	100%

Source: Calculated from data reported in Ip (1991), p. 293.

governments to the amount of C$26 billion. These intergovernmental transfers accounted for 16 per cent of provincial, territorial, and local government receipts in fiscal year 1989—90. Three types of transfers may be distinguished: general purpose grants, EPF grants and special purpose grants. Of the total transfers made in that year, EPF grants were largest (38 per cent of the total), followed closely by general purpose grants with 37 per cent. Special purpose grants amounted to 25 per cent (Table 9.7).

As discussed earlier, as of 1977, the EPF grants are provided by the federal government to provincial governments in support of two basic functions: health and post-secondary education (PSE). As these are targeted transfers, it is of interest to look at how they have evolved over time. Note that these grants come from two sources: outright grants (cash payments) and tax transfers (revenue-sharing). The significance of these two sources to funding of program objectives is given by the distribution over time of these two components of transfers. The dollar amount of EPF transfers is given in Table 9.8 for the period 1981—82 to 1990—91. The percentage distribution of funds by type of transfer and by function is indicated in Table 9.9. Focusing on grants in support of health services, we note a decline in the cash grants from an average of 55 per cent of the total during the period 1981—85 to an average of 49 per cent in the last four years (1987—90). Corresponding to this change is a rise in the tax transfers, from

Table 9.8 *Federal government transfer payments to the provinces for health care and post-secondary education under Established Programs Financing (in millions of Canadian dollars)*

Year	Cash payments[a]			Tax transfers[b]			Total[c]	Percentage change in total
	Health	PSE	Total	Health	PSE	Total		
1981–82	4,121	1,604	5,725	3,604	1,705	5,309	11,035	
1982–83	4,644	1,804	6,448	4,038	1,911	5,949	12,398	12.25
1983–84	5,466	2,027	7,493	4,123	1,951	6,074	13,569	9.40
1984–85	6,028	2,114	8,142	4,445	2,103	6,548	14,692	8.27
1985–86	6,253	2,181	8,434	4,919	2,328	7,247	15,681	6.73
1986–87	6,484	2,229	8,723	5,422	2,566	7,988	16,711	6.57
1987–88	6,489	2,194	8,683	6,092	2,883	8,975	17,658	5.66
1988–89[d]	6,668	2,229	8,898	6,626	3,136	9,762	18,660	5.67
1989–90[e]	6,944	2,303	9,247	7,165	3,391	10,556	19,803	6.12
1990–91[f]	6,370	2,015	8,385	7,972	3,773	11,745	20,130	1.65

Notes: a: Cash payments are equal to the difference between entitlements and the value of tax transfers which ensures the equalization of federal per capita contributions for funding.

b: Tax transfers are divided up according to the following ratio as established under the EPF: 67.9 per cent for health services, 31.1 per cent for PSE.

c: The total may differ because of rounding off provisions.

d: First preliminary adjustment, March 1990.

e: Second adjustment in the calculation of advance payments, December 1989.

f: Second adjustment in the calculation of advance payments, December 1990.

Source: Frechette (1991).

Table 9.9 *Percentage distribution of EPF transfers by function and by type of grants*

Year	Health		PSE	
	Cash	Tax transfers	Cash	Tax transfers
1981—82	53.34	46.65	48.47	51.53
1982—83	53.49	46.51	48.56	51.44
1983—84	57.00	42.99	50.96	49.04
1984—85	57.56	42.44	50.13	49.87
1985—86	55.97	44.03	48.37	51.63
1986—87	54.46	45.54	46.49	53.51
1987—88	51.58	48.42	43.21	56.79
1988—89	50.16	49.84	41.55	58.45
1989—90	49.22	50.78	40.45	59.55
1990—91	44.42	55.78	34.81	65.19

Source: Calculated from data reported in Table 9.8.

an average of 44 per cent to an average of 51 per cent over the same respective periods. The same pattern is observed for education support — a rise in the share of tax-transfer grants and a fall in the cash grants.

Influence of Current Events on Equalization Payments

Fiscal arrangements between federal and provincial levels of government are a reflection not only of constitutional assignments but also of how contemporary events may challenge them in meeting their assigned obligations. For example, the 1982—87 federal-provincial fiscal arrangements were heavily influenced by the recession of the early 1980s, the resulting federal deficits and accumulated debt that grew during the 1980s, and the constraints that were put on federal spending as the federal government sought to bring its spending under control. New rules imposing stricter standards on federal transfers were proposed and implemented in 1981 and 1982 as the federal government sought to save up to C$1.5 billion from its transfer program in the 1982—84 fiscal period.[12] Concern over the federal deficit also resulted in a reduction in the growth rate of transfer payments to provinces under the EPF plan. Information on EPF given earlier in Table 9.8 shows that the yearly growth rate of this type of transfer has continuously fallen. Between 1982 and 1986, the rate fell from 12.3 per cent to 6.7 per cent. Between 1987—88 and 1989—90, the growth rate was slightly higher but was cut by 70 per cent between 1989—90 and 1990—91. These reductions were a source of great frustra-

Table 9.10 *Equalization payments to the provinces (in millions of Canadian dollars)*

Year	Estimated amount of equalization entitlements	Percentage change
1981—82	4,395	
1982—83	4,865	10.69
1983—84	5,229	7.48
1984—85	5,422	3.69
1985—86	5,143	—5.15
1986—87	5,775	12.29
1987—88	6,589	14.09
1988—89	7,261 [a]	10.19
1989—90	7,820 [b]	7.70
1990—91	8,272 [c]	5.78

Notes: a: Seventh official estimate, March 1990.
b: Fifth official estimate, March 1990.
c: Third official estimate, March 1990.

Source: Frechette (1991).

tion for provincial governments throughout the latter part of the 1980s, as the governments were concerned about their medium-term impact on the quality of provincial health care and education systems. They interpreted the action by the federal government as a violation of its constitutionally assigned responsibilities to the provinces.[13] Provincial governments responded to the restrictions on EPF transfer growth by requesting compensatory increases in federal equalization payments. The federal government, on the other hand, wanted to maintain its goal of trimming the federal deficit by sticking to its program of reducing transfer payments.

The contentious relationship between the federal and provincial governments over their fiscal arrangements culminated in Bill C-44 (March 1987) 'respecting' the terms of the fiscal arrangements for the period 1987—92. The federal government, however, continued the process of 'slowing down' the growth rate of EPF transfers. The tabling of Bill C-33 (June 1987) provided for a one-percentage-point reduction in that growth rate beginning 1990—91. An earlier bill (1986) cut the rate of growth by two per cent. In its most recent budget (1991), the lower path for EPF growth was extended to 1994—95.[14] The federal government's efforts to halt the growth rate of EPF transfers are evident from the data reported in Table 9.10. As shown in the table, federal government equalization payments to the provinces over the 1987—91 period have fluctuated with percentage changes in the range of —5 per cent to +10.7 per cent.

6 CONCLUSION

This chapter has outlined and discussed the institutional, structural and operational aspects of fiscal federalism in Canada. In a dynamic world, however, federalism is challenged to make the necessary evolutionary changes in the structure of the relationships underlying multi-level government arrangements. Canada's grappling with the problems posed by its rising federal debt is a clear example of how necessary and difficult the task of change is. Canada appears committed to this process, however, and has been increasingly shifting economic policy decisions away from the federal government and to the provincial level government.[15] As it rethinks the proper (re)allocation of economic powers within its multi-level government structure,[16] Canada is trying to find the right balance between efficiency and equity goals as well as to define the responsibility and obligation of the federal government in attaining these goals.

NOTES

1. Premchand (1990) provides a more complete discussion on the structure of the Canadian government.
2. Premchand (1990).
3. See Doern *et al.* (1988) for a more comprehensive discussion.
4. See Premchand (1990), pp.217—9, and Strick (1985), pp. 32—3 for additional discussion.
5. Strick (1985), p. 82.
6. Premchand (1990), pp. 227—8.
7. Boadway (1992), p. 23.
8. See Chapter 6 for a more detailed discussion of these issues.
9. Boadway (1992), p. 31.
10. Ibid., p. 48.
11. Ip (1991), p. 143.
12. Frechette (1991), p. 93.
13. Ibid., p. 7.
14. Ibid., pp. 11—2.
15. See Wrobel (1991) for further discussion of these issues.
16. Boadway (1992) discusses this point further.

REFERENCES

Boadway, R. (1992), *The Constitutional Division of Powers: An Economic Perspective*, Ottawa, Minister of Supply and Services Canada.

Doern, G.B., Maslove, A.M. and Prince, M.J. (1988), *Public Budgeting in Canada*, Ottawa, Carleton University Press.

Frechette, J.-D. (1991), *Federal-Provincial Fiscal Arrangements*, Ottawa, Library of Congress Research Branch, Current Issue Review 86-23E (originally published 7 Oct. 1986; revised 4 Sept. 1991).

Hartle, D.G. (1978), *The Expenditure Budget Process in The Government of Canada*, Toronto, Canadian Tax Foundation.

Ip, I.K. (1991), *Big Spenders: A Survey of Provincial Government Finances in Canada*, Toronto and Calgary, C.D. Howe Institute.

Office of the Auditor General of Canada (1990), 'The Canadian Experience', in Premchand, A. (ed.), pp. 217–32.

Premchand, A. (ed.) (1990), *Government Financial Management: Issues and Country Studies*, Washington D.C., International Monetary Fund.

Statistics Canada, Public Institutions Division (1992), *Public Finance Historical Data 1965/66–1991/92*, Ottawa, Minister of Industry, Science and Technology.

Strick, J.C. (1978), *Canadian Public Finance*, 2nd ed., Toronto, Holt, Rinehart & Winston of Canada, Ltd.

Strick, J.C. (1985), *Canadian Public Finance*, 3rd ed., Toronto, Holt, Rinehart & Winston of Canada, Ltd.

Wrobel, M.G. (1991), *Fiscal Policy in Canada: The Changing Role of the Federal and Provincial Governments*, Ottawa, Library of Parliament.

10. Fiscal Federalism in the Federal Republic of Germany

Ute Schumacher

1 INTRODUCTION

The collapse of the wall separating the two German states, the Federal Republic of Germany (FRG) in the West and the German Democratic Republic (GDR) in the East, in November 1989 and the ensuing unification in October 1990 marked the end of more than four decades of division which resulted from Germany's defeat in World War II. German capitulation to the four victorious allied powers (GB, France, U.S. and Soviet Union) in May 1945 divided Germany into four occupation zones. The three Western zones were to become the Federal Republic of Germany with the coming into force of the *Grundgesetz* (GG, Basic Law), the German constitution on March 24, 1949.[1] On October 7, 1949, the creation of the German Democratic Republic followed in the Soviet occupation zone. Thus from 1949 until 1990 there were two states on German soil.

After World War II, the new West German state was organized as a federalist system. One of the pillars of this federalist administrative structure are the fiscal arrangements and relationships between the various levels of government which finds its expression in the public sector budgets. Fiscal federalism in Germany is the subject of this chapter. Section 2 provides an overview of the political and administrative system of the FRG. The fundamentals underlying German budgetary law and the phases of the budget cycle are identified in the following section. In Section 4, we spell out the assignment of powers and responsibilities to the various levels of government according to the *Grundgesetz* and summarize the fiscal relationships between the Federation, the states, and the municipalities. The chapter concludes in Section 5 with a detailed look at the public sector budgets. We analyze the distribution of expenditure functions across all government units, their revenue structure, as well as the system of intergovernmental transfers aimed at fiscal equalization.

It is important to point out at the outset that the following discussion focuses exclusively on the political, administrative, and fiscal structure of West Germany, since unification led to the absorption of the Eastern part into the West German political, legal, and economic system. In fact, the unified nation's official name continues to be that of the former West Germany: the Federal Republic of Germany.

2 THE GERMAN FEDERALIST SYSTEM

The Historical Context

When in May 1948 the Western powers commissioned a national assembly to create a democratic constitution for the part of Germany occupied by them, they demanded a federal structure primarily because it was hoped that it would prevent the kind of unfortunate concentration of power at the center experienced and abused during the Nazi period. Federalism was thus to promote and stabilize democracy in the new German state and to meet the security interests of Germany's neighbors. Unlike other federal systems, the main objective was not to integrate a geographically and historically dismembered country. In fact, the individual *(Bundes)Länder* (constituent states) were largely formed only after World War II with the involvement of the occupation powers, and in most cases boundaries were drawn rather arbitrarily without taking tradition into account. Recognizing that the *Länder* boundaries established by the occupation powers might later be perceived as senseless, the founders of the constitution inserted Section (1) into Article 29 GG which allows the federal territory to be reorganized by federal legislation in order to ensure that the *Länder*, by virtue of their size and capacity, are able effectively to fulfil the functions incumbent upon them. Such reorganization should take place with due respect to regional ties, historical and cultural connections, economic expediency, and social and cultural structure. To date, such reorganization has not yet taken place. While the *Grundgesetz* contained a provision for the reorganization of *Länder* territory, it also ruled out any violation of the federal principle as such ('eternal federalism').[2]

The FRG is a parliamentary democracy. The *Deutsche Bundestag* (House of Representatives), the popularly elected lower house of Parliament, is the decisive lawmaking assembly of the FRG. Yet the *Bundesrat* (Federal Council), the representative of the constituent states, also participates in legislation. This upper house of Parliament is not elected but composed of members of the *Länder* governments. While each *Land* dispatches at least three delegates, *Länder* with larger populations have four to six votes. A *Land's* votes can only be cast as a bloc. The *Bundesrat* has the right to object to all laws passed by the *Bundestag*. Laws affecting the basic principles of the Federation or those touching on *Länder* interests require the consent of the *Bundesrat*.[3] Bills involving an amendment to the Basic Law require a two-thirds majority in both chambers.

A Profile of the Public Sector

An overview of the administrative structure of the FRG as of January 1, 1991, is provided in Table 10.1.[4] While the *Grundgesetz* presumes a two-level structure which juxtaposes the *Bund* (Federation)[5] and the *Länder* with the municipalities being regarded as part of the *Länder*, the administrative system is based on a three-level structure in which the local government units constitute a distinct and independent sector. Among the latter, one can further distinguish between the government administrative districts (*Regierungsbezirke*), the counties and county-free cities (*Landkreise* and *kreisfreie Städte*) and the municipalities (*Gemeinden*).

The *Länder*

The territory of the former West Germany is divided into eleven *Länder*: the eight *Flachenländer* (territorial or area states) Baden-Württemberg, Bayern (Bavaria), Hessen (Hesse), Niedersachsen (Lower Saxony), Rheinland-Pfalz (Rhineland Palatinate), Saarland, Schleswig-Holstein, Nordrhein-Westfalen (North-Rhine Westphalia) and the three *Stadtstaaten* (city states) of Hamburg, Bremen and (West) Berlin.[6] Five new Eastern states were added with unification: Brandenburg, Mecklenburg-Vorpommern, Sachsen (Saxony), Sachsen-Anhalt and Thüringen.

Each *Land* is organized as a parliamentary system and has its own constitution which, according to Article 28 GG, has to abide by the four principles guiding the German constitution: those of a republican, democratic, social welfare and law-abiding state.

The local sector

The make-up of the political-administrative system at the local level is highly complex in the FRG as it varies across *Länder* and typically consists of two to three levels. At present there are 16,696 units of local government: 26 *Regierungsbezirke*, 543 *Kreise* and 16,127 *Gemeinden*.

The *Regierungsbezirk* is a middle-level administrative institution found only in the larger territorial states of Western Germany. Its main purpose is to coordinate the system of spatial administration and to supervise the counties and large cities in their execution of tasks delegated to them. The German *Landkreis* is an association of small to medium-sized municipalities. Large cities (typically defined as having more than 100,000 inhabitants) may become *kreisfrei* (county-free), also referred to as a *Stadtkreis* (city-county). *Stadtkreise* and *Landkreise*, like *Regierungsbezirke*, serve to coordinate and implement *Land* administration. Despite the fact that they perform a number of state-delegated tasks (*Auftragsangelegenheiten*), the counties are institutions of local self-government and as such they — as well as the municipalities — are guaranteed a certain independence from the states (Article 28 (2) GG). Each county has a

Table 10.1 *Administrative structure of the FRG (January 1, 1991)*

Land	RB[a]	Counties			Municip.
		Total	City-C.	*Land*	
FRG — WEST					
Baden-Württ.[b]	4	44	9	35	1,111
Bayern	7	96	25	71	2,051
Berlin	—	1	1	—	1
Bremen	—	2	2	—	2
Hamburg	—	1	1	—	1
Hessen	3	26	5	21	426
Niedersachsen	4	47	9	38	1,031
Nordrhein-W.	5	54	23	31	396
Rheinland-Pf.	3	36	12	24	2,304
Saarland	—	6	—	6	52
Schleswig-H.	—	40	5	35	1,710
TOTAL (West)	26	328	90	237	8,505
FRG — EAST					
Brandenburg	—	44	6	38	1,794
Mecklenburg-V.	—	37	6	31	1,124
Sachsen	—	54	6	48	1,626
Sachsen-Anhalt	—	40	3	37	1,367
Thüringen	—	40	5	35	1,710
TOTAL (East)	—	215	26	189	7,622
TOTAL FRG	26	543	117	426	16,127

Notes: a: Regierungsbezirk (government administrative districts).
b: Plus 12 Regionalverbände (regional associations).

Source: Statistisches Bundesamt (1991).

popularly elected council and a chief executive officer who is legally responsible to the district officer and politically responsible to the elected council.

In addition, there is a variety of functional administrative institutions which vary from state to state — from multi-purpose to single-purpose regional or local associations.[7] One example is the *Zweckverband* (special purpose association) which is a public corporation formed by two or more municipalities or counties for the purpose of executing a specific task (e.g. special education; recreation areas).

***Länder* profile**

While the principle of federalism is typically designed to take into account regional differences, in the Federal Republic of Germany *Länder* populations do not differ radically. Still, significant regional disparities in the economic and social structure exist and manifest themselves, for instance, in variations in per capita gross domestic product (GDP). In 1990, per capita GDP amounted to an average DM 39,281 in the western part of the FRG. Individual *Länder* values, however, differed significantly between a minimum value of DM 31,896 generated in the northern state of Schleswig-Holstein to a maximum of DM 67,792 in the city state of Hamburg. Unemployment rates also vary widely and so does the sectoral distribution in employment. Data illustrating these regional disparities are reported in Table 10A.1 in the appendix.

Given the constitutional mandate to promote uniformity of living conditions throughout the nation (Articles 72 (2) and 106 (3) GG), variations in economic structure and prosperity pose a particular challenge to a fiscal-federalist system as they imply an uneven development of various regions within the Federation. In order to prevent such an unacceptable drifting apart, the *Grundgesetz* provides for a number of mechanisms for fiscal equalization which are to be discussed later on in the chapter.

3 BUDGET LEGISLATION AND THE BUDGET PROCESS IN THE FRG

Fundamental Premises Underlying the German Budgetary Laws

In the Federal Republic of Germany, the budgetary law is governed by the fundamental principle expressed in Article 109 (1) GG which states that Federation and *Länder* are autonomous and independent of each other in their fiscal administration. While this independence may be in conflict with a need for uniformity and conformity in budget law, it is regarded as going hand in hand with the constitutional protection of *Länder* self-governance.[8]

Paragraph (2) of Article 109 GG, which was added in June 1967, obligates the Federation and the *Länder* to 'take due account in their fiscal administration of the requirements of overall economic equilibrium'. This amendment created the constitutional foundation for the Law to Promote Economic Stability and Growth (StWG) which spells out rules for multi-year financial planning and, at the time, provided new and expanded opportunities for anticyclical economic policy. Section (1) StWG requires the Federation and the states to adopt fiscal measures 'in such a way that they will, within the framework of the market economy, at the same time help to stabilize prices, maintain a high level of employment and achieve external balance, accompanied by steady and adequate economic growth'.

In view of this fundamental goal, Section (9) StWG states that 'Federal budget management shall be based on a financial plan covering a five-year period'. As most decisions concerning government revenues and expenditures have medium- to long-term implications, it was necessary to extend the planning horizon beyond the short length of the fiscal year (which coincides with the calendar year). Annual federal and state budgets are, therefore, to be incorporated into a five-year financial plan. The plan outlines the government's program priorities and its fiscal policy objectives in view of the anticipated spending needs and revenue estimates consistent with the projected development of the macroeconomy. Revisions to budget aggregates are made on a yearly basis adjusting for changes in the general economic conditions as well as in the status of individual programs.

The *Finanzplanungsrat* (Financial Planning Council), first established in March 1968, is assigned the task of coordinating the financial plans of the Federation, the *Länder*, and the local sector, and of establishing common budgetary policy objectives and priorities. It is composed of the Federal Minister of Finance, the Federal Minister of Economics, the *Land* ministers responsible for financial affairs, and four representatives of the local sector. Representatives of the *Deutsche Bundesbank* (the German Central Bank) attend all meetings. The Council's power is limited as its recommendations, which have to be adopted unanimously, are non-binding and are constrained by the budgetary autonomy and the right to self-governance that the *Grundgesetz* guarantees for the *Länder* and the local sector.

The Stability Law of 1967 broke new ground in two important ways. First, it implied an explicit acknowledgement of the public budget as a tool for macroeconomic management as opposed to being merely a means of funding government expenditures. Second, as a result of this recognition, it paved the way for a far-reaching and comprehensive budgetary reform package, the need for which had been obvious from the beginning of the FRG[9] and which was finally initiated in 1964 with the appointment of an independent commission of experts (*Troeger Kommission*). The Stability Law and the ensuing change of Article 109 GG was an important first step because it provided a justification for limiting *Länder* autonomy (and indirectly that of the municipalities) with a view towards general welfare. As the importance of coordinating public sector budgets and of enhancing their flexibility and adaptability to changing economic conditions had become apparent with the recession of 1966—67, these considerations became a major goal of the *Finanzreform* (finance reform).

This budgetary reform package enacted in 1969 included the Law to Amend the Basic Law enabling changes in Articles 109 to 115 GG and the Law on Budgetary Principles for the Federation and the *Länder*. The latter constituted an application of the amended Article 109 GG which gives the Federation the right to enact legislation (with the consent of the *Bundesrat*) in order to ensure uniformity in budget law. Given the greater reliance on macroeconomic stabilization policy at the time, a harmonization of economic and fiscal policy objectives of the Federation and the *Länder* was deemed imperative, which in turn necessitated comparability in planning and accounting.

Aside from laying the foundation for easier fiscal coordination and harmonization through new rules and procedures applicable to the entire public sector budgeting, the *Finanzreform* of 1969 contained other most important elements. In fact for Franz Josef Strauss, during whose tenure as Federal Minister of Finance (1966—69) this reform package was completed and enacted, it represented not simply an alteration and improvement in budgetary regulations and procedures but more importantly a 'reorganization of one of the pillars of the federalist system'.[10] In an amendment to the constitution, Article 91 GG introduced a new form of cooperation between the Federation and the *Länder*, the so-called *Gemeinschaftsaufgaben* (joint tasks). Furthermore, the reform entailed a reorganization of the system of revenue sharing between the territorial authorities. Both aspects will be explored in greater detail in Section 4 as they constitute an integral part of the FRG's fiscal federalism.

The Budget Process

In the FRG, the fiscal year coincides with the calendar year for all public sector entities. A summary of the annual budget cycle from submission of agency budget estimates to the publication of the budget law is given in Table 10.2. A more detailed outline of the individual steps involved is provided in the appendix and depicted in Figure 10.1.

The federal budget is prepared by the Federal Ministry of Finance based on expected tax revenues and estimated expenditure requirements submitted by the individual Federal Ministries and government agencies around February or March preceding the upcoming fiscal year. The resulting budget draft is debated and eventually adopted by the federal government and subsequently submitted to the *Bundestag* and *Bundesrat* for approval — usually in August. The government's budget plan receives a first reading in Parliament in September during which the Federal Minister of Finance delivers the 'budget speech' indicating the federal government's considerations underlying the proposed budget. The final *Bundestag* reading and vote on the budget (as a whole) takes place in November or December, after which it is resubmitted to the *Bundesrat* for approval. An important aspect of German fiscal federalism is the fact that the federal government's budget can only be enacted as law with the consent of the *Bundesrat*, the representative of *Länder* interests. The approved budget is comprised of: 1. the budget law (i.e. general regulations concerning total expenditures, total ceilings for guarantees, borrowing authority) and 2. the budget plan listing item by item all authorized expenditure ceilings and estimated revenues.

Table 10.2 *The annual budget cycle in the FRG*

Months before start of upcoming fiscal year (t)	Main events and activities
Year t—2	
December	Federal Minister of Finance (FMF) gives detailed instructions to Federal Ministries concerning budget preparation and adjustment of medium-term financial plan.
Year t—1	
February—March	Federal Ministries submit their bids for the budget and planning years to FMF.
February—June	FMF deliberates with each Ministry at all levels of officials up to Minister level.
June—July	Final Cabinet decision-making regarding draft budget and the Federal Financial Plan.
August	The Federal Government's budget plus financial plan is submitted to Parliament.
September	FMF delivers budget speech to Parliament at the first parliamentary reading.
November—December	Final reading and vote on Government's Budget.
December	Signing by the Federal President and publication.
Year t	
January 1st	Start of Fiscal Year t.

Source: Based on OECD (1987).

Figure 10.1 *The preparation of the federal budget*

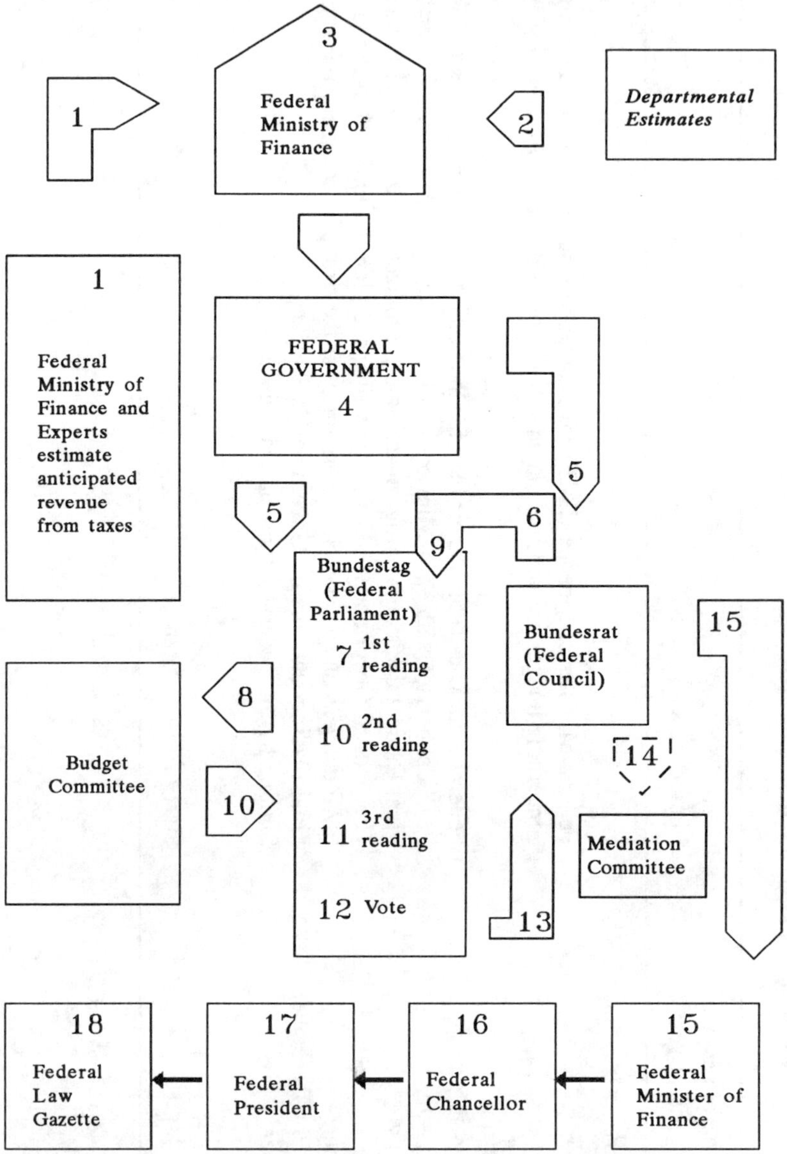

Source: Adapted from Bundesministerium der Finanzen (1987), p. 31

4 FISCAL FEDERALISM IN THE FRG

Assignment of Powers and Responsibilities

Legal assignments

In the Federal Republic of Germany, the division of governmental tasks between the Federation and the *Länder* is laid down in the *Grundgesetz*. Generally speaking, the Federation is assigned those responsibilities that are best assumed by the superior territorial authority (national government) because they are related to securing the existence of the state as a whole. More specifically, in assigning responsibilities, the *Grundgesetz* distinguishes between four major categories:

1. *Exclusively federal legislative powers*: foreign affairs, defense, currency and monetary affairs, federal railroads and air traffic, postal and telecommunication services, cooperation of the Federation and the *Länder* in matters of protection of the Constitution and law enforcement, industrial property rights, copyrights etc. (Article 73 GG)
2. *Concurrent legislative powers between the Federation and the Länder*: Article 72 GG specifies that the *Länder* have legislative powers as long as, and to the extent that, the Federation does not make use of its right to legislate. A justification for federal legislative power in this area is an inability on the part of the individual *Länder* to effectively deal with the matter; a conflict between the interests of individual *Länder* or between the *Länder* and the entire community; or because it is in the interest of legal or economic unity, especially the maintenance of uniformity of general living conditions beyond the territory of a state. This category includes areas such as civil and criminal law, legal and court system, laws regulating a variety of areas (economic matters, labor etc.), transport, environment, health etc.
3. *Federal legislation establishing a general legal framework*: applies to areas such as laws governing civil service, universities, the media, environmental protection etc. (Article 75 GG)
4. *Exclusively Länder legislative powers*: Article 70 GG stipulates that the *Länder* have legislative power to the extent that this *Grundgesetz* does not confer legislative powers to the Federation. This leaves areas such as cultural affairs, schools, police, municipal constitutions and all those areas not explicitly listed in the *Grundgesetz*.

According to those provisions, most issues of domestic policy interest fall in the category in which the Federation and the *Länder* are competing for the right to enact legislation. In practice West Germany has experienced a gradually increasing tendency toward 'unitarism' as the Federation has interpreted its role more broadly, hence expanding its legislative powers at the expense of the constituent states. In the late 1960s and during the 1970s, the expanding federal role has been justified on the basis of the constitutional mandate for 'uniformity of living conditions' throughout the Federation.[11]

Unlike for the Federation and the *Länder*, the *Grundgesetz* does not provide specific task assignments for the local sector. It does, however, expressly guarantee the right to local self-government (be it at the county or the municipal level). Article 28 GG stipulates that 1. just like the federal State, all towns, communities, and counties must be democratically organized, and that 2. the *Länder* must guarantee to local governments the right to regulate their own communal affairs (within the confines of the law). Local governments are thus free, at least in principle, to voluntarily assume any task, 'offer any service, construct any facility, or perform any other function that is within the law and not already regulated by the state'.[12]

On the basis of these constitutional guidelines, the territorial authorities have assumed the following major responsibilities: the federal government is assigned social security, defense, foreign affairs, construction of federal highways, economic development and research and development (R&D), settlement of war compensations, federal railways and postal service. The *Länder* are in charge of cultural affairs, in particular schools and education, the administration of justice, the police and health services. Finally, the local sector assumes responsibility for local utilities such as water and energy supplies, sewerage and waste disposal, the maintenance of local roads and — in conjunction with the *Länder* — the school system and cultural affairs.

The European Community (EC) as a supranational authority has been gaining increasing importance in the fiscal affairs of the FRG. Since its inception in 1957, the EC has influenced the budget allocation in particular for such areas as agriculture, regional development, social policy, research and development, energy and trade.

Implementation of functions assigned

An important distinction has to be made at this point between the assignment of legislative powers and responsibilities on one hand and the actual administration and execution of the tasks assigned on the other. For even though the *Länder* may lack in legislative power, they are the territorial authority which in practice is primarily responsible for the implementation and administration of the general policies formulated by the federal government (as well as, of course, their own).[13] Accordingly, only very few federal agencies are involved in the actual provision, the exceptions being the postal service, railways and border police. In addition there are federal agencies which perform 'specific' functions for the federal government. In accordance with the decentralized structure of the FRG, those agencies are scattered across the country, e.g. the Federal Office for Statistics in Wiesbaden, for Patents (Berlin), for the Protection of the Constitution (Cologne), for Cartels (Berlin) etc. Finally, there are a number of semi-autonomous federal agencies in charge of, e.g., the weather service and the control of air transportation.

While the responsibility for public administration rests mostly with the states, *Land* administrative agencies in turn often delegate their administrative responsibilities to the local sector. Municipalities and counties thus play a dual role of 1. self-government in all local affairs subject only to legal control (*Rechtsaufsicht*) by the *Land*, and 2. implementation of state (and more indirectly federal) legislation subject also to more detailed functional supervision (*Fachaufsicht*).[14]

To the extent that certain tasks go beyond the financial or organizational resources of small municipalities, they can be carried out by the next higher level of local government, the county. The size of the municipality represents an important constraint on its ability to execute the functions it has been assigned. This concern motivated a far-reaching reorganization of the local sector in the early 1970s. This reform has effectively reduced the number of municipalities from 24,428 in 1967 (of which more than two-thirds had less than 1,000 inhabitants) to 8,504 in 1981 (with 36.5 per cent having less than 1,000 inhabitants). At the same time, the number of counties (both *Stadt-* and *Landkreise*) was consolidated from 564 in 1969 to 355 in 1981.[15]

Joint tasks

The Federation and the *Länder*, although autonomous units of government, are not precluded from sharing in joint responsibilities. For instance, the federal government provides assistance to the *Länder* in maintaining law and order, in averting threats to the democratic system, and in dealing with natural disasters.[16] More importantly, the *Finanzreform* of 1969 introduced a new form of co-operation between the two authorities. A new section (VIIIa) with two new articles (Articles 91a and 91b) was inserted into the *Grundgesetz* concerning the so-called *Gemeinschaftsaufgaben* (joint tasks).

According to these provisions, the federal government is allowed to participate in the discharge of *Länder* responsibilities 'provided that such responsibilities are important to society as a whole and that federal participation is necessary for the improvement of living conditions'. The *Grundgesetz* specifies these jointly planned and financed activities to be: '1. extension and construction of institutions of higher education including university clinics; 2. improvement of regional economic structures; 3. improvement of agrarian structure and of coastal preservation.'[17] As to the financing of these tasks, the *Grundgesetz* stipulates that one-half of the expenditure in each *Land* related to provision in the first two categories shall be met by the federal government. As to the third, the Federation is required to cover at least one-half of the expenditure. In practice, the federal government contributes now 60 per cent for measures relating to agrarian structure and 70 per cent for coastal preservation.

Joint overall planning of a *Gemeinschaftsaufgabe* is carried out by a 'planning council' comprised of the *Länder* Ministers in charge of the issue in question and the Federal Minister of Finance. The council is chaired by the appropriate Federal Minister. Each *Land* has one vote; the Federation is assigned 16 votes which have to be cast as a bloc. Decisions can only be made with the federal and the majority of the *Länder* votes, implying that no decision can ever be taken against the Federation. This provision reveals the very centralist nature of the joint tasks. However, the inclusion of a particular project in the overall planning always requires the consent of the *Land* in which it is to be carried out. Thus while nothing can be forced upon a *Land*, the *Gemeinschaftsaufgaben* are controversial for they entail the 'meddling' of the Federation as well as other *Länder* in a particular *Land's* affairs. Especially of note is the weakening of the *Länder* Parliaments' position. A Parliament would be hard pressed to vote down a specific joint measure as this would imply the forgoing of federal matching grants. A further point of contention relates to the fact that the Federation typically shares in only the investment costs of a project, leaving the resulting long-term operating costs to the respective *Land* and therewith tying up parts of the *Länder* budgets and indirectly influencing their fiscal decisions. Thus by sharing in the financing of tasks that are primarily *Länder* territory, the Federation has (undue?) influence on state affairs.[18]

Fiscal Relationships in the FRG

The fundamental principle underlying the fiscal relationships between the territorial authorities in the FRG is that of independence and autonomy in financial administration for which Article 109 (1) GG provides the constitutional basis. Moreover, Article 104a GG, which spells out rules concerning the apportionment between Federation and *Länder* of the financial liabilities incurred in performing governmental tasks, calls for the Federation and the *Länder* to 'meet separately the expenditure resulting from the discharge of their respective tasks in so far as this Basic Law does not provide otherwise'.[19] And Article 106 GG dictates that Federation, *Länder*, and municipalities shall have separate revenue sources.

This strict separation of public finances and responsibilities is, however, at odds with the constitutionally prescribed 'uniformity of living conditions' in the federal territory.[20] In an attempt to resolve this conflict, a highly complex system of financial 'entanglement' has been developed which, in effect, undermines the separation principle. Four major areas of overlap can be identified:[21]

1. intergovernmental grants and compensation payments;
2. distribution and sharing of tax revenue;
3. financial equalization (both horizontal and vertical);
4. coordination of budgetary planning with a view towards aggregate economic management.

Intergovernmental grants and compensation payments

Aside from creating a new instrument for federal-state co-operation (the joint tasks), the *Finanzreform* of 1969 also introduced a provision for federal investment aid to the *Länder* and local governments. Accordingly, the federal government was given the right to 'grant the *Länder* financial assistance for particularly important investments by the *Länder* or communes or associations of communes, provided that such investments are necessary to avert a disturbance of the overall economic equilibrium or to equalize differences of economic capacities within the federal territory or to promote economic growth'.[22] Based on this very general formulation, a variety of programs were initiated in the 1970s, especially in the areas of urban development, local transport, housing and hospital construction.

One application is the *Strukturhilfegesetz* (Structural Assistance Law) of January 1, 1989, which calls for the federal government to provide the states (with the exception of Hessen and Baden-Württemberg) with financial assistance for the purpose of equalizing their economic differences. Given the ramifications of German unification for the federal economic and fiscal structure, the *Strukturhilfegesetz* was phased out by the end of 1991 and the *Fonds 'Deutsche Einheit'* (German Unity Fund) was established to meet the fiscal needs of the new *Länder*.[23] The Federation's mandate to assist the *Länder* in measures designed to equalize economic differences in the federal territory underlines the importance attached to the constitutional obligation to promote uniform living conditions in the FRG as one of the essential principles governing the (fiscal) relationships within the German federal system. While the main tool applied towards that end are the measures of fiscal equalization, federal grants may serve as a complementary device.[24]

In addition to structural assistance measures, the federal government provides financial support for public housing projects of the *Länder* and subsidizes private rental and owner-occupied housing and student housing construction. The *Länder* and local units also receive federal funds as compensation for financial burdens associated with special facilities such as military bases or activities.[25] Furthermore, the *Länder* are also compensated (with the consent of the *Bundesrat*) for additional burdens resulting from federally mandated expenditures or withdrawal of revenues provided that such additional burden is of a temporary nature.[26]

Tax revenue sharing

Within the German fiscal system, each government level, and especially the state and federal levels, compete over tax bases. The German system, by virtue of Article 106 GG, is one of mixed financing, where the strict division of tax sources between the Federation, *Länder*, and municipalities (*Trennsystem*) is accompanied by a 'sharing' of designated tax revenues (*Verbundsystem*).[27] The various revenue sources and their assignments to the three levels of government are listed in Table 10A.2 in the appendix. The common tax pool includes four taxes: the turnover or sales tax (VAT), the corporation and the individual income/payroll taxes, and the capital yields tax. It is worth noting that this joint tax pool accounted for DM 478.5 billion or 72 per cent of total tax revenues in 1991, underlining the fact that the *Verbundsystem* has dominated since the *Finanzreform* of 1969.

The distribution of the common tax pool is spelled out by law. The *Grundgesetz* allots to the federal government and the *Länder* each 50 per cent of the income and corporation taxes while the percentage sharing of the sales tax is to be determined by federal legislation requiring the consent of the *Bundesrat*. The *Finanzreform* also introduced a provision according to which municipalities receive a share of the income tax revenue in exchange for granting the Federation and the *Länder* a portion of their business tax revenues (*Gewerbesteuerumlage*).[28]

Fiscal equalization

With the exception of the sales tax (which is apportioned largely on the basis of population), the individual *Land* retains its share of the common taxes from the revenues collected within its boundaries.[29] Given the economic differences among the regions in the FRG, inequities in fiscal capacities would be inevitable if the *Länder* were to rely solely on this vertical transfer. As stated earlier, these inequities would violate the constitutional requirement of equalization between financially strong and financially weak *Länder*. To this end, the *Grundgesetz* contains a provision according to which the Federation may make grants 'from federal funds to financially weak *Länder* in order to complement the coverage of their general financial requirements' (*Ergänzungszuweisungen* — supplemental grants).[30]

To supplement these vertical transfers, Article 107 (2) GG calls for a system of 'horizontal equalization', i.e. transfers among the *Länder* (*Länderfinanzausgleich*) in such a way that the 'financially stronger' states provide aid to the 'financially weak' states.[31] The transfer system is based on per capita tax revenue. Its goal is to raise the revenue of the weaker *Länder* to at least 95 per cent of the average per capita tax revenue for all states. If a surplus is between 100 and 102 per cent of the average for all states, no contribution is required, while 70 per cent of surpluses between 102 and 110 per cent of the average and all of the surplus above 110 per cent are contributed to the equalization fund.[32]

The unification treaty of August 31, 1990, excludes the new Eastern states from the financial equalization measures due to the substantial differences in the tax structures of the East and the West. A partaking of the 'New *Länder*' in the *Länder* share of the turnover tax on a population basis was to be gradually introduced between 1991—94. However, in view of the desperate financial situation of the new states, the Western *Länder* voluntarily agreed to begin sharing with them the turnover tax revenue as of 1991.[33]

In 1991, the New *Länder* engaged for the first time in equalization payments among themselves. Horizontal equalization for the FRG as a whole is planned for 1995. In the interim it has been replaced by the *Fonds 'Deutsche Einheit'* with a total initial volume of DM 115 billion to benefit the New *Länder*.

Horizontal fiscal equalization occurs not only among the *Länder* but also between the *Land* and its local governmental units.[34] Clearly, constitutionally guaranteed local self-governance would be meaningless without adequate finances. Moreover, the requirement of 'uniformity of living conditions' also necessitates some degree of equalization of fiscal capacity among local governments. Therefore, aside from the *Länder* sharing their portion of the common tax revenues with the local governments as dictated by law,[35] they — together with the federal government — provide the local sector with a variety of assistance.

Federal and state grants to the local sector may be grouped into two major categories: general purpose grants and special purpose grants. Among the former, formula grants stand out as the most important form. They are designed to augment the municipalities' revenues in order to mitigate differences in fiscal capacity within the local sector and to ensure that all municipalities are able to supply a basic spectrum of services. Special purpose grants are mostly investment grants.

5 THE FISCAL STRUCTURE OF THE FRG

An Overview of Public Sector Budgets

An overview of the public sector budgets for 1988 is provided in Table 10.3. The table contains expenditure and revenue data for the federal government, the *Länder*, and the local sector — as well as for the Social Insurance Fund and a fifth category comprising a variety of special purpose funds (SPFs). The Social Insurance Fund is a separate account; it prepares its own budget and finances its expenditures primarily through social security contributions of insured employees and employers, although it receives some transfers from the federal government. The SPFs include the *Lastenausgleichsfonds* (Equalization of Burdens Fund) which provides compensation for damages and losses associated with war destructions and expulsions and the reform of the monetary system in 1948; the European

Table 10.3 *Overview of public sector budgets, 1988 (in billion DM)*

Item	Direct Expend[a]	Federal	*Länder*	Local	Soc.Ins	SPF[b]	Total
Expenditures, total	1,021.8	278.2	270.1	184.4	395.4	38.3	1,166.4
Current account	914.3	243.8	228.1	141.2	390.9	31.5	1,034.6
Capital account	106.8	34.4	42.0	43.2	5.3	6.8	131.8
Revenues, total	967.8	242.2	253.7	185.1	393.9	38.0	1,112.8
Current account	943.9	236.4	239.8	161.9	393.4	32.8	1,064.2
Capital account	23.6	5.8	13.9	23.2	0.5	5.2	48.6
Deficit (—) or surplus (+)	—53.6	—36.0	—16.3	+0.7	—1.5	—0.3	—53.6
Current account	+29.6	—7.4	+11.7	+20.7	+3.4	+1.3	+29.0
Capital account	—83.2	—28.6	—28.1	—20.0	—4.8	—1.6	—83.2

Notes: Details may not add to total due to rounding.

Column 2 indicates direct expenditures; column 8 (total) indicates the sum of expenditures in columns 3 to 7 and exceeds direct expenditures because of double counting due to intergovernmental disbursements.

a: Direct expenditures (excluding intergovernmental disbursements).

b: SPF-Special Purpose Funds; include *Lastenausgleichsfonds* (equalization of burdens fund), *ERP-Sondervermögen* (European Recovery Program), EC, and *Zweckverbände* (special purpose associations).

Source: Calculated from data reported in Statistisches Bundesamt (1991).

Recovery Program (ERP); the European Community; as well as the *Zweckverbände* (special purpose associations).

In 1988, the FRG public sector spent a total of DM 1,166.4 billion. This sum includes some double counting due to intergovernmental disbursements of DM 145.3 billion, leaving a net total of DM 1,021.1 billion. Expenditures of the Social Insurance Fund accounted for approximately one-third (DM 395.4 billion or 33.9 per cent); the federal government's and the *Länder* shares were roughly 23 per cent each. The local sector share was around 16 per cent (DM 184.4 billion), while SPFs accounted for the remainder (DM 38.3 billion or 3.3 per cent).

Unlike in budget presentations in the United States, it is common practice in the FRG public budgets (including the Social Insurance Fund) to distinguish between the current and the capital accounts. Across all public sector entities, capital expenditures accounted for DM 131.8 billion or 11.3 per cent of the total in 1988; expenditures on the current account amounted to DM 1,034.6 billion or 88.7 per cent. The importance of capital spending in the overall budget differs across levels of government. At the local level, the capital account expenditures as a fraction of total local spending were the highest with 23.4 per cent, followed by the special purpose funds with 17.8 per cent and the *Länder* with 15.5 per cent.

Total public sector revenues in 1988 were equal to DM 1,112.8 billion. Their allocation among the five public sector entities is similar to that of the public sector expenditures. Again we find the Social Insurance Fund's share to have been the largest with 35.4 per cent of the total. The *Länder* ranked second with 22.8 per cent, while the federal government's share was 21.8 per cent. The local sector accounted for 16.6 per cent of public sector revenues; the SPFs absorbed 3.4 per cent.

Comparing expenditures and revenues, we find a public sector deficit of DM 53.6 billion or 4.6 per cent of total (gross) expenditures (5.2 per cent of net expenditures). By level of government, the deficit was the largest for the federal government (DM 36 billion or 12.9 per cent of federal government expenditures), followed by the *Länder* with six per cent of their expenditures. The only government authority to have seen a balanced budget (a small surplus in 1988) was the local sector. It is worth noting that the overall deficits were almost exclusively those of the capital account. Only the federal government experienced a deficit on the current account as well.

Distribution of Expenditure Functions

For the purpose of presentation in this section, public sector expenditures for the FRG were regrouped according to the functional classification used in earlier chapters for the U.S. and Canada. Accordingly, we distinguish between allocation (public goods), redistribution, and the provision of merit goods. The results of this exercise are reported in Table 10.4. (The percentage distribution is given in Table 10A.3 in the appendix.) Across all government units, we find the most significant spending category to have been redistribution, absorbing some DM 490.7 billion or 48 per cent of the entire public sector budget. Expenditures on public goods followed with DM 311.6 billion or 30.5 per cent. The remaining DM 200.3 billion (21.5 per cent) went to the public provision of merit goods.

Among the public good expenditures, the single most significant category (aside from general administration and finance) was national defense. Given its size and importance, it may be useful to exclude national defense when analyzing the functional classification. This reduces the overall public (non-defense) expenditures to a total of DM 967,970 million of which 50.7 per cent were allocated to redistribution, 26.7 per cent funded the provision of non-defense public goods, and 22.6 per cent were absorbed by merit goods (see Table 10A.3).

Clearly, there is significant variation across government units in the relative importance of the three expenditure categories. The Social Insurance Fund, being a single-purpose institution, directs its funds exclusively towards the redistribution category. The other four sector budgets, however, contain expenditures in all three categories, even though with varying emphasis. For the federal government, the provision of public goods comes first. Even after the exclusion of national defense, 44.3 per cent of federal expenditures were allocated to this function in the 1988 federal budget. Redistribution followed as a close second with 40.7 per cent, leaving 15 per cent of federal spending for merit goods. For the *Länder*, the distribution of expenditures is quite different. The largest fraction of state funds (47.4 per cent) was used for merit goods, in particular education which is the primary *Länder* domain. Some DM 70 billion or 30 per cent of the entire *Länder* budget was allocated towards education in 1988, the single largest item in the state budgets across all functional categories. Public goods came second, absorbing 44.5 per cent of all state funds. Within this category, the general administration and finance expenditures accounted for the bulk of all spending. Redistribution was but a minor *Länder* concern, using up only 8.2 per cent of total funds.

For the local sector, too, the provision of merit goods was the primary function. As shown in the appendix Table 10A.3, 45.2 per cent of local funds were directed towards that function, most importantly to fund hospitals and schools. Public goods provision (especially sanitation) followed second with 30.2 per cent and redistribution was third with 24.5 per cent. Finally, the expenditures of the special purpose funds were almost evenly split among public goods (50.4 per cent) and merit goods (49 per cent). Less than one per cent went towards redistribution expenditures.

One may also wish to analyze the data with a different focus in mind and ask who within the public sector is the major public provider of public

Table 10.4 Functional classification of public sector expenditures, 1988 (in million DM)

Expenditure function	Total	Federal	*Länder*	Local	SPF [a]
A. NON—MARKET SUPPLY (public goods)					
General administration	37,383	7,992	13,904	15,112	375
General finance	106,795	58,848	54,498	+8,029	1,478
International relations	22,196	8,856	77	—	13,263
National defense	53,146	53,146	—	—	—
Public security/legal system	30,134	2,293	22,617	5,201	23
Science, R&D [b]	11,980	9,184	2,501	293	2
Clean air, water, soil	1,991	444	655	—	892
Sanitation [c]	21,657	56	1,423	19,196	982
sewerage	9,094	+44	540	8,094	504
refuse	5,004	+ 3	351	4,193	463
street cleaning	932	—	101	831	1
Transport & communications [d]	26,291	11,443	6 618	8,181	49
roads	21,455	7,399	5 861	8,181	13
waterways, ports	2,716	2,050	630	—	36
TOTAL	311,573	152,262	102,293	39,954	17,064
TOTAL excl. national defense	258,427	99,116	102,293	39,954	17,064

Table 10.4 continued

Expenditure function	Total	Federal	*Länder*	Local	SPF [a]
B. MODIFYING MARKET SUPPLY (merit goods)					
Education	88,179	3,746	69,677	14,731	25
schools	53,476	10	40,998	12,488	+20
universities	27,001	1,651	25,350	—	—
other educ. affairs	7,702	2,085	3,329	2,243	45
Cultural affairs	8,000	178	3,709	4,079	34
Health/sports	40,328	334	9,934	28,620	1,440
hospitals	30,092	4	7,695	20,971	1,422
health/recreation	7,997	114	1,210	6,656	17
Housing	7,825	1,353	5,202	1,263	7
(Urban) Planning	7,539	735	3,143	3,644	17
Energy/water/mining	21,228	8,418	7,835	1,641	3,334
Railways & public transport	3,673	1,787	1,886	—	—
Economic enterprises	23,513	13,744	4,103	5,369	297
Nutrition/agriculture/forests	18,509	3,243	3,449	396	11,421
TOTAL	218,794	33,538	108,938	59,743	16,575

Table 10.4 continued

Expenditure function	Total	Federal	*Länder*	Local	Social Insurance	SPF [a]
C. REDISTRIBUTION						
Social Security, war impact, reparation	490,749	90,910	18,835	32,438	348,361	205
social administration	4,920	474	1,556	2,863	—	5
social insurance	393,994	45,423	209	—	348,361	—
welfare	60,806	19,722	12,190	28,841	—	201
war, political events	16,729	13,963	1,885	733	—	148
GRAND TOTAL	1,021,116	276,710	230,066	132,135	348,361	33,844
GRAND TOTAL excluding national defense	967,970	223,564	230,066	132,135	348,361	33,844

Notes: Individual figures may not add to total due to rounding.
a: SPF — Special Purpose Funds (see explanatory note in Table 10.3).
b: Outside of universities.
c: Only major sub-categories are shown.
d: Excludes railways (see part B), but includes postal services which are not listed separately.
+ Indicates offsetting receipts.

Source: Calculated from data reported in Statistisches Bundesamt (1991).

goods versus merit goods or redistributive services. Out of DM 218.8 billion which were allocated to the provision of merit goods, half (49.8 per cent) were contributed by the *Länder*, followed by the local sector with DM 59.7 billion or 27.3 per cent (see Tables 10.4 and 10A.4). The reason again is that education is the most significant merit good and it is the major function assigned to the state and local sectors. Not surprisingly, the great majority (71 per cent) of the expenditures on redistribution services were carried out by the Social Insurance Fund. The federal government contributed 18.5 per cent (in the form of transfers to the Social Insurance Fund), and the state and local sectors shared the remainder. Since the federal government is the sole provider of national defense, the identity of the major providers of public goods depends to some extent on whether or not national defense expenditures are included in the total. Including defense, the federal government was the major provider of public goods overall, accounting for DM 152.3 billion or 48.9 per cent of the total expenditures in this category. The states came second with 32.8 per cent (DM 102.3 billion), and the local sector (12.8 per cent) and the SPFs (5.5 per cent) ranked third and fourth respectively. Excluding defense spending, the *Länder* ranked first (39.6 per cent), but were followed closely by the federal government whose share now dropped to 38.4 per cent.

Examining the more disaggregated information in Table 10.4 more closely, one can identify a number of goods and services by major provider. The provision of hospital and recreational services as well as sanitation is clearly local in nature. University education, housing, and public security are provided primarily at the state level, while national defense is obviously a federal function. Clearly, some goods and services are not characterized by one particular preferred mode of provision. Roads and welfare services, for instance, are paid for at all levels of government. Expenditures on public transport and energy and water related matters are shared by the *Länder* and the Federation, while the states and the local sector are jointly responsible for cultural affairs.

Revenue Sources

Turning now to the structure of finance, we show in Table 10.5 the revenue sources for the federal, state and local governments in 1988. Public sector revenues in the FRG are derived from four primary sources: taxes, fees and dues, receipts from economic activity, and intergovernmental transfers (grants). Taxes constitute the main revenue source for all three territorial authorities; yet we note some variation across public sector entities in the relative importance of the different sources. Tax revenues accounted for close to 92 per cent of the federal government's revenue in 1988 but made up only 36.8 per cent of that total for the local sector. As indicated in the table, local governments rely much more heavily on intergovernmental

Table 10.5 *Public sector revenue structure, 1988*

Revenue Type	Total		Federal		*Länder*		Local	
	bill DM	%	bill DM	%	bill DM	%	bill DM	%
Taxes [a]	470.3	69.1	222.7	91.9	179.5	70.8	68.1	36.8
Econ. activity	20.0	2.9	6.2	2.6	5.5	2.2	8.3	4.5
Fees & dues	57.8	8.5	2.5	1.0	16.2	6.4	39.1	21.1
Public sector grants & loans [b]	83.7	12.3	—	—	33.9	13.4	49.8	26.9
Miscellaneous	49.2	7.2	10.8	4.5	18.6	7.3	19.8	10.7
TOTAL	681.0	100.0	242.2	100.0	253.7	100.0	185.1	100.0

Notes: a: Including tax-like levies.
b: Net of transfers within the respective sector.

Source: Calculated from data reported in Bundesministerium der Finanzen (1991).

Table 10.6 *Revenues from joint taxes, 1988 (in million DM)*

Tax Type	Total	Federal	*Länder*	Local
Turnover tax [a]	123,286	80,136	43,150	—
Income tax [b]	200,693	85,295	85,295	30,103
Capital yields tax	8,732	4,366	4,366	—
Corporation tax	30,003	15,001	15,002	—
TOTAL	362,714	184,798	147,813	30,103
Business tax [c]	34,465	2,484	2,484	29,496
GRAND TOTAL	397,179	187,282	150,297	59,600

Notes: a: Includes import turnover tax.
b: Includes wages tax.
c: The business tax is a local tax and is not officially included among the joint taxes. However, the local governments may be required to share some of their business tax revenues with the Federation and the *Länder*.

Source: Calculated from data reported in Bundesministerium der Finanzen (1991).

grants as well as fees and dues than either the *Länder* or the federal government.

Tables 10.6 and 10.7 provide information on the distribution of tax receipts by type of tax. As stated earlier, the German tax system is characterized by mixed financing where the *Trennsystem*, i.e. the strict division of tax sources between the Federation, the *Länder*, and the local sector, is combined with the sharing of certain tax revenues (*Verbundsystem*). A breakdown of the joint tax pool is given in Table 10.6. As shown by the data in Table 10.7, these joint taxes constitute the primary tax source for all three public sector entities. The federal government generated 77.4 per cent of its revenues (net of the EC tax revenue share and supplemental grants to the states) from joint taxes, with only 22.6 per cent to be derived from its 'own' (non-shared) tax sources. Among the latter, the oil and the tobacco taxes stand out as the main fund raiser. In 1988, they accounted for 51.3 per cent and 27.6 per cent of all revenues from 'own' federal taxes respectively. Both the *Länder* and the local sector rely even more heavily on joint taxes than the federal government. At the state level, 85.7 per cent of tax revenues were derived from joint sources; 12.9 per cent stemmed from *Länder* taxes (most importantly the motor vehicle tax (36 per cent) and the wealth tax (24.5 per cent)). The remaining 1.4 per cent were accounted for by federal supplemental grants which are based on the turnover tax. The local sector generated 86.6 per cent of its tax revenues from shared tax sources. Of this, approximately half was derived from the truly joint income tax. The other half came from the business tax which is local in nature, but of which only about 85 per cent is retained by the local governments. A second local tax of significance is the property tax, which contributed some 12 per cent of local net tax revenues in 1988. The heavy reliance of all three public sector entities underlines the dominance of the *Verbundsystem* in the German tax system which stands in marked contrast to the U.S. system which is organized around the principle of separation.

Intergovernmental Transfers

As stated earlier, the desire to comply with the constitutional mandate for uniform living conditions and thus to minimize interregional disparities in fiscal capacity has led to a complex set of intergovernmental fiscal relationships including tax revenue sharing as well as horizontal and vertical transfers.

Horizontal transfers

An important tool used in the attempt to reduce fiscal disparities among the states is the *Länderfinanzausgleich* (LAF), the direct formula distribution from rich to poor states. In 1988, the LAF had a volume of DM 3,360 million. Table 10.8A lists the *Länder* owing equalization payments and the amounts paid for selected years. Table 10.8B conveys the corresponding information for *Länder* receiving horizontal transfer payments. Because of its special status, Berlin does not participate in the *Länderfinanzausgleich* but instead receives federal grants. During the 1970s, NRW, Hessen, Baden-Württemberg, and Hamburg, i.e. the states with significant industrial areas, have consistently been required to share some of their revenues with their financially weaker neighbors. Due to a decline in its smokestack industries, NRW dropped out of this group during the 1980s, and Hamburg's contribution decreased, especially during the second half of the 1980s. This leaves Hessen, with its significant industrial areas around Frankfurt and Kassel, and Baden-Württemberg with its industrial centers Stuttgart and Mannheim, as the main contributors. Niedersachsen, Rheinland-Pfalz, Schleswig-Holstein, Saarland, and Bremen have been on the receiving end throughout the 20-year period covered in Table 10.8B. Bayern with its large agricultural areas had been receiving increasingly less money throughout the 1980s and eventually switched to become a surplus *Land* in 1989.

As stated above, the New *Länder* do not yet take part in the *Länderfinanzausgleich*. However, in 1991, they engaged for the first time in equalization payments among themselves. The total equalization volume amounted to DM 74.7 million and was almost entirely contributed by Sachsen (DM 74.6 million); an insignificant sum was paid by Brandenburg.

Table 10.7 Tax revenues in detail, 1988 (in million DM)

A. FEDERAL TAX REVENUES	
Revenue from joint taxes [a]	187,282
./. EC share of turnover tax	—14,314
./. Supplemental grants [b]	—2,466
Subtotal	170,502
Federal taxes [c]	
Oil tax	27,032
Tobacco tax	14,555
Insurance tax	2,903
Brandy tax	3,999
Miscellaneous	4,244
Subtotal	52,733
./. EC tax based on GNP	—3,028
TOTAL FEDERAL TAX INCOME (net of EC share)	220,207
B. *LÄNDER* TAX REVENUES	
Revenue from joint taxes [a]	150,297
Länder taxes	
Motor vehicle tax	8,169
Wealth tax	5,554
Beer tax	1,254
Miscellaneous	7,693
Subtotal	22,670
Supplemental grants [b]	2,466
TOTAL *LÄNDER* TAX INCOME	175,433
C. LOCAL TAX REVENUES	
Revenue from joint taxes [d]	59,600
Local taxes	
Property tax	8,238
Miscellaneous	953
Subtotal	9,191
TOTAL LOCAL TAX INCOME	68,791

Table 10.7 continued

D.	EC TAX REVENUES	
	Customs revenue	6,325
	Share of turnover tax	14,314
	Tax on GNP	3,028
	TOTAL EC TAX INCOME	23,667
GRAND TOTAL, all authorities		488,098

Notes: For a breakdown of the joint tax revenue sources see Table 10.6.
a: Includes share in local business tax.
b: Equivalent to 2 per cent of turnover tax.
c: Excludes EC share in customs revenues (100 % = DM 6,325).
d: Excludes federal and *Länder* share in business tax.

Source: Calculated from data reported in Bundesministerium der Finanzen (1991).

Equalization payment recipients were Sachsen-Anhalt (DM 18.1 million), Thüringen (DM 40.7 million), and Mecklenburg-Vorpommern (DM 15.9 million).[36]

The commencement of horizontal fiscal equalization for the entire territory of the united FRG is scheduled for January 1995. Since per capita tax revenues in the East remain significantly below the West German level,[37] the Western states can be expected to be required to transfer an estimated DM 30 billion to the East starting 1995. This will turn most of the Western *Länder* into surplus states, i.e. owing equalization payments. Estimated per capita transfers would range from DM 136 per inhabitant in Niedersachsen to DM 1,277 in Hamburg. Bremen and the Saarland would remain as the only Western states still receiving equalization payments (DM 377 and DM 331 per capita respectively). The five Eastern states would receive anywhere from DM 1,867 per capita (Sachsen) to DM 1,934 (Thüringen).[38]

In the meantime, the eastern states receive support through the *Fonds 'Deutsche Einheit'* (German Unity Fund) with a total initial volume of DM 115 billion. Of this amount, the Federation contributes DM 20 billion; the remaining DM 95 billion are to be raised on the capital markets. The resulting debt is to be serviced jointly by the Federation (50 per cent) and the Western states and their municipalities (50 per cent). The poorer states of Bremen and the Saarland are exempted until 1994.[39]

Table 10.8A *Länder owing equalization payments (in million DM)*

Year	NRW	Bayern	B.Württ.	Hessen	Hamburg	Total
1970	316.9	—	314.4	290.0	294.0	1,215.3
1975	433.5	—	660.5	206.1	544.2	1,844.3
1980	76.3	—	1,504.1	297.7	313.2	2,191.3
1981	—	—	1,638.3	357.7	426.7	2,422.7
1982	—	—	1,788.7	279.9	430.9	2,499.5
1983	—	—	1,428.5	331.7	386.0	2,146.1
1984	—	—	1,461.0	574.8	294.4	2,330.3
1985	—	—	1,444.1	724.6	406.7	2,575.4
1986	—	—	1,742.8	783.2	198.1	2,724.0
1987	—	—	1,912.7	1,228.1	58.2	3,199.0
1988	—	—	1,920.0	1,439.9	—	3,359.9
1989	98.9	64.7	1,412.6	1,926.5	12.4	3,515.1
1990	62.9	35.9	2,471.6	1,445.6	7.9	4,023.8

Source: Bundesministerium der Finanzen (1992), p. 131.

Table 10.8B *Länder entitled to equalization payments (in million DM)*

Year	NRW	Bayern	Nieders.	Rhld.Pf.	Schl.Hol	Saarland	Bremen	Total
1970		148.2	407.3	228.4	199.1	142.8	89.5	1,215.3
1975		386.6	717.6	294.3	239.4	178.9	45.5	1,844.3
1980		402.6	753.5	246.7	323.0	287.3	178.2	2,191.3
1981		268.3	1,007.0	303.0	423.0	260.8	160.6	2,422.7
1982		162.6	1,128.6	278.3	428.1	262.7	239.2	2,499.5
1983		134.5	704.2	255.5	486.1	304.6	261.3	2,146.1
1984		41.3	835.8	284.1	524.6	333.0	311.5	2,330.3
1985	90.7	27.5	826.8	374.3	564.1	359.2	332.7	2,575.4
1986	—	48.8	854.5	378.9	614.4	381.7	445.7	2,724.0
1987	165.9	—	1,115.5	477.9	598.9	337.1	503.8	3,199.0
1988	28.4	—	1,577.8	311.9	595.8	333.4	512.7	3,359.9
1989	—	—	1,673.8	303.6	578.7	328.8	630.3	3,515.1
1990	—	—	1,926.6	489.9	601.6	366.2	639.6	4,023.8

Source: Bundesministerium der Finanzen (1992), p. 132.

Vertical transfers

Broadly interpreted, vertical fiscal equalization measures take on a variety of forms from federal (matching) grants for *Gemeinschaftsaufgaben* (joint tasks) to structural assistance grants and *Ergänzungszuweisungen* (supplemental grants).

In 1992, some DM 16 billion were allocated to the three joint tasks, thus accounting for roughly 6.3 per cent of the combined federal and state budgets. Of this amount, the federal government contributed DM 8.6 billion or close to 54 per cent. Almost half of the funds went to the *Gemeinschaftsaufgabe* 'regional economic development', and here the new Eastern states were the main recipients. Slightly less than one-third of total funds was used for the promotion of agrarian structure and coastal preservation, and the remaining 20 per cent supported the extension and construction of institutions of higher education.

As stated above, *Ergänzungszuweisungen* are federal supplemental grants designed to enhance the fiscal capacity of the poorer *Länder*. In 1991, the financially weak *Länder* receiving these federal funds were: Niedersachsen (DM 1,559 million), Rheinland-Pfalz (DM 678 million), Schleswig-Holstein (DM 603 million), and the Saarland (DM 403 million). Bayern was a member of this group until 1988. Bremen has received payments since 1986 (DM 289 million in 1991) and Nordrhein-Westfalen (NRW) from 1987 to 1990. Between 1974 and 1987, the supplemental grants were set at 1.5 per cent of turnover tax revenues; this fraction was raised to two per cent in 1988 plus an additional DM 50 million for Bremen for a total of DM 3.5 billion in 1991.[40]

The local sector is the subnational government level that relies most heavily on vertical transfers as a revenue source. In 1989, local governments derived DM 51.1 billion, more than one-fourth of their total revenues, from federal and state grants. Figure 10.2 depicts the breakdown of these funds into two major categories: general purpose grants and special purpose grants. General purpose grants were given in the amount of DM 28.2 billion in 1989 or 55 per cent of the total. In this category, the formula grants were most significant, accounting for 79 per cent of all general purpose funds. Special purpose grants were mostly investment grants amounting to DM 12.4 billion or 54 per cent of this category. The remainder (DM 10.5 billion) provided support for delegated and routine functions in the administrative budget.

6 CONCLUSION

Fiscal relations and budgeting in the FRG are governed by two guiding principles laid out in the *Grundgesetz*: that of uniformity of living conditions throughout the Federation and that of *Länder* and local self-

Figure 10.2 *Federal and Land grants to local governments, 1989*

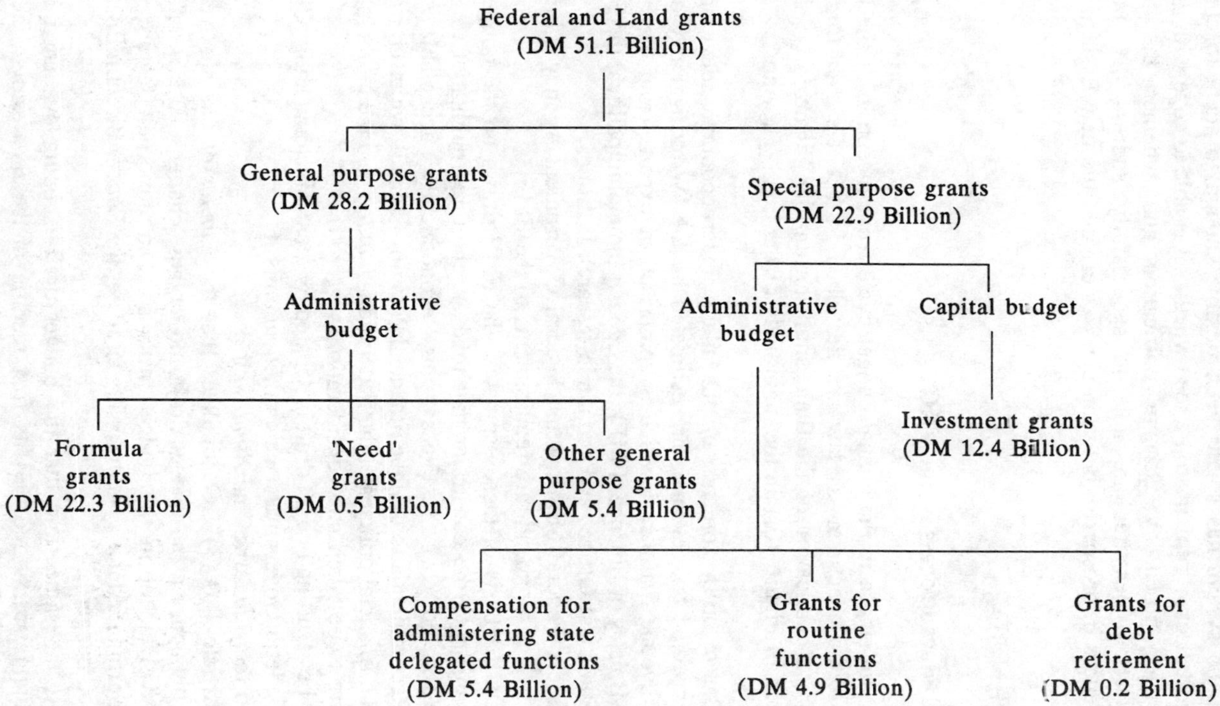

Source: Bundesministerium der Finanzen (1992), p. 139.

governance in general and autonomy in financial administration in particular. The inherent conflict between the two has resulted in a highly complex system of fiscal relationships and has given the federal government reason to expand its role, entailing greater centralization of public finances. While the system has so far been flexible enough to adapt to changing circumstances, it remains to be seen whether it is able to cope with the new challenges posed by German unification and whether the built-in equalization measures are able to successfully address the immense differences in prosperity between the Western and the new Eastern states.

APPENDIX

The Budget Process in the FRG

The main stages in the annual budget cycle from inception of the budget draft to its enactment as law are described in *The German Budgetary System*, a publication of the Bundesministerium der Finanzen (1987) and outlined in Figure 10.1 in the main body of the text. They are:

1. Based on a forecast of the likely macroeconomic development, expected tax revenues are estimated by the 'Working Party on Tax Revenue Estimates' which is comprised of experts from the Federal Ministry of Finance (FMF), the *Länder* and municipalities, the Federal Statistical Office, and economic research institutes.
2. Every Federal Ministry and Federal Government Agency submits its estimated expenditure requirements to the FMF.
3. On the basis of these estimates, the FMF draws up the budget plan subject to the constraint that total expenditures ought not to exceed estimated tax revenues plus economically acceptable loans. Recommendations of the Financial Planning Council, which coordinates the financial policies of the Federation, *Länder*, and the municipalities, are to be taken into consideration.
4. The resulting budget draft is debated by the cabinet and adopted by the Federal Government which then submits it
5. to the *Bundesrat* and *Bundestag*.[41]
6. Article 110 (3) GG stipulates that the *Bundesrat* has six weeks to comment on the budget draft and suggest changes. The *Bundesrat*'s involvement in the budget process is an important feature of the German federal system for it guarantees the *Länder* direct influence on the budget bill.
7. At the same time that the budget draft is being evaluated by the *Bundesrat*, it receives its first reading in the *Bundestag*. The FMF gives his budget speech which presents the Federal Government's

considerations underlying the proposed budget. Representatives of all political parties are given the opportunity to express their views on the subject.

8. Following the deliberations in the *Bundestag*, the budget bill is transferred to the Budget Committee of the *Bundestag* where it is examined in detail and alterations, if any, are decided upon.
9. The second reading in the *Bundestag* can take place only after the *Bundesrat* comments have been received as they are to be taken into consideration in the ensuing legislative process.
10. During the second reading, the results of the Budget Committee's deliberations are presented to the *Bundestag*. All potential alterations to the budget draft are to be discussed and decided upon one by one.
11. During the third reading the complete budget bill is discussed in summary and
12. voted upon.
13. After the *Bundestag* has passed the bill, it is transferred to the *Bundesrat* for a second round.
14. Should the *Bundesrat* raise objections to the budget bill, it may call upon the Mediation Committee which consists to equal parts of members of the *Bundestag* and *Bundesrat* and is assigned the task of working out a compromise between the two legislative bodies. If the Mediation Committee suggests any alterations to the budget, the *Bundestag* has to vote once more. Again the *Bundesrat* may raise objections according to Article 77 (3) GG, which can be rejected by the *Bundestag* with the necessary number of votes.

    The budget plan becomes law when — after passing *Bundestag* and *Bundesrat* — it has been
15. countersigned by the Federal Minister of Finance
16. countersigned by the Federal Chancellor
17. signed by the Federal President and
18. promulgated in the Federal Law Gazette.

Table 10A.1 *Länder Profile*

Land	Bundesrat Votes	km^2 '000	pop. mill.	pop/ km^2	gdp/ cap.	Sectoral Employment (%) Agric.	Manuf.	Comm.	Other	unemp rate[a]
FRG — United	68	357.0	79.1	222	n/a	n/a	n/a	n/a	n/a	n/a
FRG — West	47	248.6	61.7	252	39,281	3.7	40.9	17.9	37.5	6.1
Baden-Württemberg	6	35.7	9.6	269	40,470	3.2	47.0	15.0	34.6	4.9
Bayern	6	70.1	11.2	159	39,418	6.9	41.9	16.6	34.6	4.7
Hessen	4	21.1	5.7	268	44,128	2.6	38.2	19.6	39.6	5.7
Niedersachsen	6	47.3	7.3	154	32,513	5.8	37.8	18.1	38.3	8.2
Nordrhein-West.	6	34.1	17.1	502	36,582	1.8	43.5	18.3	36.4	8.3
Rheinland-Pfalz	4	19.8	3.7	186	34,158	4.5	41.4	16.6	37.4	6.0
Saarland	3	2.6	1.1	414	33,225	—	41.8	18.9	38.3	9.2
Schleswig-Hol.	4	15.7	2.6	165	31,896	4.5	29.9	20.8	44.8	7.5
Berlin (West)		0.5	2.1	4,437	42,893	0.8	30.3	19.1	49.9	11.7
Bremen	3	0.4	0.7	1,667	48,494	—	32.2	26.8	40.2	10.9
Hamburg	3	0.8	1.6	2,153	67,792	0.8	26.2	28.2	44.9	7.6
FRG — East[b]	21	108.3	17.4	161	n/a	n/a	n/a	n/a	n/a	13.4
Brandenburg	4	29.1	2.6	91						14.0
Mecklenburg-V.	3	23.8	2.0	82						15.5
Sachsen	4	18.3	4.9	267						12.7
Sachsen-Anhalt	4	20.4	3.0	145						14.4
Thüringen	4	16.3	2.7	165						14.1

Notes: a: As of November 1992.
b: Including East Berlin.

Sources: Based on Statistisches Bundesamt (1991); Reuter (1991); German Information Center (Dec. 11, 1992).

Table 10A.2 Tax revenue sources by territorial authority

JOINT TAXES	*LÄNDER* TAXES
Turnover tax	Personal wealth tax
Federation 65%	Motor vehicle tax
Länder 35%	Beer tax
Corporation tax	Real property tax
Federation 50%	Inheritance tax
Länder 50%	Betting & lottery tax
Capital Yields Tax	Fire protection tax
Federation 50%	
Länder 50%	FEDERAL TAXES
Income and wages tax	
Federation 42.5%	Insurance tax
Länder 42.5%	Bills of exchange tax
Municipal. 15.0%	Domestic investment tax
	Stock exchange tax
LOCAL TAXES	Transaction tax
	Customs duties
Business tax[a]	Mineral oil tax
Real property taxes	Coffee tax
Licensing tax	Tea tax
Entertainment tax	Sugar tax
Hunting and fishing tax	Salt tax
Dog tax	Spirits levies
Municipal beverage tax	Sparkling wine tax
	Light fixture tax
	Tobacco tax

Note: a: The business tax is local in nature. However, local governments are required to relinquish approximately 15 per cent of their revenues to the Federation and the *Länder*.

Source: Based on Voigt (1989).

Table 10A.3 *Percentage distribution of public sector expenditures by function, 1988*

Function	Total	Federal	*Länder*	Local	Soc.Ins.	Other
		including national defense				
Allocation (Public G.)	30.5	55.0	44.5	30.2	0.0	50.40
Merit Goods	21.5	12.1	47.4	45.2	0.0	49.00
Redistribution	48.0	32.9	8.2	24.5	100.0	0.60
		excluding national defense				
Allocation (Public G.)	26.7	44.3	44.5	30.2	0.0	50.40
Merit Goods	22.6	15.0	47.4	45.2	0.0	49.00
Redistribution	50.7	40.7	8.2	24.5	100.0	0.60

Source: Calculated from DM figures reported in Table 10.4.

Table 10A.4 *Percentage distribution of functional expenditures by public sector entity, 1988*

Function	Total	Federal	*Länder*	Local	Soc.Ins.	Other
Allocation incl. defense	100.0	48.9	32.8	12.8	0.0	5.50
Allocation excl. defense	100.0	38.4	39.6	15.5	0.0	6.60
Merit Goods	100.0	15.3	49.8	27.3	0.0	7.60
Redistribution	100.0	18.5	3.8	6.6	71.0	0.04

Source: Calculated from DM figures reported in Table 10.4.

NOTES

1. The choice of the term 'Basic Law' instead of 'constitution' was to underline the provisional nature of the text as reunification with the Soviet zone was hoped for in the near future.
2. Article 79 (3) GG. It would be misleading, however, to convey the impression that federalism was imposed on Germany for the first time by Western Allied powers. In fact, decentralization and in particular local self-government have a rich tradition in German history and date back to at least as far as the administrative reforms in Prussia by Baron von Stein at the beginning of the nineteenth century. For a more thorough exposition of the federalist and administrative tradition in Germany see Gunlicks (1986).
3. If the two chambers cannot reach an agreement, a mediation committee composed of members of both bodies must be convened and assigned the task of working out a compromise.
4. An excellent account of Germany's administrative structure with particular emphasis on the important role of the local sector can be found in Gunlicks (1986).
5. The *Grundgesetz* uses the term *Bund* — commonly translated as 'Federation' — to denote the superior territorial authority whereas the term *Bundesregierung* (federal government) refers to the executive, i.e. the Federal Chancellor and his Cabinet. In the following, we shall use the terms Federation and federal government interchangeably.
6. West Berlin had special status. For instance, its delegations to the *Bundestag* and *Bundesrat* had advisory status in committee deliberations and plenary debates but did not vote officially on legislation.
7. For further elaboration on these associations see Gunlicks (1986).
8. Articles 20, 28, 30, and 79 GG.
9. Up to the 1969 reform of the budget law, public budgeting in the FRG was governed by the Reich Budget Code of 1922. The validity of this code for the FRG was deemed temporary as implied by its name: 'Provisional Budget Code' of 1950 (Bundesministerium der Finanzen (1980)).
10. Strauss (1969), *Vorwort* (preface).
11. Rudzio (1983), ch. 12. For a detailed account of the evolution of German federalism since 1949 see Klatt (1989).
12. Gunlicks (1986), p.88
13. Article 30 GG stipulates that the discharge of all governmental functions is incumbent on the *Länder* unless the Basic Law expressly prescribes or permits another arrangement. Furthermore, according to Article 83 GG, the *Länder* execute *federal* laws as a matter of their own concern unless the *Grundgesetz* provides or permits otherwise.
14. An important issue that has emerged in recent years concerns the extent to which the local sector is able to implement on its own initiative local programs, given the multiplicity of federal and state mandates.
15. Rudzio (1983), p. 330.
16. Article 35 GG.
17. Article 91a (1) GG.
18. Reuter (1991).
19. Article 104a (1) GG. However, according to Sections (2) and (5), where the Federation delegates certain tasks to the *Länder*, the Federation is responsible for the resulting non-administrative expenditures. If the *Länder* and local governments administer certain *distributive* functions on the Federation's behalf (e.g. housing support, financial aid in education), the funds to be disbursed may 'be contributed wholly or in part by the Federation'. If the *Länder* carry 25 per cent or more of the financial burden, the consent of the *Bundesrat* is required (Article 104a (3) GG).
20. Articles 72 (2) and 106 (3) GG.
21. Rudzio (1983), ch. 12; Rothweiler (1972).
22. Article 104a (4) GG.
23. The former Western recipients of the *Strukturhilfe*-funds are to receive 'transition assistance' to the amount of DM 1.5 billion in 1992.

24. Again we encounter the likely conflict between uniformity and *Länder* autonomy as federal investment assistance is accompanied by the potential undermining of state and local independence. While the *Grundgesetz* builds in the *Bundesrat* consent requirement as a check and balance, this does not necessarily constitute a binding constraint in situations where the *Länder* are eager to compete for federal subsidies. Even though a *Bundesverfassungsgericht* (Federal Constitutional Court) decision of 1975 ruled investment assistance to be the exception rather than the rule, given the vagueness of the *Grundgesetz* formulation, it is impossible to define effective limits other than the federal government's budget constraint (Rudzio (1983), pp. 308—9 referring to BVerfGE 39, p. 96).
25. Article 106 (8) GG.
26. Article 106 (4) GG.
27. Originally, the German constitution provided exclusively for a *Trennsystem*. In 1955—56 the sharing of income and corporation tax revenue was introduced. The *Finanzreform* of 1969 added the sales tax to the *Verbundsystem*.
28. Article 106 (6) GG.
29. Up to 25 per cent of the *Land* sales tax share may be granted on the basis of financial need to *Länder* 'whose per capita revenue from *Land* taxes and from the income and corporation taxes is below the average of all the *Länder* combined' (Article 107 (1) GG).
30. Article 107 (2) GG.
31. More precisely, rather than speaking of 'strong' or 'weak' *Länder* in this context, Article 107 (2) GG uses the terms *ausgleichspflichtig* (owing equalization payments) and *ausgleichsberechtigt* (entitled to equalization payments).
32. Gunlicks (1986), p. 127.
33. Bundesministerium der Finanzen (1991), p. 124.
34. The subject of local government finance is extensively treated in Gunlicks (1986).
35. Article 106 (7) GG. *Land* legislation is to determine the percentage of the *Land* share of common tax revenue to be received by the local sector. Accordingly, there are differences in these allocations from *Land* to *Land*.
36. Bundesministerium der Finanzen (1992), p. 132.
37. Ibid.
38. The German news magazine *Der Spiegel* reported the following per capita tax revenues for 1992 (November 9, 1992):

Tax	Tax Revenue/Capita (DM) East	West
Income/Wages	980	3,630
Turnover	350	3,100
Motor Vehicles	100	180
Business	60	700

39. *Der Spiegel* (November 9, 1992), pp. 16—20.
40. Bundesministerium der Finanzen (1992), pp. 130—31.
41. Unlike other legislation where submission to the *Bundesrat* follows a bill's passing the *Bundestag* vote, Article 110 (3) GG stipulates that the budget draft be submitted simultaneously to *Bundesrat* and *Bundestag* to speed up the process.

REFERENCES

Bundesministerium der Finanzen (1987), *The German Budgetary System*, Bonn.

Bundesministerium der Finanzen (1988), *Federal German Budget Legislation*, Bonn.

Bundesministerium der Finanzen (1991), *Finanzbericht 1992*, Bonn.
Bundesministerium der Finanzen (1992), *Finanzbericht 1993*, Bonn.
German Information Center (Dec. 11, 1992), *Deutschland Nachrichten*, New York.
Gunlicks, A.B. (1986), *Local Government in the German Federal System*, Durham, Duke University Press.
Klatt, H. (1989), 'Forty Years of German Federalism: Past Trends and New Developments' *Publius*, **19** (Fall), pp. 185—202.
Organization for Economic Cooperation and Development (OECD) (1987), *The Control and Management of Government Expenditures*, Paris, OECD.
Reuter, K. (1991), *Föderalismus*, Heidelberg, Decker & Müller.
Rothweiler, R.L. (1972), 'Revenue Sharing in the Federal Republic of Germany', *Publius*, 2 (Spring), pp. 4—25.
Rudzlo, W. (1983), *Das Politische System der Bundesrepublik Deutschland*, Opladen, Leske.
Der Spiegel (Nov. 9, 1992), 'Es muss Masse in den Topf', pp. 16—20.
Statistisches Bundesamt (1991), *Statistisches Jahrbuch für das Vereinte Deutschland 1991*, Wiesbaden.
Strauss, F.J. (1969), *Die Finanzverfassung*, München, Olzog.
Voigt, R. (1989), 'Financing the German Federal System in the 1980s', *Publius*, **19** (Fall), pp. 99—113.

11. Budgeting in the United Kingdom

Peter Smith

1 INTRODUCTION

Budgeting plays an important part in securing public expenditure control at all levels of government in the United Kingdom (UK). The purpose of this chapter is to describe the budgetary process in central and local government, and to explore the impact that the very centralized structure of UK government has on budgeting. The chapter starts with an outline of the institutional framework of the UK public sector. It then describes budgetary procedures, first in central government and then in local government. The analysis concludes that there are considerable centralizing tendencies in UK political structures, and that these are severely compromising local democracy, with potential adverse consequences for allocative efficiency.

Institutional Framework

The UK is comprised of the countries of England, Scotland and Wales, together with the province of Northern Ireland. The national government develops policies for the entire UK, and there are no separate governments for the constituent countries. The supreme UK legislature is the national Parliament, which sits in London, and to which the national government is accountable. The most important component of Parliament is the House of Commons, which comprises about 650 Members of Parliament elected from all parts of the UK. No more than five years must elapse between national elections for the House of Commons, although the precise timing is at the discretion of the central government.

Beneath the national government is a structure of local government, the precise organization of which varies between different parts of the country. With trivial exceptions, local government can undertake expenditure only on services which the national Parliament has given it explicit powers to deliver. Strictly speaking, therefore, as Foster, Jackman and Perlman (1981) explain, the UK has a system of local administration rather than local government. It is usual, therefore, to describe the jurisdictions as local authorities rather than local governments. In most areas there are two tiers of local government. An upper tier (counties in England and Wales, regions in Scotland) is responsible for local services. However, in some parts of the country (London, for example), the two tiers are combined into unitary local authorities. There are 60 upper tier, 390 lower tier and 69 unitary local authorities in the UK excluding Northern Ireland.[1] Elections to most local authorities take place every four years.

In 1991—92, total public expenditure in the UK was 244.4 billion pounds, or about 41.5 per cent of gross domestic product.[2] Of this, 176.3 billion pounds (72 per cent) is spent on central government programs, and 63.8 billion pounds (26 per cent) on local government programs. The remaining 4.3 billion pounds comprises support for nationalized industries and some accounting adjustments. Table 11.1 shows how the responsibilities for expenditure on the principal programs is split between tiers of government (the table excludes interest payments on debt). Note that the central government is wholly responsible for programs such as defense and overseas programs, and that the largest program managed outside central government is education, which accounts for 24.9 billion pounds (43 per cent) of total local expenditure.

The figures in Table 11.1 refer to the entire United Kingdom. However, Scotland, Wales and Northern Ireland each has a government department, responsible for developing policies and budgets for many public services in their respective countries. The total budgets for these territorial departments are determined by the national government within the context of the entire UK budget. The territorial departments then allocate their budgets to programs within their country. These administrative arrangements confuse discussion of public sector budgeting in the UK. In order to simplify the discussion, therefore, this chapter focuses on the budgeting process for England.

Financing

The national government has available the full panoply of taxes to fund its expenditures. Local government is funded from two principal sources: central government grants-in-aid; and local taxes. The form of local taxation is determined by the national Parliament. Until 1990, the local tax was a form of property tax, known as the rates, levied on both residential and business property. In 1990 this system was changed. Residential property taxes were replaced[3] by a community charge, or poll tax, levied at the same rate on all adults in a locality. The poll tax proved unsustainable,[4] and in 1993 it is in turn being replaced by a revised form of property tax, known as the council tax, which incorporates a 25 per cent discount for one-person households.[5]

The 1990 reforms also introduced a fundamental revision to business property taxation, which was changed from being a local tax to a national tax, levied at the same rate — determined by the national government — in all parts of the country. The tax is still collected by local authorities. The

Table 11.1 *United Kingdom public expenditure on programs 1992—93*

Program	Central govt. spending (£ millions)	Other public spending (£ millions)	Total public spending (£ millions)	Central as % of total (%)
Defense	22,753	0	22,853	100.0
Overseas services	3,031	0	3,031	100.0
Agriculture, fisheries and food	3,057	107	3,164	96.6
Trade, industry, energy, employmt	5,906	1,351	7,257	81.1
Transport	3,001	6,723	9,724	30.9
Housing	3,679	2,199	5,878	62.6
Environmental services	1,760	6,346	8,106	21.7
Law, order, public protection	5,001	7,876	12,877	38.8
Education & science	6,117	24,874	30,991	19.7
Arts & libraries	653	853	1,506	43.4
Health & social services	31,652	5,666	37,318	84.8
Social security	63,375	5,918	69,293	91.5
Miscellaneous	6,589	0	6,589	100.0
TOTAL	156,674	61,913	218,587	71.7

Source: UK Government (1992).

proceeds are however sent to the central government who then redistributes the tax to local authorities in proportion to their adult populations. Thus, to local government, the business property tax is indistinguishable from central government grants-in-aid, and for the rest of this chapter we use the term grants-in-aid to include receipts from business property taxes.

Grants-in-aid are of two sorts: conditional and unconditional. Conditional grants, known as specific grants, are matching grants, related to a local authority's expenditure on specific services. Unconditional grants are known as revenue support grants. They are intended to compensate for differences in resource base and expenditure needs between jurisdictions, and are described in more detail below. Revenue support grants are lump sum, and unrelated to chosen expenditure levels.

Local authorities are obliged to produce balanced budgets, such that revenues equal expenditures, and they are not allowed to borrow to fund current expenditure.[6] Until recently, they were free to choose any level of expenditure. However, throughout the 1980s the Conservative central government pursued a wide-ranging program designed to reduce the level of local government expenditure. Full details are given by Travers (1986). Measures introduced included revisions to the systems of grants-in-aid and the abolition in 1986 of seven strategic urban local authorities (including the Greater London Council). Crucially from a budgeting perspective, in 1985 the central government assumed the power to limit the tax rates (and therefore expenditure) of individual local authorities if it thought their expenditure was 'excessive'. Two arguments were put forward to justify this power. The first was the need, for macroeconomics reasons, to restrain local government expenditure. The second was to protect individual taxpayers in what the central government deemed to be high-spending local authorities. The power of tax limitation was used selectively in a handful of local authorities until 1991. In that year, in order to moderate the unpopularity of the poll tax, the central government announced a large increase in grants-in-aid after budgets had been set, and simultaneously imposed universal limitations on the expenditure of all local authorities in England for the next fiscal year.[7] In practice, therefore, the upper level of expenditure opportunities for most local authorities is now constrained by the national government.

Conclusion

From this thumbnail sketch of the UK administrative arrangements, it can be seen that the structure of UK government is strictly unitary.[8] There is no tier of state or regional government to act as a counterbalance to the central government. And, although local government is nominally responsible for a substantial proportion of public expenditure, its powers and expenditure levels are severely circumscribed by the central government. The budgeting arrangements within this context are now described in more detail, first for central government and then for local government. The chapter ends with some conclusions about the extent of centralization in UK public sector budgeting.

2 CENTRAL GOVERNMENT BUDGETING

The central government's budgeting system has been in place in its current form since 1963.[9] It is now known as the Public Expenditure Survey (PES), and is described in detail in a series of training booklets produced by the Cabinet Office and Her Majesty's Treasury (1989). The current PES is undertaken each year, the main stages being shown in Table 11.2. First, in March the Cabinet makes a preliminary judgement on what expenditure

Table 11.2 *The public expenditure survey (PES) process*

Cabinet decides on guidelines for spending	April
Departments submit bids to the Treasury	May
Cabinet considers bids and sets total expenditure	July
Treasury negotiations with departments	Summer
Resolutions of any disputes by 'Star Chamber'	October
Publication of Autumn Statement	November
Publication of detailed spending plans	February
Publication of detailed departmental plans	February
Announcement of sources of revenue	March
Start of financial year	April

Source: Cabinet Office and HM Treasury (1989).

can be afforded, within the framework of the national government's Medium-Term Financial Strategy. A baseline level of spending is determined for each government department, based on existing levels of spending. Departments then bid to the Treasury for resources additional to those implied in the baseline. On the basis of these bids, the government decides on a firm aggregate spending limit. The Treasury then negotiates with the departments to secure conformity to the limit. If this proves infeasible, a 'Star Chamber' of Cabinet ministers is convened to resolve differences. The result of the process is the Autumn Statement, issued in November, which contains the planning totals for each government department for the financial year starting the following April, and provisional totals for the two years thereafter. Individual departments then set their own budgets conforming to the totals agreed by the Cabinet. The detailed departmental expenditure plans are published in February.

In discussing UK governmental budgeting it is important to note the important impact of inflation. Until the late 1970s, budgets were prepared in what was known as volume terms. Levels of activity were planned, and costed at current prices. Any cost increases caused by inflation were funded, and had to be found from taxation or borrowing. This system ensured that planned programs could be carried out in their entirety, and that meaningful year-to-year comparisons of activity levels could be made. However, to a government whose principle objective was control, volume planning had a number of defects. It gave managers no incentive to respond to inflation by searching for cost reduction measures, such as changing suppliers or changing the mix of inputs. It also led to uncertainty about financing requirements. As Likierman (1988, p. 14) notes, 'the argument is between giving greater priority to control, or the fulfillment of expenditure plans irrespective of cost'.

Cash planning, in which budgets are developed in cash (nominal) terms and must be adhered to regardless of cost inflation, was introduced by a Labour government in 1976 at a time of considerable fiscal crisis. The system was also attractive to the first Thatcher government, elected in 1979, which saw control of public expenditure as a priority. As a result, cash planning has been used in central government ever since, and is now also used by many local authorities.

Central government financing arrangements are announced in March, just before the start of the financial year, in what is paradoxically called 'The Budget'! This rather theatrical parliamentary event is concerned principally with the determination of rates of taxation. The confusing nomenclature is a legacy from the days before the PES, when expenditure and financing decisions were announced simultaneously. Thus, budgeting and taxation decisions are now announced over four months apart, an arrangement unusual in the developed world.

There has for some time been widespread disquiet about the separation of budgetary and financing decisions. The Cabinet must make decisions about spending in the absence of any very clear information about its implications for taxation. Citizens and their parliamentary representatives are not presented with the trade-off between public expenditure and taxation and borrowing with any clarity, and therefore the arrangements do not promote the accountability of government. In addition, the system leads to some uncertainty about tax plans for the forthcoming year, and employers — who collect many income and payroll taxes — have only a short time to implement changes. As a result of these concerns, starting in December 1993, the budgeting and finance decisions will be announced simultaneously. The main disadvantage envisaged is that taxation decisions will have to be taken without the benefit of up-to-date forecasts of future economic circumstances. However, there appears to be a consensus that this potential cost is outweighed by the benefits of the change.

Another change to the PES, proposed but not implemented at the time of writing, is that the Cabinet should agree on the aggregate government expenditure limit at the start of the budgetary process. The government training booklet is at great pains to emphasize that 'the Government must first decide what can be afforded before making plans to spend it'.[10] The proposed arrangement would therefore institutionalize this philosophy, by committing the central government to fix an expenditure limit without reference to expenditure demands. Setting of program budgets would then become a zero sum game between government departments. Again, this development reinforces the central government's overriding concern with control, at the expense of its capacity to secure efficient allocations of resources.

3 LOCAL GOVERNMENT BUDGETING

The Budgeting Framework

Local government expenditure forms an integral part of the central government PES. Local government representatives are invited to provide forecasts of future aggregate expenditure in the local government sector and take part in a consultative process with the central government. In practice these detailed negotiations reveal fundamental disagreements between central and local government about the scope for efficiency savings and expenditure reductions, with the central government continually pressing for lower expenditure levels. However, as a result of the deliberations, and other more general considerations, the central government issues a consultative document in October. This contains detailed spending assumptions and central government assessments of the need to spend in each local government, as well as details of grants-in-aid criteria to be applied for limiting expenditure. After an opportunity for local government responses, the central government then issues its formal 'Revenue Support Grant Settlement' in January.

Thus, as well as defining the legal framework for local government activity, the central government has immense influence upon the financial context within which local authorities are budgeting. In particular, the central government:

1. Determines the scope of local government activity, by circumscribing the range of services it can deliver. It also prescribes the nature of the tax instrument available to local authorities.
2. Determines the aggregate level of grants-in-aid and business taxation to be distributed to local government.
3. Announces a 'needs assessment' for each local authority, which attempts to indicate the revenue costs of delivering a 'standard' level of spending. A complex formula of the central government's own devising is used for these purposes.
4. Distributes grants-in-aid to local authorities. Conditional (specific) grants are distributed on the basis of expenditure levels, while unconditional (revenue support) grants are distributed on the basis of the central government's needs assessments.
5. Determines, on the basis of a formula, the maximum amount of current expenditure that any local government might incur.
6. Similarly, on the basis of bids received, announces the maximum amount of capital expenditure that any local government might incur.
7. Prescribes a plethora of detailed conditions on local government activity.

These considerations are now discussed in turn.

Budgeting framework

With the exception of a small discretionary sum, the central government prescribes which services local government may undertake. The major activity is education, of which the principal component is compulsory schooling for children aged five to 16. Other important services are personal social services, refuse collection and disposal, transportation, housing and police and fire. With certain exceptions, local authorities are free to determine the balance of expenditure between competing services.

The local property tax (the rates) endured from 1601 until 1990. The poll tax, which replaced the residential rates under the Thatcher government's 1990 reforms, was disastrous,[11] and it in turn will be replaced in 1993 by a 'Council Tax'. This is a form of property tax with a 25 per cent discount for one-person households. From the point of view of the budgeting process, it is important to note that local authorities have no choice about the nature of the tax instrument, and that — even with equalizing grants-in-aid — the different taxes place local authorities under different degrees of fiscal pressure. Thus, for example, under the rates, areas with high-valued properties tended to have the highest tax bills for standard spending levels. Under the poll tax, all areas should levy the same tax if spending at needs assessment. The council tax tends to yield tax bills somewhere between these two extremes. In order to illustrate the profound effect of the chosen tax instrument, Table 11.3 gives the average tax bill per adult that would have arisen in 1991—92 using four different forms of local taxation: the poll tax; its predecessor, the rates (a simple property tax); a local income tax; and the new local tax, known as the Council Tax. It is assumed that national levels of central government grants-in-aid remain constant, so that the variations between the four methods arise solely because of different equalization principles used for distributing the grant, described in more detail below.

Aggregate grants-in-aid

The proportion of local government expenditure met by central government grants-in-aid is shown in Table 11.4. Note the steep decline throughout the 1980s. This was the result of a deliberate policy on the part of the central government to place more reliance on local taxation, and thereby exert downward pressure on expenditure levels. The dramatic increase in 1990 was a result of the nationalization of the business property tax, and the 1991 increase occurred when extra grants-in-aid was injected to reduce levels of the unpopular poll tax.

The aggregate level of grants-in-aid is set by the government on the basis of political judgement. The issues taken into account include the impact on individual local authorities' budgeting decisions and the consequence for local tax rates. Clearly the grants are funded from national taxes, and therefore their magnitude also has an important bearing on national tax rates. For example, the increase in grants in 1991 was funded by an increase in the national sales tax of 2.5 per cent.

Table 11.3 *Estimates of average tax bills per adult using different tax bases (in £)*

Region	Poll Tax	Property tax	Local income tax	Council tax
East Anglia	187	189	175	177
East Midlands	200	173	181	185
Greater London	179	239	208	224
North	237	155	188	207
North West	218	184	188	197
South East	172	226	239	189
South West	197	181	174	202
West Midlands	203	206	169	183
Yorkshire & Humberside	215	143	176	193
ENGLAND	197	197	197	197

Source: Smith (1992).

Table 11.4 *Government grants-in-aid and English local government expenditure*

Fiscal year	Total expenditure (£ millions)	Government grants (£ millions)	Grants as % of total
1981—82	19,933	10,939	54.88
1982—83	21,770	11,250	51.68
1983—84	23,005	11,528	50.11
1984—85	23,900	11,946	49.98
1985—86	24,039	11,785	49.02
1986—87	26,370	11,961	45.36
1987—88	28,704	12,744	44.40
1988—89	30,877	13,204	42.76
1989—90	31,656	13,575	42.88
1990—91	32,800	23,102	70.43
1991—92	39,000	30,880	79.18
1992—93	41,811	33,106	79.18

Source: Association of City Councils (various dates), *Revenue Support Grant, England.*

Needs assessments

Every year the central government determines a needs assessment for each local authority, intended to 'represent the amount of revenue expenditure which it would be appropriate for the authority to incur [in order] to provide a standard level of service'.[12] The methodology for determining the assessments is complex. First the central government determines an aggregate level of local government expenditure for the forthcoming year which it deems to be reasonable. This is then disaggregated into broad service categories, such as education and personal social services. Working groups for each category then determine a formula to distribute the service expenditure totals between local authorities. The results of their deliberations are then aggregated to give each local authority a total expenditure needs assessment.

The methods of distributing assessments between authorities vary from the crudely judgemental to the highly technical. Over 100 indicators of needs are used, including data relating to population characteristics, road lengths, fire risks and travel movements. The weights attached to each of these factors are derived either using 'expert' judgement (as in education) or regression analysis (personal social services). The needs assessments are usually announced in December.

An overview of the regional patterns of needs assessments and local expenditures is given in Table 11.5. As shown, there is some variation between the differences between needs assessment and expenditures per head. The lowest differences are for the Southeast region and Greater London with less than 1 per cent; the highest for the North region and Yorkshire & Humberside with 5.78 per cent and 4.90 per cent respectively.

Distribution of grants-in-aid

The bulk of grants-in-aid is the unconditional revenue support grant and is distributed on the basis of the needs assessments determined as above. The central government's intention is to fix grants so that — if a local authority spends at its needs assessment — it will be able to levy the national standard rate of local taxation, regardless of its local resource base. The grant therefore seeks to equalize simultaneously for differences in needs and differences in resources between localities. The national standard rate of taxation is determined by the aggregate level of grants-in-aid fixed as explained above. Once needs assessments have been determined, therefore, the grant allocation mechanism is automatic.

Expenditure limits

The maximum level of total expenditure which a local community can incur is now determined by the central government. The formulas for setting expenditure limits are complex and vary from year to year. For example, the rules in fiscal year 1991—92 were as follows:[13]

Table 11.5 *Regional patterns of expenditure in English local government, 1992—93*

Region	Needs assessment	Net total expenditure (per head)	Variation %	Expenditure per capita (£) Education	Social Services	Police	Fire	Highways	Refuse	Total Services
East Anglia	683.54	695.52	1.75	367.61	76.49	78.74	18.18	39.22	13.18	708.05
East Midlands	724.23	750.09	3.57	394.28	89.24	83.17	17.74	39.20	14.42	760.55
Greater London	1,084.67	1,091.13	0.59	436.95	172.46	221.18	34.96	37.00	24.16	1,159.09
North	783.55	828.81	5.78	408.21	100.98	99.70	26.68	50.90	16.93	849.07
North West	816.04	843.98	3.42	415.33	107.06	105.65	25.36	51.67	18.13	859.61
South East	709.68	711.86	0.31	356.86	81.48	80.66	20.00	39.04	16.30	721.63
South West	689.02	705.03	2.32	358.79	79.91	87.99	19.29	40.96	14.41	726.33
West Midlands	785.04	810.22	3.21	404.49	98.56	94.58	21.54	42.27	15.79	811.65
Yorkshire & Humberside	766.74	804.31	4.90	402.90	101.29	96.37	23.92	51.30	13.21	818.28
ENGLAND	794.12	813.05	2.38	393.11	103.27	103.27	23.51	43.03	16.85	833.37

Source: Unpublished 1992—93 budgets.

1. if budget is greater than needs assessment, it must not be more than nine per cent greater than the previous year's budget;
2. if budget is more than five per cent above needs assessment, it must not be more than seven per cent greater than the previous year's budget;
3. if budget is more than 10 per cent above needs assessment, it must not be more than five per cent greater than the previous year's budget;
4. no budget can be more than 12.5 per cent above needs assessment.

Note the importance of two variables: the level of expenditure in the previous year; and the level of the current year's needs assessment. The importance of these variables is common to the rules set in every year. Local authorities do have the right to challenge the expenditure limits, but few choose to do so in practice, as it exposes the finances of the authority to detailed scrutiny which can result in an even lower limit being set.

Capital expenditure limits

Capital expenditure in local government is tightly controlled by the central government. First the central government decides how much capital expenditure is to be allowed in the light of macroeconomic considerations. It invites bids for capital projects from local authorities. These are scrutinized by the central government, which then announces an allocation for each local authority such that the national total conforms to the cash limit previously determined. Local authorities usually finance the capital expenditure by issuing debt. The associated interest and principal payments then form part of the annual financing requirement.

The central government has adopted a very interventionist style towards the management of local government capital resources. For example, in 1980 it gave many tenants the right to buy the property they rented from their local authority, an opportunity taken up by many households. Thus local authorities were forced to divest themselves of considerable capital stock. In addition, they were precluded by the central government from spending all but a fraction of the receipts from such sales on new capital works. Most of the receipts are placed in bank accounts, the interest payments from which now form an important part of many local authorities' income.

Other central government rules

In managing its services, local government operates within very tight legal constraints set by the central government. Thus, for example, in education a national inspectorate monitors standards of schooling, and a detailed national curriculum was put in place during the 1980s, where before local schools had considerable discretion over what might be taught. Furthermore, a system of devolved budgeting has been introduced, whereby each local authority must devise a formula with which to distribute its education budget to individual schools. The spending of a school's budget is then the responsibility of the school's board of governors, which are appointed and not elected. Indeed, individual schools can apply to 'opt out' of local authority control, and instead receive their budget directly from the central government, thereby severing all links with the local authority. At the time of writing, this option had not been pursued by many schools. However, there is a clear incentive for a school threatened with closure by its local authority to apply to opt out. The possibility of this outcome makes it difficult for local authorities to plan the overall configuration of their school system and thereby secure control of their education budget.

Equally detailed regulations exist in many other services. For example, in police, standards are monitored by a national organization, and manpower levels are controlled by the central government. In a number of expenditure categories, such as leisure, street cleaning and refuse collection, services must be put out to competitive tender. Housing rents are controlled by the central government and cannot be subsidized by local taxpayers. The level of fire service provision is closely controlled by the central government. And a whole system of standards and regulations exists for many other services.

Analysis

The discussion above indicates that the budgeting process in local authorities is profoundly affected by central government policy, which exerts two conflicting pressures. First, the system of standards and regulations tends to put upward pressure on expenditure; and second the system of finance tends to place downward pressure on expenditure. Clearly the second consideration has been uppermost in the minds of successive central governments since 1979. However, it is important to retain sight of the interest of the center in standards.

The fiscal incentives on a local authority can be explored by examining its budget constraint. Suppose that the needs assessment in locality i is given by NA_i, and the central government decides the national standard rate of taxation is at this standard level r^*. Then, when spending at NA_i, jurisdiction i should be able to levy a tax rate of r^*. The remaining financing requirement must be made up by central government grants-in-aid, G. So, that if the resource base in locality i is RB_i, spending must equal revenues. That is,

$$NA_i = r^*RB_i + G_i \quad (11.1)$$

or rearranging

$$G_i = NA_i - r^*RB_i.$$

If spending varies from needs assessment, then the entire difference falls on residential taxpayers, in the form of the local tax rate r. Thus the complete budget constraint is given by

Figure 11.1 The local government budget constraint

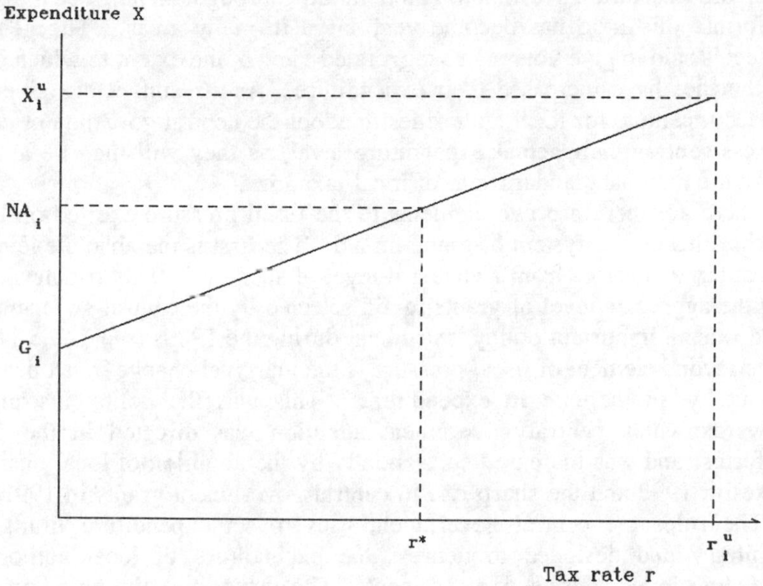

$$X_i = G_i + r_iRB_i \tag{11.2}$$

where X_i is actual expenditure and r_i actual tax rate in jurisdiction i. The budget constraint is truncated by the central government expenditure limit at a level X_i^u, which implies an upper limit to local taxation of r_i^u. Budget constraint and expenditure and tax limits are shown in Figure 11.1.

Notice that the entire burden of spending in excess of needs assessment is borne by the residential taxpayer. Thus, for a given expenditure increase ΔX in jurisdiction i, the required tax increase will be Δr_iRB_i. Equating these two gives

$$\Delta r_i = \Delta X/RB_i \tag{11.3}$$

Thus, areas with relatively low tax bases RB will require a relatively high increase in tax rate.

In the UK local authority community, much attention has been focused on the 'gearing' effect of central government grants-in-aid. The gearing ratio is defined as the percentage increase in local taxes required to finance a one per cent increase in expenditure. Algebraically, the percentage increase ΔT in local residential tax T brought about by an increase in expenditure ΔX is given by

$$\Delta T/T = \Delta X/T = \Delta X/(X—G) \tag{11.4}$$

Thus the smaller is [X—G], the larger is the percentage increase in T required to fund a given expenditure increase. Because of the substantial increase in central government grants-in-aid G brought about since the 1990 reforms, this ratio has become very large in many areas. The gearing effect is said to give voters an exaggerated view of the extent to which local authorities have increased their expenditure. As a result, it has given an added incentive for local authorities to adopt the central government needs assessment as their actual expenditure level, as they will then be able to levy the national standard rate of local taxation.

There are therefore two elements to the fiscal pressure exerted on local authorities by the system of grants-in-aid. The first is the absolute level of local tax that arises from a standard level of spending. This is determined by the aggregate level of grants-in-aid selected by the central government, and was an important policy instrument during the 1980s (see Table 11.3). The second element of fiscal pressure is the marginal change in tax brought about by an increase in expenditure. This was the policy instrument towards which central government attention was directed in the 1990 reforms, and was increased substantially by the abolition of local business taxes in 1990 and the sharp rise in central government grants in 1991.

The rules the central government uses to set expenditure limits are arbitrary and designed to depress the expenditure of local authorities spending above their needs assessments. The expenditure limitation process has two effects. First, it perforce brings down the expenditure of certain jurisdictions with expenditure well in excess of their needs assessments. However, it also introduces a perverse incentive amongst other local authorities to *increase* expenditure as much as possible. This is because with any conceivable set of limitation rules, future spending limits are likely to be highly dependent on past spending records, and so a local government wishing to avoid severe limits is well advised to keep current expenditure high. These perverse dynamic incentives are described in detail elsewhere[14] (Smith, 1989), and may explain at least in part why local government expenditure continues to grow in real terms.

Empirical Evidence

In spite of the measures described above, local government expenditure has continued to grow in real terms. Table 11.6 shows recent real term trends, and confirms the resilience of local authority budgets to the pressures to which they have been subjected. The first column shows estimates of current expenditure in cash terms, adjusted for the major changes in local government responsibilities that occurred over the 14 year period. The next column presents the figures in real terms, using the GDP deflator, and the final column shows the implied real year on year change in expenditure. The picture is of steady growth, with only one year (1985/86) showing a real reduction in expenditure. Indeed, the trend appears to have been an accelaration of growth in recent years, notwithstanding the increasingly

Table 11.6 *Real growth in local government current expenditure*

Year	Expenditure (£ millions)	Index (real terms)	Real Growth (%)
1979—80	13,605	100.00	
1980—81	16,443	101.97	1.97
1081—82	18,319	103.19	1.20
1982—83	19,975	105.12	1.87
1983—84	21,241	105.81	0.66
1984—85	22,647	107.11	1.23
1985—86	23,598	105.80	—1.22
1986—87	25,567	111.62	5.50
1987—88	27,863	115.78	3.73
1988—89	29,980	116.99	1.04
1989—90	33,226	120.73	3.19
1990—91	36,999	123.71	2.47
1991—92	41,363	129.60	4.76
1992—93	44,425	133.24	2.80

Source: Travers (1992).

stringent expenditure controls placed on local government.

A number of studies have been undertaken of the response of individual local authorities to the pressures outline above. Elcock and Jordan (1987) report the results of a series of case studies in selected local authorities, and find that the predominant approach is overwhelmingly incremental. The researchers identify a wide variety of game-playing activity by budget holders to maintain their levels of activity, and find that programs remain remarkably intact, even in times of high fiscal stress. Their conclusion is that there have been few fundamental reappraisals of budgetary practice, and little evidence of a move towards more 'rational' budgeting.

Barnett, Levaggi and Smith (1991a, 1992) explore budgeting choices by fitting standard models of household behavior to the expenditure-tax trade-off illustrated in Figure 11.1. They conclude that an incremental model, in which the arguments in the local authority utility function are changes in expenditure and change in taxes, is a better description of practice than the static model, in which the arguments are simply expenditure and taxes. Moreover, in further work, they find some evidence to suggest that the conventional model of household behavior may not be appropriate (Barnett, Levaggi and Smith, 1991b). They show that it may be the absolute level of grant support — and not the marginal cost to local taxpayers — that may be the most important determinant of expenditure choices, offering support for the 'flypaper' theory of grants-in-aid.

4 CONCLUSIONS

Budgeting is a highly developed, ritualistic activity in the UK public sector. The central government budgeting system is designed principally to secure control of expenditure rather than an efficient allocation of resources[15] (Thain and Wright, 1992b). The central government's search for control has led it to impose considerable constraints on the activities of local government. The rationale given by successive Conservative central governments for such control has been that local authorities are unaccountable bureaucracies, frustrating the preferences of citizens.

Thus, for example, the fundamental argument advanced by the central government for the introduction of the poll tax was that the property tax led to inefficient expenditure choices in local government because some marginal expenditure was borne by the (non-voting) business sector, and many adults (those not heads of households) did not pay the tax. As a result, it was argued, many citizens did not recognize the costs of their voting choices. By way of contrast, throwing the entire burden of marginal expenditure onto the local electorate, and ensuring that all voters would bear some of the marginal cost, the poll tax would lead citizens to vote for allocatively efficient levels of services. Expenditure control over local government would then be unnecessary. This argument was, of course, not borne out by events, and paradoxically the new tax led to even tougher expenditure control by the central government than had been endured before the reforms.

Similarly, the argument for the devolution of school budgets was based on the premise that local authorities were insensitive to the needs of localities, and that the school boards — although not directly accountable to local citizens — would handle school affairs more efficiently than local authorities. The rhetoric used by the central government was that of empowering parents. However, the reality appears to be different. Many localities are finding it increasingly difficult to recruit school governors, and there is evidence that some schools lack the managerial expertise to fulfil their new obligations. It is difficult to argue with the assertion that the real effect of the education reforms has been not an empowerment of parents but an enfeeblement of local government. The control of the central government over the service is now considerable, and the English education sector is becoming a national government service, albeit locally administered.

Reforms in the housing sector have led to a different sort of incapacity on the part of local government. The central government control of rent levels, and the right of tenants to buy their houses — and the refusal of the central government to allow local authorities to spend the proceeds — mean that local authorities have very little control over their housing services, and budgeting becomes an almost automatic process determined by central decree. Here the central government rhetoric is of the virtues of home ownership, and the need to allow markets to function without distortion. In practice, the outcome has been acute housing shortages in some areas, a problem which local authorities are powerless to address.

The events of recent years therefore suggest that there is a very strong centralizing instinct within UK political institutions that militates against devolution of power from the central government. In seeking an explanation, Johnson (1983) suggests four possible institutional reasons. First, as more central controls are imposed, so the caliber of local politicians declines, leading to a weak local government. This reinforces the instinct for even more central control. Second, the lack of variety in sources of finance places sometimes intolerable pressures on the local tax instrument. Third, there is a strong bias in British legal practice in favor of central authority. And fourth, the management of the economy is an important issue in UK politics, and the political imperative of being seen to be in control often overrides considerations of local freedom.

There is no evidence to suggest that the centralizing tendencies of British political institutions have led to increased efficiency in either the managerial or allocative sense. Indeed, there is considerable anecdotal evidence that local preferences are not being met by the reformed public sector. The fundamental argument for local government is that it is able to respond more sensitively to local preferences than any central authority. The UK Government's wish to secure control of the macroeconomy appears to be at the expense of such sensitivity, and has for many local authorities made the budgeting process an annual crisis. The policy severely compromises the future of UK local democracy and the ability of the public sector to respond to local needs.

NOTES

1. Local government in Northern Ireland is very weak, with only a small number of responsibilities and very low expenditure.
2. UK Government (1992).
3. Except in Northern Ireland, which retained the rates.
4. Smith (1991).
5. UK Government (1991b).
6. Subject to central government approval, they may borrow to fund capital expenditure.
7. The situation in the other three countries of the UK has varied from year to year.
8. Foster *et al.* (1981).
9. Thain and Wright (1992a).
10. Cabinet Office and HM Treasury (1988), p. 45.
11. Smith (1991).
12. UK Government (1991a).
13. Note that local government cost inflation at this time was approximately 8.3 per cent.
14. Smith (1989).
15. Thain and Wright (1992b).

REFERENCES

Association of County Councils (various dates) *Revenue Support Grant, England*, London; Association of County Councils.

Barnett, R. R., Levaggi, R. and Smith, P. (1991a), 'An Incremental Budgeting Model of Local Public Expenditure Setting in the Presence of Piecewise Linear Budget Constraints', *Applied Economics*, **23**, pp. 949—56.

Barnett, R. R., Levaggi, R. and Smith, P. (1991b), 'Does the Flypaper Model Stick? A Test of the Relative Performance of the Flypaper and Conventional Models of Local Government Budgetary Behaviour', *Public Choice*, **69**, pp. 1—18.

Barnett, R. R., Levaggi, R. and Smith, P. (1992), 'Local Authority Expenditure Decisions: a Maximum Likelihood Analysis of Budget Setting in the Face of Piecewise Linear Budget Constraints', *Oxford Economic Papers*, **44**(1), pp. 113—34.

Cabinet Office and Her Majesty's Treasury (1989), *Public Expenditure Management*, London, HMSO.

Elcock, H. and Jordan, G. (1987), *Learning from Local Authority Budgeting*, Aldershot, Avebury.

Foster, C. D., Jackman, R. and Perlman, M. (1981), *Local Government Finance in a Unitary State*, London, Allen & Unwin.

Johnson, N. (1983), 'Decentralisation in Britain: a Critique of the Case in the Light of the West German Experience', *Environment and Planning C: Government and Policy*, **1**, pp. 5—16.

Likierman, A. (1988), *Public Expenditure: the Public Spending Process*, London, Penguin Press.

Smith, P. (1989), 'Dynamic Aspects of Local Authority Expenditure Decisions', *Financial Accountability and Management*, **5**, pp. 1—18.

Smith, P. (1991), 'Lessons from the British Poll Tax Disaster', *National Tax Journal*, **44**, pp. 421—36.

Smith, P. (1992), *In Place of the Poll Tax*, London, Chartered Association of Certified Accountants.

Thain, C. and Wright, M. (1992a), 'Planning and Controlling Public Expenditure in the UK, Part I: The Treasury's Public Expenditure', *Public Administration*, **70**(1), pp. 3—24.

Thain, C. and Wright, M. (1992b), 'Planning and Controlling Public Expenditure in the UK, Part II: The Effects and Effectiveness of the Survey', *Public Administration*, **70**(1), pp. 193—224.

Travers, T. (1986), *The Politics of Local Government Finance*, London, Allen & Unwin.

Travers, T. (1992), 'Caps Push Up Spending', *Local Government Chronicle*, 31 July 1992, p. 13.

UK Government (1991a), *The Revenue Support Grant Report (England) 1991/1992*, London, HMSO.

UK Government (1991b), *A New Tax for Local Government*, London, Department of the Environment.

UK Government (1992), *Public Expenditure Analyses to 1994—1995: Statistical Supplement to the 1991 Autumn Statement*, Cmnd 1920, London: HMSO.

12. Centralized Versus Decentralized Provision and the Size of Government

with Ronald Shadbegian

1 INTRODUCTION

By conventional budget and income measures, the government's share of national income has increased in all countries of Western Europe and North America over the last century.[1] This finding is documented in numerous studies including, Tarschys (1975), Beck (1976), Borcherding (1977, 1985), Nutter (1978), Peacock and Wiseman (1961, 1979), Peltzman (1980), Ott (1980, 1983), Becker (1985), Lindbeck (1985), Musgrave (1985), and Aronson and Ott (1991).

Why should the rise in public budgets be a matter deserving of explanations? Secondly, how relevant is fiscal structure to the size of government? Discussion in this chapter addresses these two questions. The chapter begins with a brief survey of the major theories explaining the growth of government. In the next section, findings on the expanding size of the public sector are given. In the last section, the fiscal decentralization hypothesis, as a means for constraining the size of the government, is examined.

2 THE GROWTH IN PUBLIC SECTOR BUDGETS

Economists, political scientists, and philosophers hold diverse views about the role government should play in the economy. Some like Nozick (1974) believe that the government has only three legitimate roles: 1. to provide protection against foreign invasion; 2. to protect and enforce property rights; and 3. to supply those goods which the profit motive will not provide. This is the so-called minimal state of government. Others, notably Buchanan and Tullock (1962), go one step beyond Nozick's idea of the role of government, by advocating the notion that the government should be allowed to carry out any 'unanimously' approved program. 'Unanimity' is feasible when programs benefit everyone — everyone in the economy is made better off in the process. Bentham (1800s) and Rawls

(1972) do not ascribe to this somewhat limited view of the government. Bentham believes that the objective of government taxing and spending programs should be the maximization of the sum of all individuals' utility. Rawls, on the other hand, would rather the government maximize the utility of the worst-off individual.

No matter what one believes the proper role of government to be, public sector budgets have been expanding greatly. Cross-national data comparisons establish a common trend among the industrialized countries in the West — that of the growth of public sector budgets. Whether the growth is measured by changes in the ratio of expenditures or the ratio of receipts to national income, the data show that the share of the public economy relative to the private economy has been on the rise. Not everyone agrees with these conventional measures. It is often argued that the extent of public sector activities is not fully reflected in the public budget. For example, many government activities such as regulation affect businesses and consumers through court decisions affecting property rights. To the extent that governments assume different roles in different nations, the use of public budgets in cross-nation comparisons may be misleading. Measurement problems aside, the fact remains that the public sector in most countries has been expanding in size ever since the turn of the century.[2]

3 EXPLAINING THE GROWTH OF GOVERNMENT

While explaining the growth of government may be viewed as a purely intellectual exercise, the interest in this phenomenon goes beyond intellectual curiosity; it reflects the concern over both the public sector's rate of absorption of national resources, and the expanding role of government in democratic societies.

Rationale for Public Sector Growth

Over time, one would expect the size of the budget (everyone's budget) to rise in nominal magnitude to reflect the trend in prices. If the prices of the public sector basket of goods and services were to rise faster than the prices facing business and consumers, then the nominal level of spending of the public sector, absolutely and relatively to nominal national income, will rise. Differential prices or costs of public and private sector goods may reflect differences in productivity growth in the two sectors. This is the thesis of unbalanced growth which was advanced by Baumol (1967).

The basic tenet of the thesis of unbalanced growth is that economic progress, defined as the growth of output per man hour, in the public sector lags behind that of the private sector. Over time, this slow-productivity sector will experience higher per unit costs than the progressive, higher productivity sector. Since the demand for goods and services depends on relative prices and income, the expectation is that continuously rising prices in the public sector relative to those in the private sector will reduce the demand for public goods. This outcome will not be forthcoming, if the demand for public sector goods is very price inelastic, and/or when the income elasticity of demand for the public sector goods is high. The presumption that the demand for public sector goods is characterized by both low price elasticity and high-income elasticity provides a rationale for the growth of public budgets over time.

Private Demand for Social Goods

Public sector budget trends reflect the changing role of governments in society. In democratic nations, the functions assigned to governments are for the most part the outcome of the political process, where the preferences of the citizenry are expressed in voting for their representatives. Early in the history of nations, the role assigned to government was quite limited. This limited minimal state role, over time, was expanded to accommodate societal needs associated with economic development.

Wagner was the first person to note the tendency for the government budget to rise with the growth in income. Since then, students of public finance have explored the relationship between economic development, industrialization and urbanization and the trend toward a larger public sector budget.[3] According to these studies, economic development has created, in addition to public goods provision, a demand by the citizens or groups of citizens for new types of government services — the 'inter-temporal' redistribution of societal incomes.[4]

According to Lindbeck (1985), the government was asked to act 'as a mixed credit institute and insurance company by establishing publicly provided and financed old age pensions and sickness, disability and unemployment funds'. Further expansion in the role of government followed with the call for vertical distribution of income — from the top down, as well as horizontally — across groups of the population. In short, the government role has evolved over time, from the role ascribed to it in the minimal state, to one where the government is called upon to provide non-collective private goods and for guaranteeing specified levels of such goods to particular households. Lindbeck explains this shift by three factors: urbanization and the general spread of franchise increased the demand for public insurance; the changing character of the median voter; and the evolution of an extremely diversified socioeconomic structure.

A model which hypothesizes that public sector growth reflects the citizens' preference for public goods may be represented by an equation of the form:[5]

$$G = A\, P^{\eta}\, Y^{\epsilon}\, \delta^{\rho} \qquad (12.1)$$

where G is the amount of the good demanded by the voter-taxpayer, P is the price for the good G, Y is income and δ represents a number of political shift variables. The exponents η and ϵ denote respectively the demand price elasticity and the income elasticity of demand, and ρ represents a vector of socio-political elasticity of demand for the public good. The model described by equation (12.1) is rewritten for the purpose of empirical testing for which a statistical measure of G and P has to be found as neither are observable magnitudes. In the empirical literature, G is defined as per capita public spending ($G = E/N^{\alpha}$, α is the degree of publicness), while P is approximated by the taxpayers' share in the cost of the good ($P = t/PN^{\alpha}$). A useful form of equation (12.1) is given by Borcherding (1985). In log form:

$$g = (n + 1)p + (\epsilon - 1)y + [\alpha\eta + (\alpha - 1)]n + \eta t + \epsilon k + \rho\delta \quad (12.2)$$

The terms g, p, y, n, t, k, and δ refer to growth rates of the variables. The contribution of the income, price, and socio-political variables to the growth of government is captured by the coefficients.

Suppose that as income rises by say 10 per cent, the quantity demanded of public goods increases by 20 per cent, i.e. $\epsilon > 1$. The process of income growth itself would increase the share of national income absorbed by the public sector. Similarly, a fall in the individual tax share raises the demand for public services. Borcherding (1985) uses U.S. data for the period 1902—82 and demand elasticities reported in the literature to estimate the growth of public spending (g) as defined by equation (12.2). Comparing the estimated value of g with the actual growth rate over the period, he finds the model capable of explaining some 40 per cent of the actual growth rate of the public sector. The finding, according to Borcherding, clearly suggests that other things besides income, prices, and the population are behind the 'unexplained' portion of the growth rate.

Group Interests and Bureaucratic Incentives

The public choice literature offers many insights into the causes of government growth. According to this literature, the size of the public sector budget may be viewed as the outcome of the political process. Through the interactions of two sets of agents — consumer/voters who wish to maximize their own self-interest and bureaucrats, whose objective is the maximization of their political power — the level of the budget is set.

This interaction and hence the outcome is explored by different models. Stigler (1970), Peltzman (1980), and Becker (1985) offer hypotheses linking the growth of government in the twentieth century to special interest groups. Government growth is a consequence of 'rent-seeking' individuals attempting to use the political system to redistribute national income in their own favor. Although these models differ in the description of the 'process' through which the 'pressure' is applied, or which voters (rent-seekers) are responsible for the outcome, the models are unanimous in attributing the growth of government to its distributive role. Indeed, when viewing government expenditures as pure transfers from one group of the population to another under a majority rule, a 'politically dominant' redistributive strategy will ensue. This strategy will be the one that maximizes the benefits to the greatest number. According to Peltzman, there are a large number of potential public servants (politicians), and thus competition between them (for votes) will ensure that the actual policy undertaken by the government will be the politically dominant policy. Bureaucratic incentive to redistribute will determine the size of the public sector. But, why is the politically dominant strategy not the one which would equalize all the income in the economy? The reason is that the poor and the rich also meet in the labor market. In other words, the rich employ the poor. As the poor vote to tax the rich more, the rich lose some incentive to produce. If the rich decide to produce less, they would need to hire less 'poor' agents. This in turn lowers the amount of income the poor earn in the form of wages. So eventually, increases in taxes on the rich to subsidize the poor will come to the point where increases in subsidies to the poor will be more than offset by decreases in their wage income. As total income (wages plus transfers) begins to fall with each additional increase in taxes, the poor will stop voting for tax increases on the rich.

In addition to the distribution of income from the rich to the poor, Peltzman cites another distribution — between groups which affect the size of government. These two types of distributions impact on the size of government, each pulling it to a different direction. Peltzman suggests that as the income distribution of the poor becomes more equal, there is pressure for the size of government, as measured by the level of transfers, to grow. On the other hand, as incomes between poor and rich become more equal there is less pressure for it to grow.

Another model of group interest is that of bureaucrats. The effect of bureaucracy on its 'own' growth is best illustrated by Niskanen (1971, 1975). Bureaucrats, like any special interest group, behave to maximize their utility or self-interest. Maximizing self-interest is synonymous with maximization of the size of the public sector because of the 'power and prestige' that a powerful government bestows.[6] Bureaucrats' attempts to influence budget choices are posited by Mackay and Weaver (1978, 1979), Romer and Rosenthal (1978, 1980) and Fiorina and Noll (1978). In a representative democracy, bureaucrats and not voters control the public sector's agenda. Alternative mixes of expenditures and taxes are offered until the budget most preferred by the bureaucracy is chosen. Although the empirical evidence in support of this thesis is not sufficiently strong, one need only look at the U.S. experience with budget deficits in the past decade or so to realize how much the budget outcome is influenced by special interest groups.

The battle over the federal budget that is waged annually between the executive and legislative branches of the U.S. government is indicative of bureaucratic control of the agenda. Neither side has been willing to reduce the deficit, for to do this would mean resisting pressures from interest groups, and that in turn may not be in the best interest of politicians.

The Fiscal Decentralization Hypothesis

Buchanan (1975) advanced the proposition that a systematic bias exists in the fiscal system leading to an 'overexpansion' in public sector budgets. The reason such a bias prevails is to be found in the political process where in a system of majority voting, logrolling may lead to an over-sized public sector.[7]

Brennan and Buchanan (1977, 1978, 1980) expound this bias by assuming that the post-constitutional budgetary decisions do not conform to the desires of the median voter, but to those of a revenue-maximizing monolithic government ('Leviathan'). They note that this view is in 'apparent consistency with a large, rapidly growing and uncontrollable public sector'.[8] Since tax institutions are normally intended to be reasonably permanent features of a political framework within which post-constitutional budgetary decisions about the provision of public goods are made, Brennan and Buchanan ask the question: What constraints should rational voters, at the constitutional level, place on the government to ensure the provision of the desired level of public goods? In other words, after the government receives the power to raise revenues (tax), its goal will be to try and maximize those revenues and provide as few public goods as possible. Therefore, what constitutionally-derived constraints could be placed on the 'Leviathan' to ensure that, within some reasonable limits, an efficient level of public goods is provided?

One way to effectively limit the ability of the government to raise excess revenues and to provide at least some minimum level of desired public goods would be to allow the government to tax only those goods which are complements of the public goods it provides. Thus, if the government wants to raise any revenue at all, then it will have to provide at least some amount of public goods to entice people to consume those goods which it is allowed, by the constitution, to tax.

Second, and probably more feasible, would be for citizens to vote to have increased fiscal decentralization. In other words, to have a large number of small governmental units providing public goods. If this were the case, then Brennan and Buchanan contend that competition between these units and 'interjurisdictional mobility' of persons in pursuit of 'fiscal gain' can offer partial or possibly complete substitutes for explicit fiscal constraints on the taxing power.[9] In other words, they contend that if the federal government is forced to grant more power over the provision of public goods to state and local governments, then this will provide an effective constraint on the power of 'Leviathan' to extract resources from the private sector. There are two reasons for this contention. First, when decisions on the provision of public goods are made at a more local level, it will be easier for citizens to watchdog the government and thereby force a more efficient level of public good provision. Second, if the government tries to extract more resources and provide more public goods than its citizens prefer, they will be able to move to another jurisdiction which provides a more acceptable level of public good provision. Thus, Brennan and Buchanan believe fiscal decentralization will lead to a slow decrease in the growth of the public sector.

4 DECENTRALIZATION AND THE SIZE OF GOVERNMENT

Does fiscal decentralization act as a constraining force on the size of the public sector? In other words, does competition between governments, other things being equal, lead to a smaller public sector? If the answer is yes, then we would conclude that Brennan and Buchanan's decentralization hypothesis is the correct model of the public sector. The following section provides a brief review of the empirical literature on the decentralization hypothesis.

Empirical Studies of the Decentralization Hypothesis

Those who have examined the decentralization hypothesis include Oates (1972, 1985), Nelson (1987), Eberts and Gronberg (1988), Marlow (1988), Forbes and Zampelli (1989), Zax (1989), and Joulfaian and Marlow (1990). The results of these empirical studies are quite mixed due in part to the different ways the researchers defined the size of government and the proxy they employed to measure decentralization (competition between governments).

Wallace Oates (1972), using a cross-sectional sample of 58 countries, was the first researcher to test empirically the decentralization hypothesis. In contradiction to the decentralization hypothesis, Oates found a negative (but insignificant) relationship between his measure of the size of the public sector (total tax revenues as a fraction of national income) and his measure of centralization (central government tax revenues as a fraction of total tax revenues). Due to increased interest in the decentralization hypothesis, Oates (1985) again conducted a study to confirm the existence of Brennan and Buchanan's Leviathan. This time Oates used two different sets of data: one set consisted of data on the state and local governments of the 48 contiguous states in the United States, and the second (world sample) consisted of data on 43 different countries.[10] In this study, Oates also employed a different measure of the size of government and three different indices of decentralization. The measure of the size of government was the aggregate state-local tax receipts (and expenditures) as a fraction of personal income for the United States sample. The corresponding size of government measure for the world sample is total tax revenues (and expenditures) as a fraction of GDP. The first two measures of decentralization for the United States sample are: 1. state share of state and local revenues and, 2. state share of state and local expenditures. For the world sample they are correspondingly, the fraction of total tax revenues going to the central government and the fraction of total expenditures attributable to the central government. The third measure is the absolute number of local government units in the state[11] and is implied by Brennan and Buchanan's remark that 'the potential for fiscal exploitation varies inversely with the number of competing governmental units in the inclusive territory'.[12] Oates' new findings fail to discover the existence of a strong systematic relationship between the size of the government and the degree of fiscal centralization of the public sector, thus, once again, providing empirical evidence against the decentralization hypothesis of Brennan and Buchanan.[13]

Nelson (1987) takes exception to these findings. He points out that Oates' measure of competition, the absolute number of local governments in a state, assumes that each type of local governmental unit within a state has an 'analogous' influence on the size of the public sector. Nelson notes that this may not necessarily be true given that the range of government powers has a great variance at the local level.[14] Therefore, Nelson divides the number of local governmental units into two types: 1. general-purpose governments and 2. single-function governments. General-purpose governments are defined as local governments which provide a range of services (e.g. police and fire protection, sanitation, etc.). Single-purpose governments are defined to include all other types of local government units (i.e. special districts and school districts). Since the decentralization hypothesis is based on the mobility of citizens, it seems most relevant for general-purpose local governments in which the value from moving may be more significant than for single-purpose governments. Nelson employs two measures of the size of the state-local sector to see if the type (general-purpose or single-purpose) and the number of local government units has any effect on the size of the public sector: the first measure is the ratio of state and local taxes to personal income; the second is given by the ratio of state and local adjusted expenditures to personal income.[15] The second measure attempts to control for variations among states in the division of responsibilities between state and local governments that could influence the size of the state-local public sector. Nelson finds that the larger the number of general-purpose governments in a state the smaller are both his measures of the public sector. Thus, his results tend to lend support to the decentralization hypothesis. Eberts and Gronberg (1988) conduct nearly the same experiment as Nelson (1987),[16] the only major difference is that they test the decentralization hypothesis at the SMSA (Standard Metropolitan Statistical Area) level. Their results are essentially the same as those of Nelson in that they find that the greater the number of general-purpose governments, the smaller is the size of the local public sector.

Marlow (1988) tests the decentralization hypothesis using time series analysis. Marlow constructed a data set on federal and state and local levels of U.S. government over the years 1946—85. The size of the public sector is taken to be total government spending (federal plus non-federal) as a fraction of GNP. The decentralization measure employed is the ratio of state and local expenditures to total government expenditures. Controlling for income and population, Marlow finds an inverse relationship between his decentralization measure and the size of the public sector. Thus, Marlow concludes that fiscal decentralization appears to be a viable means of lowering or controlling the extent of resource extraction of the government sector.

Forbes and Zampelli (1989) test the decentralization hypothesis at the SMSA level, and their conclusions agree with Oates that there is no evidence supporting the decentralization hypothesis. Indeed, their results directly contradict the decentralization hypothesis in that they find that the greater the number of competing government units there are in an SMSA (this measure only includes the number of county governments), the larger is their measure of the size of the public sector (share of county taxes per capita).

Zax's (1989) study examines the effect of intra-county competition on the size of the county fisc. His measure of the size of government, accordingly, is the aggregated budget of all local governments within the county as a fraction of county income. Zax finds that his measure of centralism (county share of local tax revenue) is positively related to the size of the county government, and his measure of fragmentation (number of general-purpose governments) is negatively related to the size of the county government. His results support the decentralization hypothesis.

Joulfaian and Marlow (1990) note that all cross-sectional studies of the decentralization hypothesis exclude the federal sector. However, Brennan and Buchanan's view, 'Total government intrusion into the economy should be smaller, *ceteris paribus*, the greater the extent to which taxes and expenditures are decentralized'[17] implies that the federal sector should be included. Thus, in their cross-sectional study they include disaggregated federal spending on a state-by-state basis. In stark contrast to most but not all cross-sectional empirical studies, their findings suggest that the size of the public sector is inversely related to the level of decentralization. In sum, there is a wide range of evidence about the Leviathan hypothesis. Table 12.1 provides a guide to these contradictory findings.

Table 12.1 *The decentralization hypothesis: a guide to the empirical literature*

Author	Size of Government	Centralization	Sample	Time	Finding
Oates (1972)	1. TR/NI	1. CENTR/TR	58 Countries	1972	No
Oates (1985)	1. TR/PI and TE/PI	1. STR/SLTR 2. STE/SLE 3. AGOVTS	48 States (Excl. Alaska and Hawaii)	1977	No
	2. TR/GDP and TE/GDP	1. CENTR/TR 2. CENTR/TE	43 IMF Countries	1982	No
Nelson (1987)	1. SLTR/PI 2. SLTE/PI [a]	1. GPGOVTS 2. SPGOVTS	50 States	1978	Yes
Marlow (1988)	1. TE/GNP	1. SLE/TE	U.S.	1946—85	Yes
Eberts and Gronberg (1988)	1. SLTE/PI [b]	1. GPGOVTS 2. SPGOVTS	280 SMSAs	1977	Yes
Forbes and Zampelli (1989)	1. CNTYTR/POP 2. CNTYTR/PI	1. NCNTY	157 SMSAs	1977	No
Zax (1989)	1. CNTYSR/PI	1. GPGOVTS 2. SPGOVTS 3. CNTYTR/TR	3022 Counties	1982	Yes
Joulfaian & M. (1990)	1. TE/GSP	1. SLE/TE [c]	50 States	1984	Yes

Table 12.1 continued

Notes:

a: This measure includes expenditure on local schools, public welfare, fire protection, sanitation and local parks.
b: This measure is the same as Nelson (1987) except it also includes spending on police protection.
c: SLE includes federal government expenditures disaggregated by state.

AGOVTS = Total number of governmental units in the state
CENTR = Central government revenue
CI = County Income
CNTYSR = County government share of total local revenue
CNTYTE = County government expenditures
CNTYTR = County government revenue
GDP = Gross Domestic Product
GNP = Gross National Product
GPGOVTS = Total number of general purpose governments
GSP = Gross State Product
NCNTY = Total number of county governments in the SMSA
NI = National Income
PI = Personal Income
SLTE = State and Local government expenditure
SLTR = State and Local government revenue
SPGOVTS = Total number of special purpose governments
STE = State government expenditure
STR = State government revenue
TE = Total Expenditure
TR = Total Revenue

Does the Form of Government Affect the Size of Government?

In this section we provide yet another test of Brennan and Buchanan's decentralization hypothesis.[18] The test presented here differs from the empirical literature reviewed above in that it examines not only whether or not the size of government is affected by decentralization, but also whether or not the size of government is affected by the form of government (i.e. federal versus unitary government). The empirical analysis consists of two single-equation regression models similar to that of Marlow (1988):

$$\text{SIZE} = \beta_0 + \beta_1\text{DEC} + \beta_2\text{GDP} + \beta_3\text{POP} + \beta_4\text{DUMMY} + u \quad (12.3)$$

$$\text{SIZE}^* = \beta_0 + \beta_1\text{DEC}^* + \beta_2\text{GDP}^* + \beta_3\text{POP}^* + \beta_4\text{DUMMY} + u^* \quad (12.4)$$

where SIZE represents the total size of government (measured as either total expenditures or total revenues relative to gross domestic product), DEC represents the degree of government fiscal decentralization (measured as total state and local expenditures or revenues to SIZE), GDP represents real gross domestic product per capita and POP represents the population. The * over a variable signifies the growth rate (as opposed to the level) of the corresponding variable.[19]

Equations (12.3) and (12.4) above are different from Marlow's in that they contain one extra term: DUMMY. The inclusion of a dummy variable in the equation is intended to capture the difference in the relationship between SIZE and DEC for the two different forms of government.[20] The need for the dummy variables arises because unitary governments do sometimes have local units providing public goods and services, so their decentralization ratio is not zero. DUMMY just captures the difference in the intercept terms.[21]

One prediction of the decentralization hypothesis is that countries with more decentralized government will have a smaller public sector or at least it will grow more slowly (therefore it is expected that $\beta_1 < 0$). This conclusion is derived from the following reasoning presented above. First, the more control local governments have over the supply of public goods the easier it will be for citizens to watchdog the government and thereby force a more efficient provision of public goods. Second, if a local government tries to extract more resources (and thereby provide more public goods) than its citizens prefer they will be able to move to another jurisdiction which provides a more acceptable tax and spending package. Thus, the more localized (decentralized) the provision of public goods the harder it will be for the government to extract excess resources from its citizens and therefore, the more difficult it will be for government to expand.

There is both theoretical and empirical evidence to support the notion that income and population positively affect the level of spending through the public sector (therefore it is expected that $\beta_2 > 0$ and $\beta_3 > 0$). As mentioned earlier in the chapter, it can be expected that as an economy's income grows over time, the size of the public sector will grow at an even faster rate (Wagner's Law). Thus, we should expect to see countries with higher income growth having greater degrees of public spending. We also noted that as a nation's population increases, the tax price of public goods falls, and therefore we should expect to see a rise in public spending as population increases. Thus, it is expected that, other things being equal, countries with more people will have a larger-size government. However, if economies of scale are important in the provision of public goods, then population growth may have a negative effect on the relative size of government (i.e. $\beta_3 < 0$).[22]

Using annual data (for the period 1973—88) for five countries — three with federal systems and two with a unitary system of government — equations (12.3) and (12.4) are estimated.[23] The results are presented in Table 12.2. It is clear from the results that decentralization has a dampening effect on the size of government. Looking at regressions corresponding to models (a) and (b), one notes that the coefficient on DEC is negative and very significant, indicating that the more decentralized a government, the smaller will be the size of its public sector, thereby providing proof for Brennan and Buchanan's decentralization hypothesis. The coefficients on the dummy variable capturing the form of the government are both significant implying that there is a difference in the relationship between SIZE and DEC for the different form of government. The negative sign on DUMMY indicates that countries with a unitary form of government have smaller public sectors.

Looking at regressions of the models designated as (c) and (d) we find a negative and significant coefficient on DEC once again providing proof in favor of the decentralization hypothesis. However, this time the coefficients on DUMMY are insignificant indicating that there is no difference in the growth of government between the two forms of government. This result is similar to that of Oates (1972).

In both regressions (a) and (b), the coefficient on GDP is positive but only significant in (a) providing some evidence in favor of Wagner's law. In both (c) and (d) it is negative and significant (a surprising and inexplicable result). The coefficient on POP is negative in three of the four regressions and significant in two of them [(a) and (b)], indicating that there are scale economies in the provision of public goods.

In short, the above evidence is generally in favor of the Brennan-Buchanan decentralization hypothesis. In all four regressions, the coefficient on DEC is negative and significant indicating that as the public sector becomes more decentralized, it grows at a slower pace.

Table 12.2 *Testing for Leviathan*

Dependent Variable	REVGDP (a)	EXPGDP (b)	GREVGDP (c)	GEXPGDP (d)
CONSTANT	3.23*	3.31*	0.005	0.063***
	(9.96)	(7.31)	(0.18)	(1.68)
DEC	–2.18*	–1.26*	–0.237*	–0.272**
	(8.29)	(4.38)	(2.60)	(1.69)
GDP	6.16*	2.07	–0.268**	–0.939*
	(5.09)	(1.30)	(2.33)	(7.12)
POP	–0.245*	–0.257*	0.0006	–0.004
	(12.14)	(8.75)	(0.20)	(0.99)
DUMMY	–0.414*	–0.253*	0.009	–0.001
	(6.00)	(4.34)	(1.30)	(0.09)
R^2	0.93	0.85	0.16	0.49

Notes: t-statistics in parentheses.
The countries are: federal system: Canada, Germany, the U.S.; unitary government: Denmark and Canada.
For models (c) and (d) all control variables (except DUMMY) are percentage growth rates.
* Indicates significance at the 1 per cent level.
** Indicates significance at the 5 per cent level.
*** Indicates significance at the 10 per cent level.
DEC = State and local revenues (expenditures) as a fraction of total revenues (expenditures).
EXPGDP = Total government expenditure as a fraction of GDP.
GDP = Real Gross Domestic Product per capita.
GEXPGDP = percentage growth in EXPGDP.
GREVGDP = percentage growth in REVGDP.
POP = Log of population.
REVGDP = Total government revenue as a fraction of GDP.

Source: Regressions based on data reported in International Monetary Fund (1977).

NOTES

1. See Aronson and Ott (1991).
2. For a discussion of measurement problems and data on the growth of government, see Aronson and Ott (1991), pp. 525—7.
3. This is essentially the explanation offered by Peacock and Wiseman (1961, 1979) for the growth of government.
4. Lindbeck (1985).
5. For a review of the median voter models, see Atkinson and Stiglitz (1980) and Romer and Rosenthal (1980).

6. Niskanen (1971).
7. Buchanan (1975), ch. 9.
8. Brennan and Buchanan (1977), p. 256.
9. Brennan and Buchanan (1980), p. 184.
10. This group of countries includes developed, developing and underdeveloped countries.
11. This is used for the United States sample.
12. Brennan and Buchanan (1980), p. 185.
13. Heil (1991) conducts a similar study using two samples: 1. 22 OECD countries and 2. 39 IMF countries to see if the quality of Oates' international sample affected his results. Heil finds no systematic relationship between decentralization and government size in either of his two samples, thus he concludes that Oates' sample did not affect his results.
14. Nelson notes, 'For example, the United States Census Bureau (July 1978, pp. 4—6) reports that nearly one-third of all local governments in the United States are special districts, although the proportion varies considerably from state to state. Most special districts are established to perform a single function: nearly one-half do not have the authority to levy taxes and two-thirds have not full-time employees.'
15. This measure includes only expenditures which are uniformly the responsibility of either the state government or the local levels of government. The major functions include local schools, public welfare, fire protection, sanitation and local parks.
16. One minor difference is that Eberts and Gronberg include police protection in their measure of the size of the public sector, whereas Nelson did not. However, they note that the results are not sensitive to its inclusion or exclusion.
17. Brennan and Buchanan (1980), p. 185.
18. The findings are preliminary. A much larger sample is currently being used to test the hypothesis.
19. Equation (12.1) also contains a time variable to control for any time trend between government size and decentralization.
20. Two separate regressions could have been run for the two forms of government. Then it would have been possible to compare the coefficients from the two regressions to see if there is any difference. However, by using dummy variables, the regressions can be run simultaneously and the coefficients on the dummy variables indicate the difference (if any) the form of government has on the relationship between SIZE and DEC.
21. The coefficient on DUMMY is equal to the intercept term for the regression just involving unitary governments and the intercept term for the regression just involving countries with decentralized governments.
22. In other words, the average cost of a unit of public output is declining over some range of population. Therefore it will be less expensive to provide public output over that range which will lead to a smaller public sector.
23. Because the range of the dependent variable in equation (12.3) is limited between zero and one, it has been transformed using the logistic transformation:

    $$\text{SIZE} = \text{LOG}(\text{SIZE}/(1-\text{SIZE}))$$

    SIZE can now take on any value on the real number line. See Pindyck and Rubinfeld (1981), pp. 287—9. All regressions have been corrected for serial correlation.

REFERENCES

Aronson, R. and Ott, A.F. (1991), 'The Growth of the Public Sector', in Greenaway, D., Bleaney, M., and Stewart, I.M.T., (eds), *Companion to Contemporary Economic Thought*, London and New York, Routledge.

Atkinson, A.B. and Stiglitz, J.E. (1980), *Lectures on Public Economics*, Maidenhead, McGraw-Hill.

Baumol, W.J. (1967), 'Macroeconomics of Unbalanced Growth', *American Economic Review*, **57**, pp. 415—26.

Beck, M. (1976), 'The Expanding Public Sector: Some Contrary Evidence', *National Tax Journal*, **29**, pp. 15—21.

Becker, G. (1985), 'Public Policies, Pressure Groups, and Dead Weight Costs', *Journal of Public Economics*, **28**, pp. 329—47.

Borcherding, T.E. (1977), *Budgets and Bureaucrats: The Sources of Government Growth*, Durham, Duke University Press.

Borcherding, T.E. (1985), 'The Causes of Government Growth: A Survey of the U.S Evidence', *Journal of Public Economics*, **28**, pp. 359—82.

Brennan, G. and Buchanan, J. (1977), 'Towards a Tax Constitution for Leviathan', *Journal of Public Economics*, **2**, pp. 255—74.

Brennan, G. and Buchanan, J. (1978), 'Tax Instruments as Constraints on the Disposition of Public Revenues', *Journal of Public Economics*, **9**, pp. 301—18.

Brennan, G. and Buchanan, J. (1980), *The Power to Tax: Analytical Foundation of A Fiscal Constitution*, Cambridge, Cambridge University Press.

Buchanan, J. (1975), *The Limits of Liberty*, Chicago, University of Chicago Press.

Buchanan, J. and Tullock, G. (1962), *The Calculus of Consent*, Ann Arbor, University of Michigan Press.

Eberts, R.W. and Gronberg, T.J. (1988), 'Can Competition Among Local Governments Constrain Government Spending?', *Economic Review, Federal Reserve Bank of Cleveland*, **1**, pp. 2—9.

Fiorina, M. and Noll, R.G. (1978), 'Voters, Bureaucrats and Legislators: A Rational Choice Perspective on the Growth of Bureaucracy', *Journal of Public Economics*, **9**, pp. 239—54.

Forbes, K.F. and Zampelli, E. (1989), 'Is Leviathan a Mythical Beast?', *American Economic Review*, **79**, pp. 68—77.

Heil, J. (1991), 'The Search for Leviathan Revisited', *Public Finance Quarterly*, **19** (3), pp. 334—46.

International Monetary Fund (1977), *Government Finance Statistics Yearbook*, Washington, D.C.

Joulfaian, D. and Marlow, M. (1990), 'Government Size and Decentralization: Evidence from Disaggregated Data', *Southern Economic Journal*, **56**, pp. 1094—1102.

Lindbeck, A. (1985), 'Redistribution Policy and the Expansion of the Public Sector', *Journal of Public Economics*, **28**, pp. 309—28.

Mackay, R.J. and Weaver, C.L. (1978), 'Monopoly Bureaus and Fiscal Outcomes: Deductive Models and implications for Reform', in Tullock, G. and Wagner, R.E. (eds), *Policy Analysis and Deductive Reasoning*, Lexington, D.C. Heath.

Mackay, R.J. and Weaver, C.L. (1979), 'On the Mutuality of Interest Between Bureaus and High Demand Review Committees: A Perverse Result', *Public Choice*, **34**, pp. 481—91.

Marlow, M.L. (1988), 'Fiscal Decentralization and Government Size', *Public Choice*, **56**, pp. 259—86.

Musgrave, R.A. (1985), 'Excess Bias and the Nature of Budget Growth', *Journal of Public Economics*, **28**, pp. 287—308.

Nelson, M.A. (1987), 'Searching for Leviathan: Comment and Extension', *American Economic Review*, **77**, pp. 198—204.

Niskanen, W.A., Jr. (1971), *Bureaucracy and Representative Government*, Chicago, Aldine.

Niskanen, W.A., Jr. (1975), 'Bureaucrats and Politicians', *Journal of Law and Economics*, **18**, pp. 617—43.

Nozick, R. (1974), *Anarchy, State and Utopia*, New York, Basic Books.

Nutter, G.W. (1978), *Growth of Government in the West*, Washington D.C., American Enterprise Institute.

Oates, W.E. (1972), *Fiscal Federalism*, New York, Harcourt Brace Jovanovich.

Oates, W.E. (1985), 'Searching for Leviathan: An Empirical Study', *American Economic Review*, **75**, pp. 748—57.

Ott, A.F. (1980), 'Has the Growth of Government in the West Been Halted?', in Samuels, W.L. and Wade, L.L. (eds), *Taxing and Spending Policy*, Lexington, D.C. Heath.

Ott, A.F. (1983), 'Controlling Government Spending', in Stubblebine, C. and Willets, T. (eds), *Reaganomics*, Washington D.C., Institute for Contemporary Studies.

Peacock, A.T. and Wiseman, J. (1961), *The Growth of Expenditures in the United Kingdom*, New York, National Bureau of Economic Research.

Peacock, A.T. and Wiseman, J. (1979), 'Approaches to the Analysis of Government Expenditure Growth', *Public Finance Quarterly*, **7**, pp. 3—23.

Peltzman, S. (1980), 'The Growth of Government', *Journal of Law and Economics*, **23**, pp. 209—87.

Pindyck, R. and Rubinfeld, D. (1981), *Econometric Models and Economic Forecasts*, New York, McGraw-Hill.

Rawls, J. (1972), *A Theory of Justice*, Cambridge, Harvard University Press.

Romer, T. and Rosenthal, H. (1978), 'Political Resource Allocation, Controlled Agendas, and the Status Quo', *Public Choice*, **33**, pp. 27—43.

Romer, T. and Rosenthal, H. (1980), 'Median Voter or Budget Maximizers'. Unpublished manuscript.

Stigler, G.J. (1970), 'Director's Law of Public Income Distribution', *Journal of Law and Economics*, **13**, pp. 1—10.

Tarschys, D. (1975), 'The Growth of Public Expenditures: Nine Models of Explanation', *Scandinavian Policy Studies*, **10**, pp. 9—31.

Zax, J.S. (1989), 'Is There A Leviathan in Your Neighborhood?', *American Economic Review*, **79**, pp. 560—7.

PART THREE

Budget Policy

13. Budget Policy: An Overview

Public sector budgets have evolved over time as new government functions were added on top of the traditional ones of providing for the national defense and protection of property rights. The Great Depression and the Keynesian revolution in the 1930s assigned to government a more active role — that of managing the economy. Tax and expenditure changes were advocated to provide full employment and price stability. As this activist policy was embraced by many, public sector budgets reflected more and more the preoccupation with macroeconomic management. By the 1960s a consensus had developed among Keynesian macroeconomists (Bronfenbrenner, 1969) that controlling aggregate demand through fiscal actions would virtually eliminate economic fluctuations. This belief turned out to be false. Actual experience with high unemployment and high inflation during the 1970s and empirical findings from recent macroeconomic research have also cast doubt on the validity of the Keynesian prescriptions for the economy. Earlier on, Friedman (1948) was critical of Keynes' activist policies. He argued that the use of budget instruments for the purpose of finetuning the economy would not be effective. Friedman's challenge to the then accepted wisdom was based on two astute observations: our ignorance of the true structure of the economy and the presence of significant lags in causal economic relations.

The recent developments of neoclassical macroeconomics — with its emphasis on explicit recognition of intertemporal links in the economy — together with the current literature on endogenous growth have shifted the focus in budget making from short-term macro-policy to the long-term impact of budget decisions. According to this literature, budget actions are likely to impact not only current private actions but also influence future outcomes. A more fruitful avenue in the study of fiscal decisions is to focus on their long-term impact. Part Three of this volume is devoted to the study of the long-run effects of budget policy. Short-term stabilization is not addressed.

One channel of interactions between the aggregate economy and the fiscal stance is through interest rates: long-term interest rates are influenced by the demand for funds needed to finance budget deficits. Rising long-term interest rates and growing public sector dissaving are situations of concern, as they may hamper the capacity of the economy to invest and grow. Public sector dissaving cuts deeply into the economy's rate of capital formation. Future generations will suffer on two counts: because of a reduced standard of living brought about by a reduction in the economy's stock of capital and because of future taxes that will have to be levied to finance interest costs on government debt. Public sector dissaving behavior is the subject matter of Chapter 14.

The second channel of interaction is between deficits and national saving. National saving, the sum of public and gross private saving, is essential for enhancing the standard of living of the population. It is required for the replacement of the capital stock and for maintaining the level of the capital stock per head as the population increases. The neoclassical growth models provide insight into the link between savings and economic growth. According to these models, an increase in the saving rate leads initially to a rise in the capital labor ratio and to an increase in output growth per capita, provided that total future productivity remains constant. But since the production process is characterized by diminishing returns to capital, output per capita increases at a decreasing rate. The growth rate in per capita output will eventually come down to the level consistent with the (exogenous) rate of technical advance. Thus, while the growth rate of per capita output cannot be 'permanently' raised by an increase in the national saving rate, the *level* of output per capita can be permanently at a higher level.

In recent years, an alternative growth model has been advanced where technical progress is treated as 'endogenous'. The endogenous growth model postulates the existence of strong links between the rate of investment and the rate of technical progress. A higher investment rate not only will lead to a 'temporarily' higher growth rate of output per capita, but also will increase the long-term rate of growth. Externalities associated with capital accumulation, according to the endogenous model of growth, reduce the effects of diminishing returns to capital. The model cites investment in human capital, government spending on research and technology, and tax policies as example of externalities that can affect the rate of technical progress. The case for increasing public sector saving (reducing deficits) is, therefore, even stronger. Chapter 15 explores the role of public capital formation in the growth process.

REFERENCES

Bronfenbrenner, M. (ed.) (1969), *Is the Business Cycle Obsolete?*, New York, John Wiley & Sons, Inc.

Friedman, M. (1948), 'A Monetary and Fiscal Framework for Economic Stability', *American Economic Review*, **38**, pp. 245—64.

14. Public Saving and the Economy

1 INTRODUCTION

Concern over budget deficits worldwide, but especially in the U.S., has increased economists' interest in theories and evidence of fiscal policy. The harmful effects of the deficit on the economy arise from two directions of causation: from budget deficits to long-term real interest rates and domestic investment, and from the budget deficits to deficits in the external accounts. A higher budget deficit raises domestic interest rates relative to foreign rates, leading to an appreciation of the value of the domestic currency. The higher exchange rate of the national currency makes exports more expensive abroad, imports less expensive at home, thus worsening the trade balance.

Since domestic deficits (the budget and trade deficits) must be counterbalanced by surpluses elsewhere, either domestic private savings have to rise, or the net acquisition of domestic financial assets by foreigners must increase. This chapter explores these interrelationships, in particular the link between the budget deficits and the national saving rate. An important element in the link is the Ricardian equivalence paradigm — the extent to which private saving increases to offset public dissaving. Another focal point in the discussion is the intergenerational effects of deficit finance. The chapter begins with a brief discussion of deficit measurements and provides comparative statistics of public sector deficits based on these measurements. Section 3 develops the links between the deficit and the aggregate economy within the standard model of budget deficits. In the following section, the Ricardian and the neoclassical paradigms are stated. Empirical evidence linking the fiscal stance to the macroeconomy is cited. The chapter closes with a few comments about fiscal policy stance in the global context.

2 PUBLIC SECTOR SAVING AND THE ECONOMY

The public sector may incur budget deficits for two reasons: as a temporary measure to stabilize the economy; and, secondly, as a 'permanent' feature of fiscal stance. Permanent deficits may be the outcome of a deliberate fiscal decision to shift part of the cost of financing certain expenditures to future generations. The alternative is clearly a case of policy failure — the failure to balance current claims on the budget against current budgetary resources. A temporary deficit is not a matter for concern. What concerns economists and the public at large is the permanency of public sector deficits. A permanent deficit, defined as the addition to the stock of public debt, raises the ratio of the national debt to aggregate output. The rise in the deficit/output ratio is said to crowd out private investment and to adversely affect the well-being of future generations. These adverse consequences are attributed to the persistent trend of higher deficits. This issue — effects of temporary versus permanent deficits — goes hand in hand with the way the deficit has traditionally been measured.

Deficit Concepts and Measurements

The term budget deficit is commonly used when making reference to an excess of expenditure over receipts. In regard to public sector deficits, one needs to be a bit more specific, since a public sector budget may be presented in several ways. As outlined in Chapter 3, the U.S. federal budget is on a unified basis, hence the federal deficit is the unified budget deficit which combines deficits or surpluses in the federal funds and the trust funds. Other budget presentations are used in the U.S. by the state and local sectors and by countries elsewhere. State governments' budgets make distinctions between the general government accounts and trust fund accounts. Since state governments are prohibited from running deficits to finance current expenditure, borrowing or lending activities of the state-local sector are associated with financing capital expenditures or accumulation in the pension funds.

Budget presentation for European countries, i.e. the European Community (EC), is similar to that of the state-local sector of the U.S. The budget balance (for most members) is represented by net lending (+) or borrowing (—) of the general government. This balance reflects transactions in the current and capital accounts, but not the trust funds. The fiscal stance measured by the difference between general government receipts and general government expenditures is said to be 'inappropriate' as it incorporates feed-back from the aggregate economy. During business cycles, certain items in the budget behave counter-cyclically with changes in income. Hence, an adjustment to the deficits is needed to remove the cycle effects on budget receipts and expenditures. The adjusted deficit is a better measure of the fiscal stance than the unadjusted deficits.

The cyclically adjusted deficit

Fluctuations in economic activities cause changes in budget expenditures, receipts, and correspondingly the budget deficit. When the economy contracts during a recession, the budget deficit increases for two reasons: revenues fall as incomes fall; and secondly, government expenditures for unemployment compensation and welfare payments increase. Similarly, in periods of expansion, tax receipts grow with the growth in incomes.

Recession-induced expenditures also decline during economic expansion as the need for such expenditures is reduced. Unemployment insurance claims fall with the fall in the unemployment rate and the number of eligible recipients for income support programs decline with the growth in personal income.

Changes in the deficit that occur 'automatically', i.e. as a result of cyclical behavior of the economy, are temporary and are to be distinguished from deficits that are the result of deliberate fiscal action. Since the deficit is measured by a 'single' number — the difference between overall receipts and overall spending — there is a need to separate these two components. By eliminating these 'automatic' — (temporary) influences on the budget, the structural deficit is measured. This measure reflects the true relationship between budget commitments and budget resources embodied in fiscal decisions. In the U.S., the Department of Commerce provides estimates of the cyclically adjusted deficit. Starting with the NIPA deficit, the cyclically adjusted budget is constructed under the assumptions that: 1. existing tax laws and programs are in effect, and 2. the economy experiences no cyclical fluctuations — i.e. a constant six per cent unemployment rate has been maintained. Thus, the cyclically adjusted budget in effect removes the cyclical components from both receipts (+) and expenditures (—).

In a similar fashion, the European Commission calculates adjusted budget balances for the community as a whole and for individual member states. Their calculation is informative in that it shows first the change in fiscal stance between two periods. Next, it subtracts from this change the effect of economic activities on the budget balance. The residual, the adjusted budget balance, is used as a 'proxy' for the change in the discretionary fiscal policy stance.[1] Table 14.1 presents estimates of the effect of economic activity on the budget balance between 1989—90. As shown in the table, there is evidence of a 'loosening' of the discretionary component of the budget by 1.3 percentage points of GDP for the European Community and 0.7 percentage points of GDP for the U.S. For both the EC and the U.S., discretionary fiscal policy was more expansionary than indicated by the change in the actual size of the deficit. In other words, the economic condition was better (in the U.S. the unemployment rate was below six per cent), than that which would induce 'automatic' deficits adjustments in the budget. The only exception to this pattern was for the U.K. where the impact of economic activities was negative — the discretionary fiscal stance was more restrictive than was indicated by changes in the budget balance.

In addition to removing the cycle effects from the budget two other adjustments are proposed: correcting for inflation effects on interest payments and/or changes in the value of the public debt. Both of these adjustments are relevant to the measurement of public sector savings as discussed below.

Table 14.1 *Budget balances: adjusting for the cycle effects 1989—1990 (as a percentage of GDP)*

Item	1989	1990	Change in fiscal stance
European Community (EUR 12)			
Net lending (+) or borrowing (—)	—2.9	—4.1	—1.200 [a]
Impact of economic activity (CA)			+0.100 [a]
Adjusted budget balance [b]			—1.300
Germany			
Net lending (+) or borrowing (—)	+0.2	—1.9	—2.100
Impact of economic activity (CA)			+0.900
Adjusted budget balance [b]			—3.000
United Kingdom			
Net lending (+) or borrowing (—)	+1.2	—0.7	—2.000
Impact of economic activity (CA)			+0.900
Adjusted budget balance [b]			—1.100
United States			
Federal fund deficits, NIPA bases	—2.2	—2.9	—0.700
Impact of economic activity (CA)			+0.003
Adjusted budget balance [b]			—0.697

Notes: a: A plus sign indicates an improvement, a minus sign indicates a deterioration associated with the fluctuations in the aggregate economy.
b: Adjusted budget balance gets larger when CA(+), smaller when CA(—).

Source: For the European Community: Commission of the European Communities, *Annual Economic Report, 1991—1992*, No. 50 (December 1991), p. 189; for the U.S., *The Economic Report of the President* calculates the cycle adjustment for 1990 to be equal to —\$18.2 billion (p. 268). The NIPA deficit excluding social insurance fund and GDP figures are from *The Economic Report of the President* (February 1992), Statistical Tables.

Measurement of government saving

Goldsmith's (1962) and Kendrick's (1976) approach to measuring saving is perhaps the most useful indicator of the saving or dissaving activities of the public sector. Essential to this approach is the application of the system of accounts used in the private sector to the public sector. Accordingly, public sector saving is defined as:

Gross Saving = change in tangible assets + change in intangible assets — change in liabilities and

$$\text{Net Saving} = \text{Gross Saving} - \text{Depreciation.}$$

This concept would require the annual valuations of assets and liabilities of the public sector. A less comprehensive measurement of public sector saving, one which avoids the need for such valuation, is derived from the sector's accounts as recorded in the budget. Gross saving would be measured as the difference between general government income less general government consumption expenditures. Net saving would be equal to gross saving less depreciation of public sector capital (capital consumption allowances).[2]

Gross or net saving of the public sector, measured by changes in the sector balance sheet or the sector's account, reflect the net accumulation of public sector assets. Government deficits on current accounts (dissaving) add to the liability of the sector while public investment financed by borrowing increases both the assets and liabilities of the public sector. Except for minor differences, the treatment of inventory investment and errors in measurement of public sector assets, the two concepts of public sector saving — from the balance sheet versus the sector's account — should amount to the same thing.[3]

Nominal changes in public sector net worth reflect real as well as inflationary effects. Just as changes in the value of the assets and the liabilities of the sector have to be adjusted for inflation in calculating the public sector's net worth, the nominal budget deficit derived for the sector account also needs to be adjusted to remove the effects of inflation on budget transactions. One approach would adjust nominal interest payments by removing from the deficit an amount equal to the inflation premium on interest payments. Another approach is to reduce the deficit by an amount corresponding to the change in the market value of the public debt. Both of these involve flow-stock adjustments.

To adjust nominal interest payments for the inflation premium component, the premium first has to be calculated. Cagan (1981) proposed estimating an equation of the form:

$$i = \alpha \sum \beta_j P_{t-j} + e \qquad (14.1)$$

where i is the government bond rate, P_t is the inflation rate, β_j is the coefficient associated with P_{t-j}, and e is the error term ($N(0, \sigma^2)$). The estimated inflation premium is then multiplied by the stock of interest-bearing debt to obtain the inflation adjustment.

The second adjustment requires the valuation of the stock of debt to reflect changes in the price level. Changes in the GDP deflator are commonly used for this purpose. The difference between the two valuations is then deducted from the current deficit. Neither of these adjustments have been adopted by the federal government in its presentations of the budget, although several economists and CBO have provided measures of their magnitudes.[4] Based on CBO calculations, the inflation adjustment makes little difference to the trend value of the federal deficits in relation to the economy. For example, the inflation premium added, on average, \$5.1 billion to the deficit between 1960—69; \$23.6 billion during 1970—79, and \$48 billion during 1980—89. Adjusting the deficit/income ratio by these amounts reduced the unadjusted deficit/income ratio by 0.008 in 1960—69; by 0.018 during 1970—79, and by 0.015 during 1980—89. When both adjustments are subtracted from the deficit, again the trend remains — higher ratios of deficits to national income in the 1980s compared to the earlier periods.

A somewhat different approach has been followed by the Commission of the European Community in measuring fiscal stance and public sector saving. Beside the cyclical effect on the deficit, the Commission applies two budget criteria in evaluating the deficit: the 'primary balance' and the 'Golden Rule'.[5]

The primary balance (PB) is defined as the required budget balance before payments of interest on the debt to ensure (given a specified growth rate of output and interest rate) the long-term stability of the ratio of public debt to GDP.[6] That is,

$$PB = (i - g)\, d \tag{14.2}$$

where i is the nominal rate of interest, g is the nominal growth rate of output, and d is the derived debt/GDP ratio. When $i = g$, the primary balance is zero, d is unchanged. Assuming both i and g are constant, the change in the debt is equal to the deficit.

Since interest on the outstanding stock of debt is part of the deficit, one may decompose the changes in the debt as follows:

$$D_t - D_{t-1} = E_0 - T + ip_{t-1} \tag{14.3}$$

or

$$(D_t - D_{t-1}) - id_{t-1} = (E_0 - T) \tag{14.4}$$

where E_0 is expenditures net of interest payments and D_t is the stock of debt in period t. The term $(E_0 - T)$ is referred to as the primary deficit — the net addition to the stock of debt (excluding servicing requirement of the debt outstanding). The ratio of the primary deficit to GDP may be taken as a measure of the fiscal stance.

The second criterion — the golden rule — permits government borrowing only for investment purposes; it 'forbids' dissaving, that is increasing deficits to finance government consumption. Adherence to the golden rule would mean adjusting public sector saving to reflect public capital formation. This criterion is appropriate in the European setting in that the budget presentations there allow for capital budgeting. This practice is not followed in the U.S. budget presentations, hence there would be no incentive to adhere to it. Nonetheless, for data comparisons, this criterion will be applied to the federal budget.

Table 14.2 *Public deficits, alternative measurements, 1988 (as a percentage of GDP)*

Item	EC	Germany	U.K.	U.S.	Canada
1. Net lending (+) or borrowing (—) adjustment	—3.7	—2.1	1.1	—3.7[a]	—3.0
a) Interest payments	4.8	2.8	4.0	3.2	4.0
b) Capital formation	2.7	2.4	1.2	1.9[b]	0.4
2. Primary balance = (1—a)	1.1	0.7	5.1	—0.6	1.0
3. Gross saving = (1+b)	—1.0	—0.3	2.3	—1.8	—2.6
4. Gross public debt[c]	59.6	44.6	49.2	42.6	37.4

Notes: a: U.S. deficit for federal budget excluding social security accounts.
b: Federal investment in federal government fixed capital. It does not include grants-in-aid to state-local government for investment projects.
c: Debt held by the public.

Source: Except for the U.S., Commission of the European Communities, *European Economy,* vol. 39—42, study no. 3, p. 148; for the U.S., *Survey of Current Business* (November 1991) and *The Economic Report of the President* (February 1992), pp. 385 and 387.

Applying the above concepts to the public sectors in the U.S., Canada, and the EC, we show in Table 14.2 gross savings and public sector debt in 1988. In Table 14.3 the recent trend in the permanent deficit (measured by changes in the ratio of gross debt to GDP) is shown along with the ratio of primary deficit to GDP.

The data in the tables clearly show a difference in budget behavior among the countries considered. While Canada and the U.S. exhibit consistent patterns of dissaving (reducing national saving), the U.K. has consistently augmented private saving by accumulating surpluses in the budget, reducing the ratio of debt to GDP throughout the 1980s. Germany's public sector saving posture began to erode at the end of the early 1980s. Contrasting the trend of the primary deficit (as a measure of permanent deficit) to changes in debt/GDP ratio, we find a correspondence between surpluses (+) in the primary deficit/GDP ratio and reductions (—) in the debt/GDP ratio or vice versa for the U.K. and the U.S. This correspondence is not evident for Germany where addition to the public debt has taken place even when the primary deficit was in surplus. Overall the trend in the primary deficit shows a worsening position for all three countries since the mid-1980s. To stabilize the debt/GDP ratio, an increment of primary balance is needed on the order of two to four per cent of GDP.

Table 14.3 *Permanent deficits (as a percentage of GDP)*

Year	Germany	U.K.	U.S.	Canada
		Primary Deficit		
1982	–0.5	2.6	–1.10	2.33
1985	1.9	2.2	–0.5	1.70
1986	1.7	2.1	–2.5	0.18
1987	1.0	3.0	–0.8	–1.09
1988	0.9	5.0	–1.0	–1.05
1989	2.9	4.6	–0.9	–1.22
1990	–0.6	3.1	–1.9	N.A.
1991	–1.5	2.4	–2.4	N.A.
		Change in gross public debt [a]		
1982			2.9	4.43
1985	0.7	–1.4	2.6	2.42
1986	0.2	–0.9	3.3	1.07
1987	1.1	–2.0	1.3	–0.80
1988	0.7	–5.0	0.2	0.15
1989	–0.9	–5.3	–0.2	N.A.
1990	0.1	–2.7	1.7	N.A.
1991	1.5	–1.2	3.6	N.A.

Note: a: Debt of general government; U.S. federal debt held by its public.

Source: Commission of the European Communities, *European Economy*, 46—1990, Statistical Appendix; for the U.S. calculated from *The Economic Report of the President.*

3 PUBLIC SAVING, NATIONAL SAVING, AND THE ECONOMY

National saving consists of three components: personal saving, business saving and public saving. A reduction in any one of these three, unless offset by changes in the others, reduces national saving.

As shown in the tables, mostly for the U.S., there has been a consistent erosion in the saving position of the public sector, measured either by the primary deficit or changes in the debt/GDP ratio. If neither component of domestic saving were increased to offset public sector's dissaving, lower national saving would be the outcome, which in turn would cause: a reduction in investment (domestic and foreign) and, secondly, by reducing the rate of capital formation, retardation of living standards in the long run. The long-run implications of public sector deficits clearly depend on the response of the private sector to the public sector's behavior. Neoclassical economists such as Diamonds (1965), Phelps and Shell (1969) and Bailey (1972) offer one hypothesis; Keynesians hold an alternative view; the Ricardian equivalence paradigm offers still another.[7] To sort these out, we begin with the standard (textbook) model of budget deficits.

The Budget Deficit and the Crowding Out of Private Capital Formation

The much debated link between the budget deficit and the rate of capital formation is not a simple one to resolve. Crowding out of domestic investment can take one of two forms: an ex post crowding out via the rise in the equilibrium rate of interest or ex ante when private debt issues are displaced by government bonds. In the latter case, total demand for funds will be equal to the supply of saving, leaving the equilibrium rate of interest unchanged.

To prove or disprove such a link, two key elements have to be uncovered. One is the magnitude of the elasticities of saving and investment with respect to real rates of return and secondly, the net wealth effect of government bonds on households. The conventional or textbook argument states the issue in the following way. In an economy at or near full employment, the rise in government deficit, given a 'stable' national saving rate, will give rise to higher real interest rates. Since the government's demand for funds is totally interest inelastic whereas private demand exhibits an elasticity greater than zero, the sale of government bonds absorbs resources which otherwise would have been devoted to private capital formation. This view has been rejected on two grounds: when the economy is below full employment, it is the 'job' of the deficit to absorb private saving and thus keep aggregate demand from falling; secondly, in a fully integrated world capital market, the total saving schedule (domestic plus foreign) is highly interest inelastic — the increased borrowing by the public sector would be accommodated without a rise in the equilibrium rate of interest. Crowding out of domestic private investment in this scenario would not occur.

The Ricardian equivalence paradigm offers theoretical foundation for rejecting the crowding-out thesis. Barro (1974, 1979, 1987) theorizes that, in a lifecycle model, household consumption plans internalize government actions: a reduction in current taxes entails future taxes equal to the present value of the current deficit. In a full employment economy, if expenditures were to remain unchanged, taxes cut, and the deficit financed by issuing bonds, then replacing tax finance by issuing debt will leave the real interest rate unchanged. In this scenario, households will not regard the deficit as contributing to their permanent private disposable income — they will save rather than spend the deficit. Saving will rise by just enough to offset the extra tax liability needed to service the extra debt.

Put simply the Ricardian equivalence theorem suggests that: government dissaving leads to an offsetting increase in desired private saving, hence, no change in desired national saving.[8] The Ricardian equivalence view of the deficit, although appealing, is not 'sensible'. Objections to it have been summed up by Barro (1989); all of which question the validity of its underlying assumptions. The five assumptions and critiques are:

1. infinite horizons — since people do not live forever, it would not be expected that they care about taxes levied after their death;
2. perfect capital markets — capital markets are not perfect; they do not provide opportunities for intertemporal substitution at the government bond rate;
3. perfect foresight — this is not realistic in view of uncertainty about future incomes and taxes;
4. government taxes are lump sum — this is contradicted by the fact that government taxes are distortionary; and
5. full employment — when the economy is not at full employment, deficits raise consumption and income.

The neoclassical paradigm explores the long-term implication of the permanent deficit in the context of a lifecycle model. Diamonds' model (1965) is the most often cited in this regard. According to Diamonds, a persistent rise in the debt to GDP ratio (permanent deficit) depresses the steady-state capital/labor ratio. At the original rate of interest, individuals would be unwilling to hold new debt issues, given the initial distribution of the portfolio between physical capital and bonds. To induce them to hold more government bonds, interest rates have to rise. Rising interest rates reduce investment until capital market equilibrium is re-established. Hence, permanent public sector deficits 'crowd out' private capital formation.[9] This outcome need not happen in the Keynesian framework.

In the standard Keynesian model, a bond-financed increase in government spending leads to an increase in output (by a multiple of the rise in expenditure through the multiplier effect), a rise in the interest rate, and subsequently a crowding out of investment. However, if the rise in demand were to increase the profitability of investment, then the rate of investment may not be reduced.[10] Alternatively, if government expenditures were viewed by households as providing goods that were perfect substitutes for other (private) goods in their consumption basket, then households' saving will rise; crowding out need not occur.[11] Since the Keynesian 'deficits' are 'temporary' — they are incurred in periods of unemployment — the Keynesian framework is not appropriate for investigating the long-run implications of persistent deficits.

One way of validating the prediction of the theoretical model is to turn to empirical findings. The Ricardian view predicts no effect of budget deficits on real interest rates; the standard view predicts a positive effect. The neoclassical view which is concerned with permanent deficits cannot be tested against the empirical findings since the tests do not distinguish between permanent and temporary deficits.

A considerable number of studies have been done examining the relationship between a change in the actual deficit and long-term interest rates. As one may expect, with many studies come a variety of results. Studies by Feldstein and Eckstein (1970), Bradley (1983), Frankel (1983) and Barth *et al.* (1985) found a significant positive relationship in the 0 to 0.25 percentage point range to exist between a change in the deficit and long-term interest rates. Positive ranges of 0 to 0.25 (Kudlow, 1981) and 0.75 to 2.25 (Muller and Price, 1984) were also reported as the influence of the deficit on long-term rates. Feldstein and Chamberlain (1973), in a later study, found an uncertain relationship to exist between the two. This conclusion was supported by research done by Tatom (1984) and a U.S. Treasury study (1984) which found the relationship to be in the —0.25 to 0 percentage point range. Studies by Giannaro and Kolluri (1985) and Evans (1985) lend further support to the uncertain influence conclusion as they found the relation to be either a positive or negative one. As the evidence linking budget deficits to the real rates of interest is mixed, it is interpreted by some to be in support of the Ricardian equivalence (Barro, 1989), while others (Bernheim, 1989) find the estimated relationship too poorly specified to take the evidence seriously. In Table 14.4, a summary of the findings is given.

If there is one conclusion that may be agreed upon on the basis of the evidence, it is that the effects of budget deficits on interest rates do not warrant strong conclusions. While one may accept or reject the implied relationships, one aspect of the budget deficit that ought not be overlooked is the ever rising share of the budget devoted to the servicing the public debt. Over the 1970—90 period, the debt service requirement (interest only) more than doubled in the EC from 1.9 per cent of GDP during 1970—74 to 4.8 per cent of GDP in 1987—90. Similarly, in the U.S. the interest/GDP ratio rose from 1.4 per cent in 1970—74 to 3.3 per cent in the later period. In Canada the interest payment/GDP ratio almost doubled since 1980, from 2.5 (in 1980) per cent to 4.8 per cent in 1989.

In the U.S. and Canada, nominal GDP growth — while exceeding the effective rate of interest on the debt during the 1970s — has fallen behind the rise in interest cost during the 1980s. The rise in interest cost is a matter of concern particularly for the U.S. public sector. As discussed earlier (Chapter 3), the federal government has yet to adopt a system of account which allows it to budget, on an annual basis, enough of its income to service the debt. In the absence of current tax increases to meet current

Table 14.4 *Estimates of the interest rate effects of a $50 billion increase in the deficit*

Percentage Points	Type of Data	Studies
	Effect on long-term interest rates	
0.00 — +0.25	monthly	Bradley (1983)
	quarterly	Carlson (1983), Feldstein & Eckstein (1970)
	annual	Barth *et al.* (1985), Frankel (1983)
0.00 — +0.50	quarterly	Dewald (1983)
0.00 — +0.75	annual	Kudlow (1981)
+0.25 — +0.75	annual	de Leeuw & Holloway (1985), Hoelscher (1986)
+0.75 — +2.25	quarterly	Muller & Price (1984)
—0.25 — +0.25	quarterly	Feldstein & Chamberlain (1973), U.S. Treasury (1984)
	annual	Tatom (1984)
—0.25 — +0.50	quarterly	Giannaro & Kolluri (1985)
—0.25 — 0.00	monthly	Evans (1985)
	quarterly	Mascaro & Meltzer (1983)
	Effect on short-term interest rates	
0.00 — +0.50	monthly	Bradley (1983)
	quarterly	Makin & Tanzi (1984)
0.00 — +0.75	annual	Barth *et al.* (1985)
0.00 — +1.25	annual	Hutchinson & Pyle (1984)
—0.25 — +0.25	quarterly	Makin (1983)
—0.25 — +0.50	quarterly	Hoelscher (1983)
—0.75 — +0.75	monthly	Motley (1983)
—0.25 — 0.00	monthly	Evans (1985)
	quarterly	Mascaro & Meltzer (1983)
—0.50 — 0.00	quarterly	Dewald (1983)
—0.75 — 0.00	annual	Tatom (1984)

Source: Congressional Budget Office (1987), pp. 100—101.

interest payments, some expenditures will have to be cut. Given the current budget practice in the U.S. which favors 'across the board' cuts in federal spending to meet deficit reduction targets (i.e. the GRH Act), additional sources of inefficiency in budget allocation are introduced to the budget process.

Budget Deficits and the Current-Accounts Balance

Large and unprecedented deficits in the U.S. current accounts since 1983 concurrent with deficits in the federal budget gave the impression (at least in popular writing and newspaper columns) that the two must somehow be linked. At the accounting level they are; a deficit gap in the current account (external imbalance) is mirrored by a deficit gap between domestic saving and domestic investment (internal imbalance). From the national income identity, this link is observed

$$Y = C + I + (G - T) + (X - IM)$$

$$(Y - C) - I = (G - T) + (X - IM)$$

or

$$S - I = (G - T) + (X - IM) \qquad (14.4)$$

where: Y = Gross National Product
C = consumption
S = domestic saving
I = gross domestic investment
(G — T) = government expenditure less taxes, or budget balance
(X — IM) = current account balance

A necessary implication drawn from equation (14.4) is that the domestic saving gap (excess of domestic saving or domestic investment) must be large enough to cover the budget gap plus the current account gap.

If the domestic private saving gap is set at zero (S = I), then the government deficit has to be exactly equal to the deficit or current account. That is,

$$(T - G) = (X - IM) \qquad (14.5)$$

Budget deficit (—) = Current account (—)

Budget surplus (+) = Current account (+)

In other words, when total national saving (S + T — G) falls short of total domestic investment, I, the current account is in deficit and capital flows into the country. Conversely, when national saving is in surplus, capital flows out.

The existence of a budget deficit is neither necessary nor sufficient for the existence of a current-account deficit. A current-account deficit could coexist with a fiscal surplus or a fiscal deficit with a current-account surplus; what matters is the size of the domestic saving gap in relation to the other two gaps. The identity given by (14.5) does not imply specific behavioral relationships between the variables. Behavioral assumptions concerning the determination of the variables are needed to explain causation between budget deficits and current-account deficits, between national saving and the interest rate, the exchange rate and so on.

As is widely known by now, the standard model explanation links the budget deficit to the current-account deficit via a series of sequential outcomes. As discussed earlier, the standard model postulates a link between budget deficits and interest rates. An increase in the budget deficit raises interest rates. Higher interest rates at home attract foreign capital, and this leads to an appreciation of the domestic currency. Imports become less expensive at home, exports more expensive abroad, thus generating a trade deficit. The above explanation is simplistic and partially incorrect (Somensatto, 1985). To understand these interrelationships, a more comprehensive model of the economy is needed. At a minimum, one needs to know how an exogenous shock to G (government spending) influences the time path of the other variables — whether the shock effects are permanent or transitory. As Somensatto put it, to obtain a proper measure of the effects of budget deficits on the trade balance requires a general-equilibrium framework for analyzing these relationships. In short, the co-movement of trade deficits and budget deficits, although 'interesting', does not by itself make a strong case in support of the linkage.[12]

4 CONCLUSION: DOES THE DEFICIT MATTER ?

The evidence on the effects of budget deficits on key macroeconomic variables does not provide an answer to the troubling (at least to some) question about public sector deficits. On theoretical grounds, one tends to lean towards either the neoclassical position or reject it in favor of the Ricardian equivalence paradigm. Both models have their ardent supporters as well as antagonists. Unfortunately, neither the theoretical logic nor the mathematical complexity of the overlapping generations model (perhaps because of it) have succeeded in convincing policy makers or swaying public opinion towards the model prediction that public deficits do not matter. As to the neoclassical model's prediction that permanent deficits matter, the model according to Bernheim is yet to be tested since evidence on the effects of permanent deficit is 'almost nonexistent'.

In the absence of consensus about causality, one is left to ponder the issue, if not question the predictions theoretical model. In the U.S. the body of politics seem to have resolved the deficit issue — deficits indeed do matter. Because of that, and that alone, economists should examine the political economy of this implication. The fact that deficits are increased during recessions is no longer the issue — what is at issue is the persistence of deficits.

Budget making in the U.S. has been turned over to deficit cutters at the expense of budget planners and managers. The budget process is no longer a process for articulating the nation's budget priorities, for examining the efficient operation of the federal fiscal system, rather it has become a battleground pitting one interest group against another. The significance of the budget deficit debate in the U.S. lies not so much in proving or disproving which theory prediction is the correct one, but in focusing the nation's attention to the need for restoring the integrity of the budget process.

NOTES

1. This adjustment is calculated by the EC for member countries. See Commission of the European Communities, *Annual Report 1991—1992*, p. 191.
2. See Ott and Yoo (1980), pp. 177—80.
3. Ibid.
4. See Congressional Budget Office (1985), Eisner and Piper (1984) and Ott (1983).
5. The concept of the 'Golden Rule' is derived from growth models aiming at maximizing consumption per capita. According to these models, there is a particular golden-rule saving rate that, if maintained, would maximize consumption for all generations. For other models, see Ott, Ott and Yoo (1975).
6. For methodology, see Commission of the European Communities, *European Economy*, no. 22 (November 1984); also see Congressional Budget Office (1985).
7. An excellent review of the alternative hypotheses is provided by Bernheim (1989).
8. Barro (1989), p. 39.
9. Bernheim (1989), p. 37.
10. David and Scadding (1974).
11. Ibid.
12. Barro (1989), p. 50. Barro cites Evans' (1988) study which suggests that no such links exist as proof for the Ricardian equivalence prediction.

REFERENCES

Bailey, M.J. (1972), 'The Optimal Full Employment Surplus', *Journal of Political Economy*, **80**, pp. 649—61.

Barro, R.J. (1974), 'Are Government Bonds Net Wealth?', *Journal of Political Economy*, **82**, pp. 1095—117.

Barro, R.J. (1979), 'On the Determination of the Public Debt', *Journal of Political Economy*, **87**, pp. 940—71.

Barro, R.J. (1987), 'Government Spending, Interest Rates, Prices, and Budget Deficits in the U.K., 1701—1918', *Journal of Monetary Economics*, **20**, pp. 221—47.

Barro, R.J. (1989), 'The Ricardian Approach To Budget Deficits', *Journal of Economic Perspectives*, no. 2, pp. 37—54.

Barth, J.R. and Bradley, M.D. (1985), 'Rational Expectations and the Effects of Federal Debt: Some Empirical Results', George Washington University, processed.

Barth, J.R., Russek, F.S. and Iden, G. (1985) 'Federal Borrowing and Short Term Interest Rates: Comment', *Southern Economic Journal*, **52**, pp. 554—9.

Bernheim, D. (1989), 'A Neoclassical Perspective on Budget Deficits', *Journal of Economic Perspectives*, no. 2, pp. 55—72.

Bradley, M.D. (1983), 'Federal Debt Surprises and Real Interest Rates: Whither Crowding Out?', George Washington University, processed.

Cagan, P. (1981), 'The Real Federal Deficit and Financial Markets', *The AEI Economist*, November, pp. 1—8.

Carlson, J. (1983), Statement before the Joint Economic Committee, October 21, 1983.

Commission of the European Communities (1984), *European Economy*, no. 22, Luxembourg, CES.

Commission of the European Communities (1989), *European Economy, Annual Economic Report (1989—1990)*, Luxembourg, CES.

Commission of the European Communities (1990), *European Economy*, Luxembourg, CES.

Commission of the European Communities (1991), *European Economy, Annual Economic Report (1991—1992)*, Luxembourg, CES.

Congressional Budget Office (1985), *Measuring the Federal Debt and Deficit: Adjustments and Rationales*, Staff Papers, April, Washington DC, U.S. Government Printing Office.

Congressional Budget Office (1987), *The Economic and Budget Outlook: Fiscal Years 1988—1992*, Annual Report, 1987, Washington DC, U.S. Government Printing Office.

David, P. and Scadding, J. (1974), 'Private Savings: Ultrarationality, Aggregation, and "Denison's Law"', *Journal of Political Economy*, **2**, pp. 225—49.

de Leeuw, F. and Holloway, T.M. (1985) 'The Measurement and Significance of the Cyclically Adjusted Federal Budget and Debt', *Journal of Money, Credit, and Banking*, **17** (2), pp. 232—42.

Dewald, W.G. (1983), 'Federal Deficits and Real Interest Rates: Theory and Evidence', Federal Reserve Bank of Atlanta, *Economic Review*, January, pp. 20—9.

Diamonds, P. (1965), 'National Debt and Neoclassical Economic Growth', *American Economic Review*, **55**, pp. 1125—50.

Eisner, R. and Piper, P. (1984), 'A New View of the Federal Debt and Budget Deficits', *American Economic Review*, **74**, pp. 11—29.

Evans, P. (1985), 'Do Large Deficits Produce High Interest Rates?', *American Economic Review*, **75** (1), pp. 68—87.

Evans, P. (1987), 'Interest Rates and Expected Future Budget Deficits in the U.S.', *Journal of Political Economy*, **95**, pp. 34—58.

Evans, P. (1988), 'Do Budget Deficits Affect the Current Account?', Unpublished, Ohio State University, August.

Feldstein, M.S. and Chamberlain, G. (1973), 'Multimarket Expectations and the Rate of Interest', *Journal of Money, Credit, and Banking*, November, pp. 873—902.

Feldstein, M.S. and Eckstein, O. (1970), 'The Fundamental Determinants of the Interest Rate', *Review of Economics and Statistics*, **52** (4), pp. 363—75.

Frankel, J. (1983), 'A Test of Portfolio Crowding-Out and Related Issues of Finance', National Bureau of Economic Research, Working Paper Series, No. 1205.

Giannaro, D.S. and Kolluri, B.R. (1985), 'The Budget Deficit Debate: A Review of the Recent Empirical Studies', University of Hartford, processed.

Goldsmith, R. (1962), 'The National Wealth of the United States in the Post-War Period', National Bureau of Economic Research, Princeton, distributed by Princeton University Press.

Hoelscher, G.P. (1983), 'Federal Borrowing and Short Term Interest Rates', *Southern Economic Journal*, **50**, pp. 319—33.

Hoelscher, G.P. (1986), 'New Evidence on Deficits and Interest Rates', *Journal of Money, Credit, and Banking*, **18** (1), pp. 1—17.

Hutchinson, M. and Pyle, D.H. (1984), 'The Real Interest Rate/Budget Deficit Link: International Evidence', Federal Reserve Bank of San Francisco, *Economic Review*, Fall, no. 4, pp. 26—35.

Kendrick, J. (1976), 'The Formation of Stocks of Total Capital', National Bureau of Economic Research, New York, distributed by Columbia University Press.

Kudlow, L. (1981), Statement before the Senate Budget Committee, statistical appendix (October 20, 1981).

Makin, J.H. (1983), 'Real Interest, Money Surprises, Anticipated Inflation and Fiscal Deficits', *Review of Economics and Statistics*, **65** (3), pp. 374—84.

Makin, J.H. and Tanzi, V. (1984), 'Level and Volatility of U.S. Interest Rates: Roles of Expected Inflation, Real Rates and Taxes', in Tanzi. V. (ed.), *Taxation, Inflation, and Interest Rates*, Washington D.C., International Monetary Fund, pp. 110—42.

Mascaro, A. and Meltzer, A.H. (1983), 'Long- and Short-Term Interest Rates in a Risky World', *Journal of Monetary Economics*, **11-12**, pp. 484—518.

Motley, B. (1983), 'Real Interest Rates, Money and Government Deficits', Federal Reserve Bank of San Francisco, *Economic Review*, Summer, no. 3, pp. 31—45.

Muller, P. and Price, R. (1984), 'Public Sector Indebtedness and Long-Term Interest Rates', paper presented for the World Bank/Brookings Institution Seminar on the International Consequences of Budgetary Deficits and the Monetary-Fiscal Policy Mix in the OECD, September 1984.

Ott, A.F. (1983), 'Controlling Government Spending', in Stubblebine, W.C. and Willet, T. (ed.), *Reaganomics: A Midterm Report*, ICS Press, pp. 79—107.

Ott, D.J., Ott, A.F. and Yoo, J. (1975), *Macroeconomic Theory*, New York, McGraw-Hill.

Ott, A.F. and Yoo, J. (1980), 'The Measurement of Government Saving', in Von Furstenburg, G.M. (ed.), *The Government and Capital Formation*, Ballinger, **1**, pp. 177—242.

Phelps, E. and Shell, K. (1969), 'Public Debt, Taxation, and Capital Intensiveness', *Journal of Economic Theory*, **3**, pp. 330—46.

Somensatto, E. (1985), 'Budget Deficits, Exchange Rates, International Capital Flows, and Trade', in Cagan, P. (ed.), *Essays in Contemporary Economic Problems*, Washington D.C., American Enterprise Institute, pp. 223—79.

Tatom, J.A. (1984), 'A Perspective on the Federal Deficit Problem', Federal Reserve Bank of St. Louis, *Review*, **66**, June/July, pp. 5—17.

U.S. Treasury Department (1984), *The Effects of Deficits on Prices of Financial Assets: Theory and Evidence*, Washington D.C., U.S. Government Printing Office, March.

15. Public Capital Formation and Growth

1 INTRODUCTION

An important objective of fiscal policy is controlling the trend of public finances so that resources are allocated efficiently over time. This means that the budget balance must be consistent with the capital growth requirements of the economy.

In Chapter 14, the interrelationships between public sector saving (or dissaving) and key economic variables were examined. In this chapter the focus is on the contribution of public sector capital to economic growth. Capital accumulation is one of the principal sources of economic growth. What has been overlooked until recently is the role of public sector capital in the growth process.

The slowdown in productivity growth worldwide since 1970 has renewed interest in the discovery of sources of economic growth. Studies by Aschauer (1987, 1988a, 1988b, 1990), Munnell (1990b), and Garcia-Milia and McGuire (1987) have tried to quantify the effect of public capital spending, in particular public infrastructure capital on private economic performance. Others attempted to link investment in human capital (Denison, 1985), (Hanushek, 1986), and research and development (Griliches, 1988), to economic growth.

Recent research (Romer, 1986; Grossman and Helpman, 1989; Krugman, 1988; Barro and Sala-i-Martin, 1990) which is identified by the title 'endogenous growth theories' emphasizes the endogenous linkage between changes in the investment rate and the rate of technical progress. According to these models, there are externalities associated with capital accumulation that reduce the effects of diminishing returns. Investment in physical and human capital, research and development, and tax policies are examples of externalities that affect the rate of technical progress. Endogenous growth models seek not only to demonstrate that the growth rate can be permanently raised through an increase in investment, but also to explain sustained differences in growth rates among industrial countries.

This chapter begins with a brief discussion of the relationship between capital formation and growth. Empirical evidence on the role of public capital (infrastructure capital) in the growth process is cited. The next section gives a review of models that link public asset formation with long-term growth. Concluding remarks are given in the last section.

2 CAPITAL FORMATION AND ECONOMIC GROWTH: THE TRADITIONAL MODEL

The contribution of capital to economic growth is well documented in studies of production functions. The growth of output is given by:

$$g_y = ag_n + (1-a)g_k + q \tag{15.1}$$

Assuming constant returns to scale, economic progress, according to Solow (1970), can be decomposed according to the following sources:

$$(g_y - g_n) = (1 - a) / a(g_k - g_y) + (1/a)q \tag{15.2}$$

where g_y, g_n and g_k are the growth rates of output, labor and capital respectively; a is the share of labor in output, (1 — a) is the share of capital, and q is the residual. The residual, referred to as multifactor productivity, is that part of output growth that cannot be explained by either the growth in labor or capital. Equation (15.2) is instructive in that it shows that per capita output growth can occur even if the residual q is zero provided that the capital output ratio increases.

Using U.S. data for illustrative purposes, it is estimated that the capital stock in the U.S. private sector has grown at a rate roughly equal to that of output since 1950. The relative constancy of the capital output ratio ($g_k - g_y$) in equation (15.1) means that multifactor productivity plays a significant role in the growth process. According to the data reported by the President's Council of Economic Advisers (1989), approximately one-half of the growth in the private economy in the U.S. since 1950 has been attributed to the residual q. The U.S. Department of Labor calculates measures of multifactor productivity for the U.S. between 1950 and 1986. From the data a distinct break in the growth rate of total factor productivity appeared around 1974. Over the 1951—73 period, the average growth in total factor productivity was equal to 1.8 per cent compared to 0.2 per cent for the 1974—82 period.[1] Where this residual comes from, why it is higher in certain periods compared with others is yet to be explained despite the extensive work in this area by Denison (1974, 1979, 1985), Darby (1981), and Baily and Gordon (1986, 1988) among others.

The worldwide slowdown in productivity growth (see Table 15.1) has produced a number of hypotheses. One explanation is the rapid increase in energy costs that occurred in 1973 and 1979. Other factors mentioned include changes in the composition of the labor force, inflation, regulation, mismeasurement of output or input, a levelling off in the rate of growth of R&D expenditures, as well as a decline in public investment.[2] The CBO (1987) and the Council of Economic Advisers (1989) reviewed the contribution of some of these factors to the productivity slowdown in the U.S. A summary of the findings is given in Table (15.2). According to the studies reviewed by the CBO, the most significant factor contributing to the slow-

Table 15.1 *Average annual output/man-hour growth rates in the Group of Seven countries*

Country	1960—73	1973—79	1979—86	Change 1973—79 minus 1960—73	Change 1979—86 minus 1973—79
United States	3.2	1.4	3.1	—1.8	1.7
Canada	4.5	2.1	1.4	—2.4	—0.7
Japan	10.3	5.5	5.6	—4.8	0.1
France	6.5	5.0	3.6	—1.5	—1.4
Germany	5.8	4.3	2.8	—1.5	—1.5
Italy	7.3	3.3	3.3	—4.0	0.0
United Kingdom	4.3	1.1	4.4	—3.2	3.3

Source: Adapted from data cited in Griliches (1988), p. 10.

down is a slower rate of capital formation (accounting for 20—30 per cent of the slowdown). Slower capital formation is said to have lowered U.S. productivity in the following ways:

1. by failing to maintain the capital labor ratio in response to the rapid growth in the labor force;
2. by slowing down the rate of adoption of new technologies embodied in new plant and equipment; and
3. by reducing the learning-by-doing that accompanies new investments which feeds back into the rate of technical innovation.

The slowdown in the rate of capital formation has been attributed to the decline in both the rate of private and government capital formation. The decline in public investment is said to have resulted from a shift in budget priorities from investment to consumption.

The importance of public capital to the growth in productivity has been analyzed in two types of models: 1. the production function approach where public capital enters as an input, just like labor and private capital, and estimates of its contribution are derived, and 2. cost-benefit analysis, which calculates the contribution of public capital projects to the growth of private output. Both of these approaches are discussed below.[3]

Public Capital and Productivity Growth

An example of studies using the production function approach to estimate the contribution of public capital to growth is that of Aschauer (1987). He

Table 15.2 Estimates of the importance of selected factors in the productivity slowdown

Factor and Researcher	Periods Compared	Percentage of slowdown attrib. to factor
Capital Formation		
Capital/Labor Ratio Growth		
Denison (1979)	1948—73/1973—76	4
Kendrick	1948—66/1973—78	21
Clark	1948—65/1965—73	35
Denison (1984)	1948—73/1973—81	8
Vintage Effect		
Kendrick	1948—66/1973—78	10
Clark	1948—65/1965—73	14
	1965—73/1973—78	9
Energy Price Effect		
Denison (1979)	1948—72/1972—76	3
Norsworthy *et al.*	1965—73/1973—78	16
Hudson & Jorgenson[a]	1948—72/1972—76	20
Labor Quality		
Hours Worked (efficiency-adjusted)		
Denison (1979)	1948—73/1973—76	10
Denison (1984)	1948—73/1973—81	6
Education		
Denison (1979)	1948—73/1973—76	—12
Denison (1984)	1948—73/1973—81	—3
Research & Development		
Denison (1979)	1948—72/1972—76	3
Griliches	1965—73/1973—77	10
Kendrick	1948—66/1973—78	13

Note: a: Percentage contribution based on Denison's estimate of a 2.97 percentage-point decline in overall productivity growth. 20 per cent figure is approximate.

Source: Reported in Wolff (1984), pp. 50—1, and in Congressional Budget Office (1987), pp. 86—7.

puts forth two propositions: 1. public sector investment increases the stock of private capital by raising the return on private investment, and 2. public capital investment devoted to 'core infrastructure' is complementary to private capital in the production process. Thus, an increase in the stock of public capital increases private capital productivity. In support of these propositions, Aschauer looked at the trends in public spending and public net investment and compared these trends with the profit rate. He points out that during the period 1958—84, public capital formation 'tumbled' from two to three per cent of GNP during the 1965—69 to 0.4 per cent of GNP during the 1980—84 period. The profit rate fell drastically from 13.3 per cent in 1965—69 to 7.9 per cent for the period 1980—84.

Based on this evidence, Aschauer asks: What would have happened if the government maintained the rate of investment of the earlier period? The response to this question was obtained through simulation. Holding the rate of public investment constant, at 2.1 per cent of GNP, throughout the period 1970—84, Aschauer finds initially a surge in the profit rate and private capital accumulation followed by a decline in both rates in later periods. This leads him to look further. In his next two papers, Aschauer investigated the link between public investment and private capital formation. Using regression analysis, he tested for statistically significant relationships between public nonmilitary capital, public infrastructure, public investment, and productivity of private capital.

Using data for the Group of Seven (G-7) industrial countries for the 1966—85 period, Aschauer finds a significant relationship between the ratio of public investment to GDP and labor productivity. According to the study, a one per cent rise in public investment/GDP ratio raises productivity growth by 0.4 per cent per annum. From U.S. data for the period 1949—85, Aschauer found a statistically significant coefficient on public nonmilitary capital. His regression results suggest that a one per cent rise in nonmilitary capital raises the productivity of private capital by an amount in the range of 0.34 to 0.39 per cent.[4] Aschauer also presents estimates which suggest that private output would increase by twice as much in response to increases in 'core infrastructure' than other types of investment.[5]

In her 1990a study, Munnell updated and reestimated in a slightly different form the productivity equation estimated by Aschauer. Using U.S. data for the period 1948—87, the regression results she obtains seem to be in line with those of Aschauer. Both total nonmilitary capital and infrastructure capital enter with coefficients in the range of 0.31 to 0.39. From the regression coefficients Munnell recalculated multifactor productivity to uncover the link between the decline in public capital and the slowdown in productivity. Her calculations lead her to conclude that much of the decline in multifactor productivity growth after 1969 can be attributed to the decline in public investment.

The positive and statistically significant coefficients obtained by Aschauer and Munnell, however, were not supported by findings in other studies (Barro, 1989, 1990; Eberts and Fogarty, 1987). Barro investigated the relationship between government spending and economic growth using a sample of 72 countries spanning the time period 1960—85. Two public expenditure variables were used: consumption and investment. Government consumption was measured by consumption purchases excluding spending on national defense and education. This variable proxied for public services that enter into consumer utility functions. In the empirical analysis, this variable turned out to be negatively related to the growth rate of per capita GDP.

Public investment was taken as a proxy for those government activities which enter into the production function. Barro's empirical findings show little relationship between the ratio of public investment to GDP and economic growth, especially when the ratio of private investment to GDP was held constant. Based on these findings, he concluded that public investment is not very important for economic growth. He suggests instead that the government is optimizing and is going to the point where the 'marginal effect of public investment on the growth rate is close to zero.'[6] This conclusion is also reached by Douglas Holtz-Eakin (1993). In a National Bureau of Economic Research working paper, he states, 'The best data available indicate that the best estimate of the impact of state and local [government] capital on private output or productivity is zero'.

In a recent study, CBO (1991) is critical of the use of production-function models to estimate the contribution of public capital to growth. The study highlights three problems: 'Their very breadth . . . the broad scope of production function studies would make them poorly suited for assessment of the relative contribution of changes in one type of capital versus another.' A second problem, common to all regression models, is that they only examine relationships that prevailed in the past, hence giving little information on 'changing' returns to public investment opportunities. Lastly, production function studies fail to capture those 'non-quantifiable' social goals of public investment. The cost-benefit approach to study the contribution of public capital, according to the CBO, would avoid this last critique.

Cost-benefit analysis entails the identification, in addition to private benefits, of all these social goals which could not be captured by measurements of private benefits. Thus, this approach (assuming it can be done without all the known pitfalls of the technique) offers a better measure of the contribution of public sector capital to society's welfare than the measure provided from studying production functions. Evidence from studies done in the U.S. and elsewhere on the cost-benefit of public projects show this approach to have as many problems as those encountered in production function studies. More significant is the fact that most of these studies' findings support a bigger role for the public sector. In effect the CBO's review of the cost-benefit studies of public infrastructure projects suggests that only a modest, even a negative, payoff has resulted from this type of investment.

Capital Formation and Long-Term Growth

The traditional output growth decomposition discussed in the previous section is said to understate the contribution of capital accumulation to economic growth and therefore overstates the role of the residual.[7] If this view is accepted, then slower output growth may be attributed to slower growth in capital accumulation. Moreover, since slower growth in capital accumulation accompanied the slow growth of total factor productivity (the residual), a linkage between the two might even be established.

The 'new growth models' emphasize the possible 'endogenous' linkages between a change in economic efficiency (multifactor productivity) and the change in long-term growth rate. Endogenous growth models, as they are referred to, are all based on the proposition that if the marginal product of a factor (capital or labor) does not diminish when its stock evolves, then any innovation (policy or other factor) that causes a rise in the rate of accumulation of that factor may lead to a 'permanent' increase in the rate of growth of output. This conclusion is in direct contrast to the fundamental model where an increase in the rate of accumulation of (say) capital leads to a rise in the level of output, but after a while, it settles back to its former equilibrium (steady-state) rate of growth.

Although the new theories vary in approach depending on the choice of factor which accumulates, all are based on the fundamental assumption that the accumulating factor is not subject to diminishing returns to scale. In other words, the presence of economies of scale is essential for the new models' conclusions.[8]

Production function studies give the output—input relation in its most simple form as:

$$Y/N = AK^{\Phi}(K/N)^{a} \tag{15.3}$$

where: Y = output
K = stock of fixed capital
N = labor
Φ = measure of economies of scale (in traditional model = 0)
a = elasticity of output with respect to labor ($0 < a < 1$)
A = measure of economic efficiency (total factor productivity)

In the new growth model $\Phi \neq 0$, that is, scale economies exist. If there are increasing returns to scale on an economy-wide basis, the marginal product of capital depends on the total amount of factors employed as well as on the capital—labor ratio. Hence, capital accumulation and growth depend on the total amount of factors employed. In the new growth model, increasing returns to scale replaces the 'exogenous' time path trend as an explanation of growth. Rewriting equation (15.3), we obtain:

$$Y = AK^{(\Phi + a)}N^{(1-a)} \tag{15.4}$$

In the new growth model $\Phi > 0$.

To facilitate the discussion, suppose N = constant. To see how output grows, suppose that a given shock (innovation) causes A to rise. This means that any combination of capital and labor will produce more output than before. If $(\Phi + a) < 1$, the growth of output will eventually fall back to its previous (steady-state) level. The only way to have a permanently higher rate of growth of output is if the scale economies are large enough such that $(a + \Phi) \geq 1$.

The case where $(a + \Phi) > 1$ may be dismissed, as it leads to accelerating growth in the limit reaching infinity. On the other hand, if $(a + \Phi) = 1$, this will guarantee a permanently higher rate of growth.[9] The literature offers several endogenous growth models. The critical accumulating factor is the stock of knowledge (Romer, 1986), innovation (Krugman, 1988) and human capital (Lucas, 1988; Barro and Sala-i-Martin, 1990).

Basically, there are two ways in which budget policy parameters may be incorporated in endogenous growth models. First, if the social rate of return on investment exceeds the private rate of return, then tax policies that stimulate investment raise the growth rate and households' utility. The learning-by-doing models with 'spillovers' (Romer, 1986) provide examples where attaining the social optimum requires tax incentives for investment (i.e. investment tax credits) so that the private rate of return is equated to the social rate. Second, publicly provided goods enter as productive inputs in private production functions. Growth models of this type are used by Lucas (1988) and Barro and Sala-i-Martin (1990).

Briefly, the learning-by-doing model assumes that output per worker for firm i, y_i, depends upon the firm's capital per worker, k_i, as well as on the average (or the aggregate) of the capital stocks of other firms, k. (In the human capital growth model, for example Lucas, this component, k, corresponds to the average person's human capital.) Using essentially a production function similar to that given by equation (15.4), Romer postulates that the firm's production function exhibits diminishing returns in k for fixed k_i, but constant returns in k_i and k together.

Since the firm's demand for capital depends on private rates of return, Romer shows that when 'spillovers' are present, the model solution yields a growth rate of output that falls short of the Pareto optimal rate. This optimum is found by using the social rate of return and not the private rate. Government policies that subsidize producers of capital goods or subsidize producers of knowledge (with nondistortionary taxes) reduce the cost of capital and the private rate of return is equated with the social rate.[10]

Barro and Sala-i-Martin's model treats government spending as an input in private producer production functions. Three versions of the model are presented, each dealing with a specific type of public good. One version of the model deals with those public services that may be rival but not excludable. Examples include highways and streets, water and sewer systems, and so on, in short, infrastructure capital services. This version of the model allows for congestion of the public good. Again, the production function for each producer is similar to that given above, except that it includes as an input the public good.

The production function for each producer in Barro and Sala-i-Martin's model exhibits constant returns to scale with respect to private capital input as long as government maintains a fixed level of congestion (i.e. a constant ratio of the public good to private output or G/Y). Equivalently, the aggregate production function exhibits constant returns with respect to the private capital stock and the public good, but diminishing returns to private capital for a given level of the public good. An interesting implication of the model is that a fall in the G/Y ratio either because of an expansion in any one individual producer's output or because of a fall in the level of the public good, G, congests the facilities available to the other producers, hence diminishing returns to private input. The model's conclusion does not necessarily imply that government spending on infrastructure should increase. As Barro and Sala-i-Martin have shown, user charges can be used to internalize the congestion distortion, thereby equalizing the private and social rates of return on investment.

3 CONCLUSION

By way of conclusion, the following quotation is appropriate. In a paper that was published in 1949, Buchanan states, 'The government is part of an exchange nexus. As such, one needs to evaluate the exchange process by examining the total impact of government on the individual.' Resurging interest about the effects of government parameters on the rate of economic growth is one such evaluation. What comes across from the recent as well as from the old literature is that the way governments spend private resources, and not simply how much of these resources they have used, affects living standards of present and future generations.

The theoretical and empirical work reviewed in this chapter suggests that public sector capital may have an effect on private capital productivity and on long-term economic growth. In both the Romer and Lucas models, public sector investment in human capital, or government subsidies for the purchase of education, raise the rate of growth by raising the productivity of private capital. Congestion of infrastructure in the Barro and Sala-i-Martin model affects productivity of private capital also. It must, however, be pointed out that as yet few empirical studies have been carried out to support the new growth theories. As noted by Baldwin, 'the estimates of long-term growth effects are derived from models that have a long way to go before they become part of the received wisdom of economics'.[11] One issue that needs to be resolved is the importance of scale economies at the economy-wide level as long-term growth effects depend on such magnitudes.

NOTES

1. Blanchard and Fisher (1989), p. 3.
2. See contributions by Fischer, Griliches, Jorgenson and Olson to Symposium: 'The Slowdown in Productivity Growth', *Journal of Economic Perspectives*, Fall 1988, pp. 3—97.
3. For a discussion of these studies, see CBO (1991).
4. Aschauer (1989a).
5. Aschauer (1989b).
6. Barro (1989).
7. See, for example, Hatsopoulos, Krugman and Summers (1988), p. 15.
8. See Baldwin (1992a and 1992b) for a review of growth models with economies of scale.
9. Romer (1987).
10. Barro and Sala-i-Martin (1990), p. 5.
11. Baldwin (1992b), p. 35.

REFERENCES

Aschauer, D. (1987), 'Is the Public Stock Too Low?', Federal Reserve Bank of Chicago, *Chicago Fed Letter*, No. 2, October.

Aschauer, D. (1988a), 'Government Spending and the "Falling Rate of Profit"', *Economic Perspectives*, **12**, May/June, pp. 11—17.

Aschauer, D. (1988b), 'Does the Public Capital Crowd Out Private Capital?', Federal Reserve Bank of Chicago, Staff Memoranda, SM-88-10.

Aschauer, D. (1989a), 'Public Investment and Productivity Growth in the Group of Seven', *Economic Perspectives*, **13**, pp. 17—25.

Aschauer, D. (1989b), 'Is Public Expenditure Productive?', *Journal of Monetary Economics*, **23** (2), pp. 177—200.

Aschauer, D. (1990), 'Infrastructure and America's Economic Future', Presentation to the Committee on Public Work and Transportation, U.S. House of Representatives.

Baily, M.N. and Gordon, R. (1986), 'What Happened to Productivity Growth?', *Science*, **234**, October, pp. 443—51.

Baily, M.N. and Gordon, R. (1988), 'The Productivity Slowdown, Measurement Issues and the Explosion of Computer Power', in *Brookings Papers on Economic Activity*, **19**, (2), pp. 347—420.

Baldwin, R. (1992a), 'Measuring 1992's Median-Term Dynamic Effects', National Bureau of Economic Research, Working Paper no. 3166.

Baldwin, R. (1992b), 'On the Growth Effect of 1992', National Bureau of Economic Research, Working Paper no. 3119.

Barro, R. (1989), 'Economic Growth in a Cross-Section of Countries', National Bureau of Economic Research, Working Paper no. 3120.

Barro, R. (1990), 'Government Spending in a Simple Model of Endogenous Growth', *Journal of Political Economy*, **98**, part 2, pp. s103—s125.

Barro, R. and Sala-i-Martin, X. (1990), 'Public Finance in Models of Economic Growth', National Bureau of Economic Research, Working Paper no. 3419.

Blanchard, O. and Fischer, S. (1989), *Lectures on Macroeconomics*, Cambridge, MA, MIT Press.

Buchanan, J. (1949), 'The Pure Theory of Government Finance', *Journal of Political Economy*, pp. 496—506.

Commission of the European Communities (1990), *European Economy*, no 46, Luxembourg, CEC.

Congressional Budget Office (1987), *The Economic and Budget Outlook: Fiscal Years 1988—1992*, Part I, Washington D.C., U.S. Government Printing Office.

Congressional Budget Office (1991), 'How Federal Spending For Infrastructure and Other Public Investments Affect the Economy', Washington D.C., U.S. Government Printing Office.

Council of Economic Advisers (1989), *Economic Report of the President 1989*, Washington D.C., U.S. Government Printing Office.

Darby, M.R. (1981), 'The U.S. Productivity Slowdown: A Case of Statistical Myopia', *American Economic Review*, **74** (3), pp. 301—22.

Denison, E. (1974), *Accounting for United States Economic Growth 1929—1969*, Washington D.C., The Brookings Institution.

Denison, E. (1979), *Accounting for Slower Economic Growth: The United States in the 1970s*, Washington D.C., The Brookings Institution.

Denison, E. (1984), 'Accounting for Slower Economic Growth: An Update', in Kendrick, J.W. (ed.), *International Comparisons of Productivity and Causes of the Slowdown*, Cambridge, Mass., Ballinger.

Denison, E. (1985), *Trends in American Economic Growth, 1929—1982*, Washington D.C., The Brookings Institution.

Department of Labor, Bureau of Labor Statistics (1983), 'Trends in Multifactor Productivity, 1948—81', Bulletin 2178, pp. 27—8.

Eberts, R. and Fogarty, M. (1987), 'Estimating the Relationship Between Local Public and Private Investment', Federal Reserve Bank of Cleveland, Working Paper no. 8703.

Furstenberg, G. (1980), *The Government and Capital Formation*, vol. 2, and *Capital, Efficiency, and Growth*, vol. 3, Cambridge, MA, Ballinger Publishing Company.

Garcia-Milia, T. and McGuire, T. (1987), 'The Contribution of Publicly Provided Inputs to States' Economies', unpublished manuscript, dated July 10.

Griliches, Z. (1988), 'Productivity Puzzles and R & D: Another Nonexplanation', *Journal of Economic Perspectives*, no. 4, pp. 9—21.

Grossman, G. and Helpman, E. (1989), 'Comparative Advantage and Long-run Growth', National Bureau of Economic Research, Working Paper no. 2809.

Gurley, J. (1953), 'Fiscal Policy in a Growing Economy', *Journal of Political Economy*, December, pp. 523—35.

Hanushek, E. (1986), 'The Economics of Schooling and Efficiency in Public Schools', *Journal of Economic Literature*, **24**, pp. 1141—77.

Hatsopoulos, G., Krugman, P. and Summers, L. (1988), 'U.S. Competitiveness: Beyond the Trade Deficit', *Science*, **241**, no. 4863 (July 15), pp. 299—307.

Holtz-Eakin, D., quotation from *The Wall Street Journal*, January 4, 1993, p. 1.

Kendrick, J.W. (ed.) (1984), *International Comparisons of Productivity and Causes of the Slowdown*, Cambridge, Mass., Ballinger.

Krugman, P. (1988), 'Endogenous Innovations, International Trade and Growth', Working Paper, unpublished, presented at SUNY-Buffalo Conference on Development.

Lucas, R. (1988), 'On the Mechanics of Economic Development', *Journal of Monetary Economics*, **22**, pp. 3—42.

Mourmouras, A. and Tiferina, J. (1992), 'Public Asset Creation and Future Generations', unpublished manuscript.

Munnell, A.H. (1990a), 'Why Has Productivity Growth Declined? Productivity and Public Investment', Federal Reserve Bank of Boston, *New England Economic Review*, January/February, pp. 3—22.

Munnell, A.H. (1990b), 'How Does Public Infrastructure Affect Regional Economic Performance?', Federal Reserve Bank of Boston, *New England Economic Review*, September/October, pp. 11—32.

Office of Management and Budget (1990), *Budget of the United States Government, Fiscal Year 1991*, Washington D.C., U.S. Government Printing Office.

Olson, M. (1988), 'The Productivity Slowdown, The Oil Shocks, and The Real Cycle', *Journal of Economic Perspectives*, no. 4, pp. 43—69.

Ott, D.J., Ott, A.F. and Yoo, J. (1975), *Macroeconomic Theory*, New York, McGraw-Hill.

Romer, P.M. (1986), 'Increasing Returns and Long-Run Growth', *Journal of Political Economy*, **94**, October, pp. 1002—37.

Romer, P.M. (1987), 'Growth Based on Increasing Returns to Scale Due to Specialization', *American Economic Review, Papers and Proceedings*, **77**, pp. 56—62.

Solow, R. (1970), *Growth Theory: An Exposition*, Oxford University Press.

Solow, R. (1991), 'Growth Theory', in Greenaway, D., Bleaney, M. and Stewart, I.M.T., *Companion to Contemporary Economic Thought*, London, Routledge, pp. 393—415.

Wolff, E. (1984), 'Comments', in Kendrick, J.W. (ed.), *International Comparisons of Productivity and Causes of the Slowdown*, Cambridge, Mass., Ballinger.

Name Index

Subject Index